Hamptons survival Guide

The Inside Scoop on Life in the Hamptons for Visitors, Newcomers, and Residents

5th Edition

Phil Keith

CITY & COMPA

D1410499

Library of Congress Cataloging-in-Publication Data is available upon request.

ISBN 1-885492-98-7

Fifth Edition

Printed in the United States of America

Acknowledgements

To all the merchants and service providers listed herein, thank you for making The Hamptons a
special place in which to live, work, and play. And, my special appreciation to: Marina Van,
Executive Director of the East Hampton Chamber; Laurie Costello, Executive Director of the
Montauk Chamber; and Millie Fellingham, Executive Director of the Southampton Chamber.

Dedication

To my wonderful and adored Myra—
the one woman who finally
made a difference in my life.
All my love is yours, Princess.

ABOUT THE COVER ARTIST

Carol Wilson is founder and proprietor of The Island Gallery on Shelter Island, New York, where
she formerly headed the art department at the Shelter Island School. She is widely respected for her
sensitive portrayals of the people, animals, houses, beaches and landmarks of eastern Long Island.

ABOUT THE ILLUSTRATOR

Doug Keith lives in Seattle where he runs his own studio. He happens to be the author's brother,
but don't hold that against him. He's really a good guy.

PUBLISHER'S NOTE

Neither City & Company nor the author has an interest, financial or personal, in the locations listed in this book. No fees were paid or services rendered in exchange for inclusion in these pages.
While every effort was made to ensure accuracy at the time of publication, it is always best to call
ahead to verify current addresses, fees, and other details.

CONTENTS

631

Please note
that the new area
code for the
Hamptons is 631.

C

d

q

r

S

t

u

v

w

x

y

z

INTRODUCTION

This Guide is a "Guerrilla Guide" to "The Hamptons." It has been written for summer visitors, newcomers, and full-time residents alike. Even those of you who have been here more than ten years (and thereby qualify as "semi-natives") may find a tidbit or two that is useful. It is not an all-encompassing, all-inclusive guide. As you will see, we concentrate on the information that we believe will be most useful to you. In particular, we showcase what we think are the best of the best places and service providers in hundreds of different categories. We will give you specific opinions and recommendations, something most guidebooks will not do.

We are not going to rate ALL the restaurants, visit ALL the stores, check out EVERY antique shop and farm stand. We're going to cut right to the chase and tell you, in our humble opinions, where you should be spending your time and money: Who's got the best Sunday brunch? What's the best bed and breakfast in The Hamptons? Who can you call for those tables and chairs you need for your next party? We're also going to give you as much practical advice as we can on services that you'll need at one time or another. Stuff like: How do you get a pothole filled? Who do you call to get those pesky wild cats out from under your porch? The obnoxious renter is driving you nuts, what can you do?

If you're spending weekends out here, you have only so much time to race around and find the best eateries, the hottest night spots, the most accommodating hardware store, and so forth. If you're a new resident, you need to find out quickly where to locate the goods and services that are going to be most useful to you. That's what this book is all about: telling you what we think is worth your time and your money.

If a commercial enterprise is listed in this Guide it's because it has passed our tests of quality, service, and value. We've tried to single out the best of the best. If a place or service isn't listed here it either didn't make the grade with us or we didn't personally visit or use it. If someone isn't listed here, maybe they'll try harder and be in the next edition. We've also included a great deal of information concerning various public service organizations, community activities, and the like. We've tried to do our best to sort out what's most necessary for you to know.

We will probably leave something out that should have been put in. You'll have experiences different than ours—good and bad. If any of the above occurs, write or e-mail us. We're already working on the next edition.

We'll begin with "Our Rating System" and move on to some basic background on The Hamptons. This will be a crash course in what you need to know about this wonderful community.

OUR RATING SYSTEM

We have decided to give you only what we think is the best of the best. I mean, you only have so much time to spend out here, why waste it on less than the best, or trying to read through pages and pages of reviews?

Consequently, and very subjectively, we are only listing those places that we feel are worth your time and your money. This list will change from year to year, and that's part of the fun: fun for you as well as the establishments listed (or not listed as the case may be!).

If a place is not listed here it does not mean that it isn't worth your while—it just means that it didn't make it onto our radar screen for the current season. What does cause a "blip" on our radar is a place that would probably receive three to five stars from the Michelin Book, Mobil Guide, Zagat's, or whomever: a truly exceptional spot that is more than worth your time and money.

We will list a maximum of eight establishments or entries within a category (except for "Accommodations" and "Restaurants"). Once in a very great while, we'll award a Platinum Medal (5 Stars). Last year there were only a handful of Platinum awards in the whole Guide. Platinum simply means that the product, service, and people associated with this award are the finest in these parts. These are the places that you should go to in The Hamptons if you go no place else. Gold Medals (4 Stars) are awarded to the best of the best within a category. Gold, too, is to be coveted. We do not give Gold awards lightly. You really have to be good to get a Gold. A Silver Award (3 Stars) is nothing to sneeze at either. Silver means that you're very close to Gold. Just like in the Olympics, it could be a difference of teeny fractions between Silver and Gold. Hey! Bronze (2 Stars) is part of the Winner's Circle, too! It means you're in the Top Tier and with just a little more polish, you could move up to Silver, Gold, or maybe even Platinum. No one should be disappointed with a Bronze. Heck, I would have been thrilled to just go to the Olympics as a kid. I would have been rapturous to win a Bronze in my sport! Trouble was, bowling was not an Olympic sport then.

We also award some Honorable Mentions (listed as "HM"—1 Star). These are product or service providers that are just about ready to break into the Top Tier. Some are new establishments that have burst onto the scene and are beginning to make a mark. Some are older operations that have, perhaps, been through a rough period or a major restructuring and are coming back. These winners are also worth a look.

I think our system is working. I am getting more and more calls, letters, e-mails, and faxes from people listed in the Guide. You should hear the complaints when someone gets Silver or Bronze instead of a Gold! I have to remind them of a couple of things: First, as I said above, you have to be among the best-of-the-best to even get in the Guide's winning circle! Secondly, you're in great company! Thirdly, this is a society that measures and grades everything. Someone has to get the "A+" and someone has to get an "A-." If you're not happy with your grade, what do you do? You try harder next time—and that's also what the Guide is about, getting those people that really care about their patrons to work harder. It benefits us all.

NOTES ON THE FIFTH EDITION

In addition to listing the "Best of the Best" in each category, we list 'THE 10 MOST FUN THINGS TO DO IN THE HAMPTONS. This category appears immediately after the alphabetical index. For Kids (and frazzled parents!): look under the category, "Kids! Kids! Kids!"

I wish to assure all of our loyal Guide readers (and our new fans) that the insertion of advertising absolutely in NO way influences our decisions as to who gets into the Guide. You cannot buy your way into this book (although a few have tried)! In fact, all of the insertion decisions are made well in advance of the advertising copy deadlines. I know it sounds screwy, as it has to my friends in the advertising business, but it makes no difference whether you advertise in the Guide or not as far as whether you get listed in the Guide. If we think you're among the best-of-the best, you'll be in the Guide no matter what. This does not make me an advertising genius, but it's the way I want it, thank you!

To you special folks who have advertised with us this year, my personal and heartfelt thanks. We couldn't have produced this book without you. In exchange, I'm going to tell all our readers (Listen up, now, please!) that you are very special. I would hope that our faithful readers will make an extra effort to patronize your businesses!

COMMUNITIES OF THE HAMPTONS

When we refer to "The Hamptons" we are specifically referring to the communities along the South Fork that stretch from Westhampton Beach to Montauk. Specifically, we're going to talk about and describe establishments and services in Amagansett, Bridgehampton, East Hampton, Hampton Bays, Montauk, Sagaponack, Sag Harbor, Shelter Island, Southampton, Springs, Wainscott, Water Mill, and Westhampton Beach. And, for the first time, we are going to start giving you some information on the North Fork, too.

Each community has a very distinct personality. Here's our very biased "take" on what you can expect to find in each of these unique spots. (And boy, will I get in trouble here, right off the bat!)

Amagansett

Yes, the Baldwin's live here (as in Alec and Kim), as do the Patricoff's, Billy Joel, and some of the richest folks in The Hamptons, but Amagansett is still somewhat "undiscovered." In other words, it hasn't been totally painted by the brush of its more well known neighbor, East Hampton. Amagansett stretches from the dunes to the Pine Barrens and has some pretty darn expensive places tucked away here and there, but you can still find land or a reasonably priced home here if you look hard. One phrase to describe the place?: "Quietly Unconcerned."

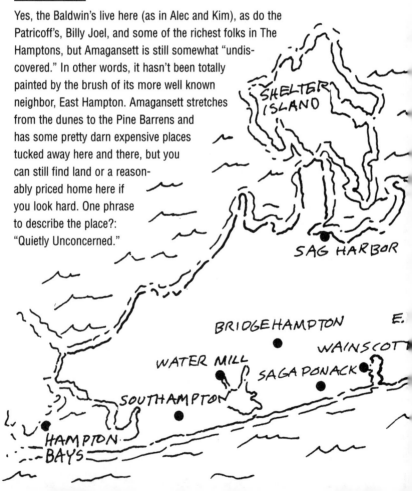

Bridgehampton

Truly a "bridge-Hampton," acting, as it does, as a bridge between Southampton and East Hampton. Bridgehampton has qualities of both. There's still some of the old family, old money feel of Southampton as you ease into town along Main Street. By the time you get to The Monument at the other end of town, however, you begin to feel the quicker pace of new-moneyed East Hampton beginning to grip you. The town has a surface serenity, to be sure, but just below the surface there's something more fast-paced boiling there. It's "Fame" and it's looking for a weak spot in the crust from which to erupt. For current buyers of homes and land, that's good news. Bridgehampton still has some bargains left. But you'd better pay attention before the place does erupt and become, as I feel it will, "East Hampton–West."

East Hampton

Some famous magazine, I forget which one, called Main Street in East Hampton "the most beautiful Main Street in America." I couldn't agree more. It is a truly beautiful place, ergo, that's where the beautiful people must be, right? Well…maybe…. But there's no question East Hampton is the epicenter of Money and Power in The Hamptons. After all, it's where the Spielbergs reside, as does Martha Stewart and many other movers and shakers. It's the home of the

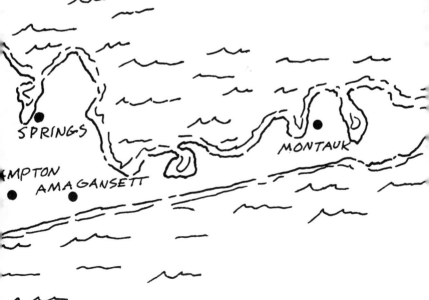

Hamptons International Film Festival, the Maidstone Club, and Georgica Pond. East Hampton boasts about having the most expensive beachfront property in America. East Hampton celebs vie for seats at Nick & Toni's, Della Femina's and The Farmhouse.

Now, don't shoot me. I love East Hampton. There are many fine shops, restaurants, beaches, and historical sights to visit. It's just that the town seems to have an "edge." And the edge seems to come from the new-moneyed folk. They arrive here all summer from The City or "the Coast." They roar in by limo or drop from the sky by helicopter or private jet. They are moving so fast that they don't have time to decompress before they arrive. The hard edges of their lives are still with them on Saturday mornings, I guess, as they push and shove their way to the front of the line for bagels. They seem to be always yelling "Hey! Hey, you!" to get the attention of exasperated sales people at any shop they happen to blow into. These folks are the ones barreling down Newton Lane leaning on the horn. (You can always tell the neurotic City and L.A. types. They're the only ones using horns out here.) Well, "if you got it, flaunt it" as they say. And if you've "got it," East Hampton's your town.

Hampton Bays

Originally settled in the 1600's as "Good Ground." Really! That was the name of the town for many years. Must have been the Puritan penchant for understatement. Anyway, it's now Hampton Bays. And I love this little place. It's like, "Huh?! We're a 'Hampton.'" Yes, you are, even if you haven't discovered that fact yet. Main Street is still populated by quaint little shops, five-and-dime-type stores, cozy bars, and tiny, home-style restaurants. If you get off of Main and go back down toward the Bay and Ocean, you'll find a lot of beach places originally built thirty and forty years ago as summer cottages. They probably cost about $10,000 each then, including the land, and they go for $250,000 today! Well, things are changing. A big United Artists Cinema just opened and land prices are going up. The Yuppies who don't care about the Southampton old-money label or the cachet of new-moneyed East Hampton are buying in Hampton Bays.

Montauk

As the bumper sticker says, "Montauk—The End." Here, at the very end of the Island, we have the "People's Hampton." Folks here are more laid-back and there's a definite family orientation, especially among the vacationers. Montauk has some of the most spectacular scenery and some of the finest beaches. And it comes without the neurotic pace gripping some other parts of The Hamptons. It's the most affordable Hampton in terms of land, homes, and rates for motels, hotels, and cottages. It's too far out for folks who need to be close to the tempo of the City. But it's not too far out for those who really want to get away. One of these years prices to the west will force more people out to this end of Paradise. The wonderful simplicity of what is still a true family, beachfront community will begin to disappear. Enjoy it while you can.

Sagaponack

To some, Sagaponack is a blip on the Globe-sat navigation system in the Cadillac or Jaguar. If you're cruising from Bridgehampton to East Hampton, you'll miss it if you blink, and that's the way the people in Sagaponack would like to keep it. Sagaponack is a wedge of land that straddles both sides of Montauk Highway, but the most desirable part is the beachfront south of the highway. There is no "town." It's all residences, horse farms, and a few scattered businesses. If you want to live here, better hurry. And bring a fat checkbook. The super rich have found Sagaponack. Folks like Ira Rennert, the reclusive billionaire who is building—hope you're sitting down—the most expensive home ever built in America, are right here in Sagaponack. Yes, it's going to be even more expensive than Bill Gates' house. Mr. Rennert's home, sitting on 64 prime waterfront acres, will cost something in the neighborhood of $100 million.

Sag Harbor

In the last century they tell me that this used to be a rip-roaring whaling village to rival New Bedford. Tall ships, wild women, salty sea captains and drunken sailors. Sounds like fun! Well, since the whaling industry collapsed, Sag Harbor hasn't been doing much "roaring," and that's just fine with the folks that like to call Sag Harbor their haven. It is, by far, the quaintest of all The Hamptons. It's a bit of Nantucket or the Vineyard here in The Hamptons.

Shelter Island

If we could live anywhere we wanted to in The Hamptons, or the world for that matter, it would be on Shelter Island. This is truly paradise, here on this "sheltered island." It sits in Gardiner's Bay, between Sag Harbor and Greenport, between the South and North Forks. You can't get here except by boat. Once you do get here it's better, I think, than Nantucket or Martha's Vineyard: peaceful, restful, and full of fun things to do if you're an outdoors type. If you don't visit Shelter Island, you'll miss, in my view, the best part of The Hamptons. But please don't stay. We're negotiating for some land there right now and we want to keep the price down!

Southampton

This is the site of the oldest English settlement in New York State (founded in 1640). Fourteen generations of Hildreths—who own the best department store in The Hamptons, the oldest department store in America (1842)— have lived here. As East Hampton is new money, this is where the old money resides. The tranquil beaches of Southampton spawned an exodus of the Victorian rich from New York City at the turn of the century. These are the folks who founded Shinnecock Hills Golf Club and had Stanford White build their homes. They built palazzos on Gin Lane and around Agawam Lake. Southampton is the "Cornerstone Hampton." It's where all the Hamptons mania started. Jobs Lane, Gin Lane, the Southampton Bathing Club: they're all here. Snobbish? Well, there can be some of that. Actually, I think Southampton has done a very fine job of integrating the old families with the "new settlers." It's a pleasant, peaceful town with a lot going for it. Let me try to put it in context: If East Hampton is "tony," Southampton is "sophisticated." A subtle difference, perhaps, but that's all the difference....

Springs

Some people who live out here don't even know where Springs is. It's located just north of East Hampton and is an enclave of old families who've been here a long time, plus a lot of new people who are discovering the joys (and the positive economics) of living "in the woods," north of the Highway. A lot of the "Bonnackers," the old fishing families, lived here. A few still live here, but unfortunately, fewer, what with the cost of land and the decline of the fishing industry. Jackson Pollack, the famous, and some-what infamous painter lived here. I understand he started flinging paint onto canvas in Springs while cloistered in an old, unheated shack with out-door plumbing. Now he's on a postage stamp and his canvases are worth millions. Go figure....

Wainscott

I've always wondered if this was where "wainscoting" was invented. I don't know. Maybe someone knows.... Anyway, Wainscott is a small community that sits by the highway between Sagaponack and East Hampton. The East Hampton Airport is actually in Wainscott. There's no town, or Main Street, just a mile or so of motels, cottages, antique dealers, delis, a pizza place and some pretty good restaurants.

Water Mill

Water Mill is officially designated a "hamlet" and is part of Southampton Town. It's tucked into a spot bordered on the west by Southampton Village, on the east by Bridgehampton and on the south by Mecox Bay. Until last year, if you drove through you'd be on the other side of Water Mill before you knew it. A local joke has the Water Mill Marker painted with "Welcome to Water Mill" on one side and "Now Leaving Water Mill" on the other. Not anymore. Water Mill now has its first stop light. It made summer traffic on Montauk Highway even more miserable, but, you know, I think it made things safer. People used to go tearing around the curve by the actual mill racing to points further east. Now, you have to slow down a little. If you do slow down, you'll see a neat and tidy little "town-let" with a working water wheel, a good museum, and a growing community of fine shops and restaurants.

Westhampton Beach

A "Fringe-Hampton." Yes, I know, Westhampton Beach really wants to be a true Hampton, but its more like a proto-Hampton, i.e., it's not quite there yet. First of all, it's still very much a summer town. By late October, the town has all but closed, except for a few hardy businesses that gamely soldier on through the winter: places (mentioned in this book) like the Beach Street Bakery, the Post Stop Café, O*Suzanna, the Westhampton Playhouse, and so forth. I mean, the Golden Pear, of all places, even shuts down in October! But there's good news in this, too. Westhampton is a Hampton without some of the staggering Hamptons prices. It's worth your time to check things out here—just don't expect to find crowd comfort on Main Street at Christmas.

More than anything else, The Hamptons are, collectively, a state-of-mind kind of place. If New York City is the center of the universe (and it is), The Hamptons are where those who live at the center of the universe go to get away from everything. But not too far away.... As we've mentioned, the epicenter of the Hamptons is barely 90 miles from Midtown.

Some people—a growing number—actually commute to work from The Hamptons. The 5:20 AM Jitney from Southampton to The City, for example, is generally pretty packed. Some people are coming out on Thursday nights, staying until Monday night, and working here Fridays and Mondays. There's also a thriving "cyber population," folks who are wired up along the information superhighway and never leave here except by fax, e-mail, and phone.

For the rest of the world, The Hamptons is a place to "see" and "be seen" or just a total escape: a place to look forward to going to on weekends or a place to unwind in during the summer.

Someone once said that the greatest pleasures in life are the ones we create in our own expectations. Once achieved, these dreams are not as fulfilling or pleasurable as we imagined them to be. Perhaps, but in my view, The Hamptons are as good and as grand as we imagine them. And no matter where I am, I always, always, look forward to coming home—to The Hamptons.

The North Fork

Recently, I've been spending a great deal more time on the North Fork. Part of it is work related, but I'm also looking toward the future and thinking, "Hmmm. Wonder if it's time for a North Fork Survival Guide?" My answer is, "Not yet," but we should all be paying more attention to what's going on there. It's a beautiful, wonderful place and more and more visitors to the South Fork are tripping over to the North Fork.

The North Fork stretches from Riverhead to Orient Point. It's mostly rolling farmland that has been in the hands of a few farming families for many generations. But just like on the South Fork, all that is changing.

The most noticeable change to the North Fork is the one that has been wrought by the relatively new but definitely burgeoning wine industry. It started in 1973 when two intrepid pioneers, my friends Alex and Luisa Hargrave, decided to "plant some grapes." Twenty-seven years later there are twenty-one operating wineries on the North Fork with five or six more in various stages of development. It's big business, folks, and phrases like "Napa of the East" are already being tossed around freely. Actually, we spend a great deal of time talking about this growing business in the "Wineries" section of the Guide, so I will refer you there for more information.

Many folks who are sick and tired of "Hamptons prices" in everything from real estate to the price of a burger are checking out the North Fork. But you have to like the rural life. There are no main street "scenes" on the North Fork like you're going to find on the South Fork—and the sidewalks truly are rolled up at night.

For the first time this year, we are going to feature some of the best places on the North Fork, especially those related to the wine business, restaurants, and other recreational attractions.

PEOPLE OF THE HAMPTONS

Full time (old) residents

Southampton is the site of the oldest existing residence in New York State. The Halsey Homestead, built in 1648, stands on South Main Street. The oldest families on the South Fork were, at first, primarily transplants from the Massachusetts Bay Colony. They included the Halseys, as well as the Herricks, Hildreths, Corwiths, and many others. These folks were here long before the British invaded Long Island during the Revolutionary War. (An old British fort site is commemorated in Southampton.) After the British invaded Long Island, some of the early settlers fled to Connecticut. Working with other "Rebels" some of them snuck back across the sound in rowboats to wage a guerrilla war on His Majesty's troops. Sag Harbor, in fact, was raided and nearly burned to the ground. That's a sixteen-mile row... they must have worked out!

These first non-native families of the Hamptons came to plant crops and become fishermen. After the Revolution they turned the South Fork into miles of farms, mostly potatoes, corn, and veggies. Their work provided food for their own tables as well as produce for sale in New York and New England. Water Mill is the site of a farm stand today called The Green Thumb that first opened in the 1640's!

But let's not forget that these pioneers were not the first people to inhabit Long Island. As became true in the Midwest and Far West, mostly European, white settlers displaced a thriving Native American population. It was less brutal here and not as bloody, but the original Americans were forced nonetheless to retreat further and further westward. Some stayed, however, and today there are several Indian enclaves scattered around the Island. The Shinnecock Tribe has a rather large reservation bordering Southampton. Each year, around Labor Day, the tribe has a grand Pow-Wow. The festivities are probably as much in celebration of the "palefaces" going back to Manhattan after the summer as it is a tribal rite.

The oldest settler surnames still grace street signs and many of our businesses here in the Hamptons: Herrick's Hardware on Main Street in Southampton is down the block from Hildreth's, America's oldest department store, which, in turn is right near Corwin's Jewelry. There are also many Indian names scattered around The Hamptons: Paumanok Winery, the villages of Aquebogue, Quogue, etc. This is an area of enduring tradition as well as a modern retreat.

To see the Hamptons turn into what they have become is, I am sure, bittersweet for the first families, and many other long-time residents (and, no doubt, the Indians). On the one hand, many of them have become very wealthy from the sale of the land that has been in their families for generations—precious land—sold off piece by piece, acre by acre. And many sell because the age-old ways of making a living are no longer profitable. Iowa can grow more corn and sell it cheaper. Idaho is now more famous as well as more productive with the potato. And so it goes.

The oldest fishing families used to haul in an enormous bounty from the waters in and around the Hamptons. Catches included striper and mussels, lobster and clams. These hardy souls have been severely hampered in recent years by restrictive fishing laws, "brown tides," and declining populations of seafood stocks due to over-fishing.

As we have mentioned, wineries have replaced some of the farms. Summer homes have replaced many of the oldest family homesteads. The quiet, country life only happens now during December and January when, for the most part, "the summer people" don't come out. But by and large, the first families and the full-timers have borne this invasion with a great deal of stoicism and grace. There is no obvious "us versus them" mentality between the full-timers and the part-timers. Each depends on the other.

Full time (new) residents

I guess that includes me. This will be my 10th year of full time residence in The Hamptons. I am now officially a "semi-native"! Or so they tell me. I've also been on the waiting list for Southampton Golf Club for five years and they said it would take "about five years." Let's hope so.

Well, there are beginning to be a lot more of "us." And I hear more and more friends and acquaintances pining for full-time residency status. Balancing a job in The City with spending more time out here is what that really means, I think. It's do-able. Myra and I have done it, and I think we've done it well. There are some cautions, though. First, to live here full time, you have to "lose the attitude." Hedges don't get trimmed over night. The busted chair can't be fixed by the time your party starts at seven. The pool heater is leaking but they can't get here until Thursday. The Bay Street Theatre will never show *Rent*—or *Showboat*. You get the idea. This place is becoming populated by a lot of ex-Manhattanites, but it's not Manhattan. If you use "the attitude" or "The Look" nothing will be taken care of any sooner: in fact, probably later. And if you don't think the good folks who service our accounts don't trade stories on whom to avoid, no matter how rich they are, you're dreaming! They do!

Secondly, and of equal importance, maybe greater importance if you're going to be a full-timer, be a good citizen, too. What does that mean? It means becoming involved somehow in protecting what we've got. Volunteer. Does that mean signing up for 1,000 hours at the Hospital or running for School Board? That would be nice, but, no, that's not necessary. It could be as simple as taking a small trash bag with you on your walk to the beach and picking up a few pieces of litter as you stroll along. It could be just joining one of the many worthy organizations we have out here dedicated to the Arts, the environment, or whatever. You'll feel better, too.

"Summer People"

"Summer people" are those that begin to flock to The Hamptons starting in April. (In case you hadn't noticed, "The Season" has really changed: it's no longer Memorial Day through Labor Day. It's now more like Easter through Columbus Day). The Hamptons are, without question, a tony, sophisticated place to escape. But this is not a recent phenomenon. It's been happening for decades. After all, Jackie Kennedy was born out here while the Bouvier's were "summering" in East Hampton.

There is no question that a great deal of the local economy is now centered on the folks who begin arriving in late spring and retreat after the first cool days of fall. These folks tend to come out on Friday, and return late on Sunday night—most of them coming from The City.

Our summer visitors fall into four basic types: The Stratospherics, The Atmospherics, The Gentle Cloud Layers, and The Dark ThunderClouds (I'm using cloud similes in honor of our wonderful summer weather).

The Stratospherics

Stratospheric clouds are those wispy, gossamer strands that are so high up they are almost out of sight. So are the "Stratospherics." They are the super rich and/or the super famous. This lofty and mostly out-of-reach-for-the-rest-of-us group, encompasses more than a fair number of City luminaries from the entertainment, financial, and political worlds. But there is an impressive number of Stratospherics beginning to come from the West Coast, too. Many of Hollywood's most famous have discovered The Hamptons.

By and large, though, the Stratospherics (from either Coast) seek only a quiet retreat here. The Hamptons are, for them, not a place to be seen, but a place to be. The folks who live and work here intrinsically know this and, in an unspoken truce, the lives of these "rich and famous" are left mostly undisturbed. In exchange for this planned indifference, you will see many more of our luminaries out and about in The Hamptons, strolling freely, eating casually, enjoying "the life" just as the rest of us do. It's just plain fun to see Christie Brinkley at the Bridgehampton Antique Show, husband Peter hovering nearby, kids in tow. And guess what: Christie's kids have runny noses just like our kids have! Jack Nicholson will sign your hot dog napkin at 7-11 if you aren't too obtrusive about it. Robin Leach comes often, but not with a film crew. He is here as a welcome party guest. Even Robin needs a break once in a while.

Mostly, though, the Stratospherics hide behind their hedgerows or play polo in Bridgehampton. They rent huge tents, have big parties, and entertain kings and Presidents (and charge the rest of us $2500 to shake hands with Bill and Hillary).

The Atmospherics

The "Atmospherics" make up the largest segment of summer people and create most of our summer atmosphere. Most of them tend to be nouveau riche, nearly rich, or rich wannabes. But they have not yet achieved Stratospheric status. Many of them are Wall Streeters who tend to take a big chunk of the yearly bonuses that come along in January and plunk that chunk down on a summer rental. It is not unusual for people to spend $50,000–$75,000 for a modest property rented from Memorial Day to Labor Day. Of course, many of these renters then break the rental into "shares" with some of their friends. Shares are allotted by weekends, rooms, specific dates, or sleeping arrangements. The logistical efficiency would have made Napoleon proud.

The Atmospherics are the young-to-graying professionals that really make this place hum in the summer. They are out-and-about, party seeking, and dining to a fare-thee-well. And a bunch of them are a lot of fun to be with. Some of them will become Stratospherics, though, so have fun with them while you can.

The Gentle Cloud Layers

These are the families that come for the summer or, more likely, just a small segment of the summer. Usually they can only come for a week or two. Families are expensive propositions and this is not an inexpensive place; so, they drag their kids off to "the shore" just like our folks did when we were kids. Most of these folks gather in Montauk, Hampton Bays, or Westhampton Beach, where there are many more motels and cottages that accommodate families. They are most welcome here. They add a lot to the economy, to be sure, but they also add a lot of character and generate tons of great nostalgia.

The Dark ThunderClouds

The "Dark ThunderClouds" worry me. I have to study them more, but just like the weather phenomena they are named after, they can pop up anytime and spoil your day. And like the storms they represent, they are mostly hot air and noise. But occasionally, lightning can strike, and someone will get hurt. Who are these folks? Well, you've seen them. It's the idiot with the new Boxter who simply has to go 50 MPH down Jobs Lane, scattering pedestrians and strollers in his wake. He's also the jerk blaring the hip-hop music at 150 decibels, like he really understands what hip-hop is all about. Dark ThunderClouds can appear as scantily clad young women who absolutely have to crash your party. They usually come in groups of three and have some sort of drug-du-jour tucked safely into their clutch bags. If they don't arrive by broom, they're usually driving an old Honda. Dark ThunderClouds can also be the big, fat idiot who shoves his way into the hottest new restaurant in town, trophy wife in tow, demanding to be seated. A $100 dollar bill appears and he gets your table—the one you've been patiently waiting to get for the last hour. He then lights up the biggest cigar you've ever seen and proceeds to abuse the wait staff for a couple of hours over trivialities—usually in a loud voice. Dark ThunderClouds can also appear in the guise of the perfectly coifed, over-dyed matrons shouting at some poor service person just trying to do his or her job. If they shout any louder their faces will crack. Most of them are already stretched to the breaking point anyway from the fourth or fifth face-lift.

Oh, well. Our summers rarely have more than a handful of storms, either real or personal.

SEASONS OF THE HAMPTONS

Summer

Of course, there's summer...the main reason most folks venture out this way. Parties, packed beaches, bumper-to-bumper traffic...ah, what fun!

But there is something truly different about the atmosphere out here in summer. It begins with the sunshine itself; or, perhaps better put, how the sun shines. The light is brighter, the glow mellower, the sunsets more brilliant, and the sunrises (which far too few of us get up to see!) are spectacular. Hollywood lighting directors go nuts for this kind of natural light.

I am told that the differences in our natural lighting are due to a couple of fortunate environmental factors. First, the earth, as it wobbles on its axis, puts our face to the sun in summer at such an angle that it favors the production of this beautiful, natural light. Second, the East End is sandwiched between Long Island Sound to the north and the Atlantic to the south. The sunlight gets trapped between these two giant reflectors. It then bounces across the Sound and the Ocean, eventually coming ashore to skip and shimmer across the fields and farms of our fair East End.

Then there are the breezes. In summer we have a gentle, prevailing northwesterly wind that never seems to ebb. Most of the time it's only a few miles per hour, providing an almost constant natural air conditioning that softly cools even the hottest of days.

The net result of all this is a combination of earth, sky, sea, and breeze that justifies the money we pay to enjoy life here: even if we can't afford it.

Summer is "party time" and it's not unusual for hardy partygoers to jump around to three and four soirees a night. The festivities run the gamut from black tie and crystal to casual beach blasts with "beer and dogs." On Saturday nights in summer, from Hampton Bays to Montauk, there's a constant hum of muted music carried on gentle breezes. Along with the music you'll often catch the scent of a cool, crisp Chardonnay or perhaps the lingering hint of some designer perfume-of-the moment.

The summer officially begins (you can almost fire a starting gun!) on Memorial Day weekend. There are a few warm-up festivities prior to the end of May, but that's the weekend the summer really kicks off. The traffic almost instantly becomes unbearable the Friday afternoon prior to Memorial Day, and it stays gridlocked until Labor Day Weekend (around September 1st). In recent years, however, summer has begun to stretch a little. I have noticed that many more people are beginning to come out in mid-April and stay until mid-October. Most rentals, however, are still priced from Memorial Day to Labor Day.

Autumn

Autumn is actually my favorite season in The Hamptons. I guess my feelings about the fall arise partly from the lessening of the crowds of summer, but September still has many glorious days left after Labor Day has passed. The sun is still warm, the beaches are still eminently swimmable, and the light—that glorious light—turns just a little more to burnished gold.

Truth be known, October is usually spectacular. It is one month wherein you can sometimes experience all four seasons in just thirty-one days. There can be damp days of warm rain scented with late roses and early autumn flowers; so, it'll feel like spring. There can be days of brilliant summer sun and warm breezes. In recent years we've had some spectacular October beach days and, believe me, we've taken advantage of the uncrowded sands. But October is surely fall, too. The first apples are ripe (just as good as Vermont's!) and the pumpkin patches are brim to overflowing. The grapes are harvested and the winemakers are just beginning to get a clue as to what sort of vintage the year will bring. The leaves are turning and there are some spots out here where the display of colors will rival Upstate. October can even bring a few harbinger days of winter. Although, in our experience, it has yet to snow during October, it is still possible. You will wake up one October morning and think it has snowed when you go outside to get the paper and there's a heavy frost covering the ground. You'll race back inside for hot coffee and the first blaze of the season in your fireplace (don't forget to open the flue!).

November gets chilly, but it's still OK. There's always Thanksgiving to think about and plan for, and if you haven't had a Hamptons Thanksgiving, with farm-fresh Long Island turkey, or a duck or goose from North Sea Farms, you don't know what you're missing. Even if you're not a resident, you can still come out and pitch into one of the many fabulous Thanksgiving meals prepared by a number of our local restaurants. Best of all: no dishes to wash! And it could snow a little by Thanksgiving. It has done so on two Thanksgivings since I've been here.

Now having told you how wonderful it is out here after summer, and into the fall, I've revealed quite a secret that will probably get me in trouble with many of the local folks who like the peace and quiet of the fall season. That's the problem with writing a Guide like this, I guess. So let's just keep this to ourselves...

Winter

Christmas, Chanukah, and Kwanzaa all fall in December and this, too, is a special month out here. With luck, we'll have just a little snow on the ground. It'll definitely be nippy. But it won't be dull. There's actually a very festive atmosphere to enjoy here in December, with Holiday lights, tree-lighting ceremonies, Santa parades, and whatnot. And many more of The Hamptons food and beverage spots are staying open year round, most at least through Christmas and the New Year. You'll always be able to find a warm, cozy bar; a hot toddy; and, in many cases, a welcoming hearth.

If we ever "close down" any more, it's in January and February, and after the '95-'96 winter, you could see why! The Blizzard of '96 dumped 26 inches on us in just one January day. Most East End towns are semi ghost towns during these two months. Local business owners will take their vacations during this time and many a store will be displaying signs like: "See you in the Spring"; or "Visit our shop in Palm Beach!"

But this, too, is changing. As mentioned previously, many more professionals are moving the locus of their activities to where they most want to be: here. If you have a phone, fax, and access to the Internet, does it really matter any more that you physically show up in your Manhattan office every day? (I guess it's easier, though, if you own the business.) With more full-timers to count on, more businesses are staying open year-round.

One last note on winters: they are totally unpredictable. The weather can range from one extreme to the other. Several recent winters have been very mild: only once or twice did we have enough snow to actually stick to the ground for more than a day and temperatures rarely got below 20°. The winter of '97-'98 was even bizarre for its mildness. We didn't have a winter at all! Temperatures in the 60's were not uncommon, and the daffodils were popping up in January. But don't count on that! Just remember the winter of '95-'96. Total snowfall: a record 70 inches, including 26 inches of white stuff that we got in one whack. Temperatures dipped to zero several times that winter, too. Well, I've seen nine winters out here now, of all types, and—frigid or fair—it really doesn't matter as long as you have enough firewood and someone with whom you can enjoy the fire.

Spring

Spring starts about mid-March. If you don't have your peas planted by St. Patrick's Day, your garden is behind schedule. The ground is generally workable right about the first of March. Which brings me to another comment about our climate and its blessings: We reportedly have the longest growing season in the Northeast here on the East End. As an avid gardener—mostly vegetables for our own table and tomatoes for our own "jars"—I can tell you this soil is incredibly rich and it produces far longer than most other areas. I have had baby lettuce by the end of April, I get tomatoes into October, and I have even harvested some peppers, onions, and greens for the Thanksgiving table. Martha Stewart (who lives part time in East Hampton) will tell you that with just a little extra effort, you can harvest vegetables from your garden through the winter—Brussels sprouts being a good example. Personally, after putting up eight to ten cases of tomato sauce, harvesting the last squash, cutting the corn stalks for decoration in October and getting in the last dried flowers in November, I'm ready for a couple of months off! I like to give the soil a peaceful winter's rest, too.

The daffodils and crocuses should be up by the end of March or the first of April. The tulips will not be far behind. The first robins will noisily return as soon as they can poke their beaks into the soil and get those juicy worms (ugh!). April can—and should—be rainy. Remember the old "April showers bring May flowers" ditty? It's appropriate out here. Consistently warm days will come in late April and there will be the scent of fresh-plowed earth all around as our local farmers plant corn and potatoes. The first of May will bring a renewed burst of lawns, flowers, and bright sun—and, of course, people.

So, there they are, our Seasons of The Hamptons. Every one of them is full and rich, each with its own distinctive merits. Come out for the summer, to be sure, but if you come out only during summer, you're missing a big piece of the total.

GETTING HERE

The greatest challenge, by far, to being in The Hamptons is simply getting here. Unless you are wealthy enough to charter your own jet, you'll have to suffer with the rest of us. Ninety-nine percent of us get to The Hamptons by train, jitney, or "POV"— privately owned vehicle. In my mind, the most relaxing and stressless

way to get here is to jump on the jitney (see "Buses"). This bus service picks up all through Manhattan and gets you to The Hamptons in an average of 2 hours—maybe 3 hours—in the very worst traffic. The train, even given that it is run by the notorious Long Island Railroad System, is an alternative (see "Trains"), but the schedules are much less flexible; and, if you're coming from the city you may have to change trains in Jamaica (the station, not the Island!).

Even with trains and buses, most of us still get here by car—and that means you have to negotiate the dreaded parkways and expressways in and around the city. By the way, do you know the difference between a parkway and an expressway? Trucks (BIG trucks) are not permitted on parkways. Just thought you'd like to know.

To get to The Hamptons by car you have only three choices: the ineptly named Long Island "Expressway" (we call it the "Long Island Distressway"), the Northern State Parkway, or the Southern State Parkway. No matter which one of those three arteries you take, you'll eventually end up on the Sunrise Highway, which, in turn, feeds into Montauk Highway. Having traveled these notorious highways and byways for, lo, these many years, and having spent countless miles and hours ranting at my windshield, let me give you some advice on how to do this trek.

Special Hint #1: As you leave the City, tune in WCBS News Radio 88 (880 on your AM dial). Every ten minutes WCBS does a traffic update. Now, I have found that their reports, just like everyone else's, lag the real scenario on the roads by as much as an hour or more. If you hear there's a "three-car fender-bender by the side of the road at Exit 49 off the LIE, traffic is backed up for three miles," would that mean avoid the LIE? Not in my opinion. That report is "old news" and it's probably long gone by the time you get there; besides, it's a minor accident that should be off the road. Any delays are likely to be "gawker blocks" and they clear up fairly rapidly. If, however, you hear one of the dreaded "closure" reports or a "major accident" report, it's time to take evasive action.

Special Hint #2: If you have a cellular phone, bring it with you. Most of the local services offer special traffic avoidance reports by dialing a "star" something number.

Special Hint #3: If you live on the West Side, or start your trip from thereabouts, you might consider taking the Brooklyn-Battery Tunnel to the Brooklyn-Queens Expressway (the "BQE") to the Belt Parkway to the Southern State Parkway. This "back door" route to the Sunrise/Montauk Highways (and thus The Hamptons) is barely 10 miles longer than going via the LIE. If the LIE is loaded down, believe me, it'll be faster. If it's bad on the Belt, you can even jump off onto Sunrise Highway just about anywhere after Kennedy Airport, starting at Exit 23. You can actually take this local artery all the way to Montauk Highway. I don't recommend it unless it's really, really bad traffic, because there are a bazillion stoplights along this route.

Special Hint #4: As if you needed this advice! Avoid the LIE at peak travel times. Naturally, that's any time between midnight and midnight seven days a week! No, seriously, there are times that are far worse than others. Certainly Fridays between 3 PM and 8 PM are the worst. Going the other way, it's Sundays between 3 PM and 8 PM. If you can get away Friday at noon, you'll be fine. Otherwise wait until 9 PM. If you want to stretch your weekend, and you have the mental discipline not to party another night, stay over on Sunday, leave at 5 AM Monday and you'll breeze into the City by 7:30 or 8:00 AM. Just tell your secretary to keep people out of your office between noon and one: you'll be taking a nap!

Special Hint #5: OK, OK, so you've got to take the LIE. Well, is there a way to survive the experience? Yes. Now I know that some enterprising author has actually written a book on avoiding the LIE by taking the frontage roads that run parallel to the LIE. It is possible to leave Queens and get to Exit 70 (the terminus of the LIE that dumps you into the Hamptons) without even getting on the LIE. To do this, you'd use the frontage roads. I've tried it.

And you know, it's an even nastier experience (if that's possible) than squirming in your hot, plastic seat during a July afternoon on the LIE. Even under the best of circumstances, traveling the frontage road route, you might save 15 minutes over staying on the LIE. Is it worth it? To race down a few side roads, slip-slide your way through the orange construction cones that grow from the pavement everywhere on Long Island? To sit there, motor revving, at every stop light while you mutter, "C'mon, c'mon, c'mon, c'mon, c'mon!"? Nah, I don't think so. But what you can and should realize is that the frontage roads are available to you. It is a fact that no matter where you are on the LIE you can get off at virtually any exit and within a mile or two you can slip back on the LIE. If you're in a traffic delay of 5 MPH magnitude or if you can see flashing lights way off in the distance, get off and stick to the frontage roads for an exit or two. Will it make a lot of difference? Probably not, but as we all know, simply experiencing movement in your vehicle is psychologically less stressful than sitting still as waves of pavement heat float up and over your sweaty brow.

Special Hint #6: The only thing worse than being stuck on the LIE in the middle of a traffic snarl is being stuck in a traffic jam on the LIE with a full bladder! Where the $#@%^&* are the bathrooms?! Well, there aren't any—at least not any operated by the State or the Counties. That may be changing, but it'll be way into the New Millennium before you see any results and I'd hate to "hold it" that long! The State passed legislation in 1997 to allow fast-food chains to set up and operate roadside rest stops along the LIE and the Southern State. In a couple of years you may see a Golden-Arched Potty or a Bob's Big Boy Bathroom but first a State transportation committee must recommend spots for the restrooms. (Isn't that a wonderful use for our tax dollars! A Potty Committee!) The rumor is that 11 potential sites have been recommended but ultimately only 4 or 5 stops will be built. There are supposed to be 2 to 3 each on the LIE and Southern State. As of this writing, nothing has happened. Are you shocked? More importantly, what do you do in the meantime?

If you can hold it long enough to get to Exit 51 off the LIE, you'll see the Long Island Convention and Visitors Bureau Center just off the side of the expressway. Their offices are in an old railroad car that's visible from the highway. There are no permanent restrooms here, but there are some port-a-potties. The Southern State Visitor's Center in Valley Stream does not have bathrooms, just bushes, and these have been very popular. The center does intend to have portable toilets, though, by the time you read this. (We said the same thing in last year's book and it hasn't happened yet!)

All of you experienced travelers know that you can no longer count on the ubiquitous gas station for a bathroom. (Notice I didn't say "service" station, since most of them no longer know the meaning of that word.) Many a grimacing driver, back teeth floating, has stopped at a beckoning marquee to face an uncomprehending or uncaring face behind three inches of bullet-proof glass who smirks and says, in muffled tones, "Sorry, Pal. We don' got no rest rooms (Snort!)."

Let me assuage your fears and relieve your (bladder) pain. Herewith listed, by LIE or Southern State, are the very best and most traveler friendly relief stations. If you use one of these mercy stops, please be sure to thank the kind-hearted souls who operate them—and it wouldn't hurt to patronize them, either. Most of them are in hotels that are convenient to the highway:

Rest Stops along the LIE:

Exit 40: Howard Johnson's
Exit 46: Howard Johnson's and Holiday Inn
Exit 49: Marriott (north service road)
   Hilton (Rte 110 southbound)
Exit 52 (eastbound): Hampton Inn
Exit 53 (westbound): Hampton Inn
Exit 57: Hampton Inn (south of the expressway)
Exit 58: Marriott Hotel
Exit 63: (Bathroom Heaven!)
   Best Western
   McDonald's
   Burger King
Exit 70: Mobil (a really nice Mobil!)
   Grace's Restaurant
   McDonald's

Rest Stops on the Southern State:

   Uniondale: the Marriott just off the Meadowbrook State
   Parkway, going west on the Hempstead Turnpike
   Route 110: McDonalds, just south of the parkway
   Seaford-Oyster Bay Expressway: McDonald's at
   Old Country Road

Rest Stops on the Sunrise: (near The Hamptons)
   Hampton Bays Diner, exit 64 (east)

There now, don't you feel better already?

HOW THE HAMPTONS ARE GOVERNED
(Who's in Charge Here?!)

All of The Hamptons are contained, of course, in Suffolk County. More precisely, the very eastern tip of Suffolk County. Our Congressman is currently Rep. Mike Forbes, a member of the Republican Revolution Class of '94 (and whatever happened to that "revolution"?!). Inexplicably, Mike had the temerity to switch parties last year. He's now a practicing Democrat in a Congressional district that is overwhelmingly Republican. I won't pretend to try and understand why a bright guy like Mike would make such a move, but if I were him, in this election year, I wouldn't be buying any green bananas for my apartment in D.C., if you catch my drift. The "long knives" of the burned Republican leaders are out and they are honing them to a fare-thee-well.

County Executive Bob Gaffney (R) is serving his third four-year term (having been handily re-elected last year). We have strong roots in county government because counties were an essential early element of local rule. Suffolk County has always been closely tied to the soil. Remember the terms "County Agent" and "County Agricultural Extension"? The traditions stretch back 300 years. County government is still powerful here. State government, on the other hand, is commonly referred to as "Those bastards in Albany."

Since we are geographically and politically as far from Albany as we are from Mars, we even have our own county legislature. It is relatively weak, but it is separate and distinct from the State Legislature and it is predominantly Republican.

Our current representative in Albany is a local boy and former Southampton Town Supervisor, Fred Thiele, who is (need I say it?) a Republican. Mr. Thiele took over from long-time local Representative, John Behan, who is Gov. Pataki's former Secretary for Veteran's Affairs. John is a combat-wounded veteran of Vietnam and after his State service has come home to Montauk. Rumor is he's contemplating another run for something. I hope so. He's a great guy.

Below the Federal, State, and County levels, each of the incorporated Towns and Villages has their own government and this is where 75 (+)% of what really matters to us, from a governmental standpoint, seems to happen. But there is one more interesting movement afoot centered at the county level: a proposal to create a new county just for the East End of Long Island. This new county would be called Peconic County. The proposal to create Peconic County has actually passed several organizational hurdles and did get on the local ballot, in 1997, as a referendum issue. It passed by a margin of 3-1 in favor.

Why Peconic County? The five incorporated towns of the East End (East Hampton, Southampton, Shelter Island, Riverhead, and Southold) are leading this drive. The officials running the East End feel that we have issues that are unique and different from the rest of Suffolk County; and, for once, the politicians may be right. Western Suffolk deals with the issues of urban sprawl, rapid population growth, provision of social services, and immigration. These issues are very different from eastern Suffolk's concerns, which are, primarily: agriculture, fishing, and tourism. With 8% of Suffolk's total population the East End pays 23% of the county's property taxes and 12% of the county's sales taxes. And taxes are a big issue for those of us who live here. Peconic County would, the "experts" predict, lower our property and other taxes substantially.

Will there ever be a Peconic County? Hard to say…even though the referendum passed, there's not much support for a new county in the State Legislature. The head of the State Senate, Sheldon Silver, has blocked every move to bring the bill to the floor of the Legislature. Why? Unclear, but his photo is beginning to appear on dart boards at local bars. Congressman Forbes told me that he felt nothing would ever happen with the creation of Peconic County until the State Legislature resolves the issue of Staten Island. The Staten Islanders have wanted to secede from New York City for many years and have voted to do so. Apparently, that issue is at the head of the queue.

Here on the South Fork, local government is vested in the incorporated Towns of East Hampton, Southampton, and Shelter Island. The Towns take care of the majority of the issues that affect us at the local level but there's more! To preserve the character and identity of the original settlement of the East End, there are still several Village governments, including, making matters even more confusing, East Hampton and Southampton. There are also Village governments for Sag Harbor, North Haven, Dering Harbor (on Shelter Island), and Westhampton Beach.

Now, where are Water Mill, Bridgehampton, Springs, Sagaponack,

Amagansett, Hampton Bays, and Montauk in all of this? These areas are known as "hamlets" and are overseen by the larger Town government most closely associated with each hamlet. Hampton Bays, Water Mill, Bridgehampton, and Sagaponack are hamlets of Southampton. Likewise, Springs, Amagansett, and Montauk are part of East Hampton. The residents of Montauk have been presented with ballot proposals on creating their own town but have voted them down consistently. There is a rumor afoot that Sagaponack, of all places, is trying to form its own town. Petitions are circulating. This is mostly in response to Mr. Ira Rennert being allowed to build his 29-bedroom, 30-bathroom, 58,000-square-foot "cottage."

It's sometimes confusing. There are two police departments in Southampton, one each for town and village. Does it all work? Actually, it works pretty well. There's a powerful incentive to make it work. We are a tourist-driven economy and we would soon come to grief if the services provided by police, fire protection, ambulances, building permits, beach safety, marriages, dog licensing, and so weren't done in a swift and efficient fashion.

That reminds me to say a few words on some people who never get enough credit: our local police and fire departments—including the County Sheriff. We can't say crime is non-existent out here. We certainly have our challenges, especially as our population grows. All in all, though, this is a very safe environment. Many people still leave their doors unlocked when they go to King Kullen. One of the most amusing sections of *Dan's Papers* is the Police Blotter. This weekly report will give you a pretty fair idea of what we're up against on the local crime scene. There's the weekly urination in a pubic place; the occasional theft of a pie cooling on a window sill; the usual "DUI's"; some petty juvenile vandalism; and, of course, there's the annual streaker in his Mercedes convertible. This guy shows up every year, zips around town, top down, wearing nothing but a pair of shades and a total-body sunburn.

There is a serious side to crime out here, and I'm not making light of that. I only wish to point out that with all the people, wealth, parties, and potential for abuse, we have very little cause for concern and this is attributable to the quality of our law enforcement.

There is one concern I will share with you, though. And it's something that our police struggle with every day. It's the war against drugs. It's such a problem and such a struggle, because the enemy is us. We bring the stuff out here, use it, abuse it, and create problems of our own making. There are, of course, no border checkpoints, and we can't station drug-sniffing dogs on Route 27 at Exit 65.

I don't believe we have a huge problem with illegal drugs in The Hamptons, but we sure have a concern. This societal scourge has, indeed, made its presence known here. Those who are foolish enough to do drugs elsewhere are not likely to stop doing it here just because the sun is out and the air is clean. But for those of you foolish enough to enhance your self-esteem chemically, be warned: tolerance for that sort of activity is very, very low out here. And the police have been well trained and they are looking for you. It's not just a matter of public safety, either. You must remember that The Hamptons are a tourist destination—one that does NOT want to become a drug haven. If you're inclined to this sort of stupidity, you are not welcome in our Paradise. And if that leaves you snickering, next time you're out, stop by the Suffolk County Jail and take the guided tour. Go ahead...it's free.

Our fire departments, depending on the Town or Village, tend to be mostly volunteer units. Your pool person may be the local assistant fire chief. But do not be "alarmed," to use a bad pun. Some of these men and women may be part-timers, but they are no less professional than the best full-time departments.

If you need evidence of that, all you'd have to do is review the news from the Westhampton Fire of the summer of '95. Tinder-dry conditions caused by the worst drought in years sent a large section of the local Pine Barrens spiraling toward the sky in dark clouds of fire, smoke, and ash. It could have been a disaster of epic proportion. Thanks to the superb, quick, and total efforts of these volunteers a tragedy that could have erased a large section of The Hamptons was avoided. And these folks did it all themselves. Not that they didn't ask for help. They did, principally in the form of U.S. Forest Service's aerial tankers. Remember that old joke, "Hi! We're from the government and we're here to help!"? Well, due to bureaucratic wrangling and sniping between Federal jurisdictions and the typical dithering characteristic of the Clinton Administration, the "help" never arrived. But that's another story. The important facts are that when it was all over, including fires that literally burned to the back doors of several Westhampton businesses, our local fire-fighting heroes got the job done. A grateful community hosted a parade and Appreciation Day for all 2,000 firefighters. When was the last time you heard about something like that being done?

REAL ESTATE IN THE HAMPTONS

Do the math! (1) We're running out of available acreage and (2) this is a very popular place. It's going to be expensive. First, a little history: The East End went through a raging boom market in the mid '80s. Then the recession at the end of the '80s and early '90s cooled things down considerably, even depressing prices some. But the resurgent economy of the last five years has reversed that slump and prices have taken off again. Building lots that you could have gotten in Water Mill four years ago for $125,000 are

now selling for $250,000. Homes that sold in Bridgehampton then for $750,000 are now $1.25 million. Many homes have doubled in value in the last few years, which is great, but what do you do if you want to sell? You'd have to buy something that has also doubled in value.

The market for homes and land this past year has been, in a word, nuts. It's been a season of full-price offers, all-cash deals, and very little inventory. Not even Jerry Seinfeld could get the first house he wanted. He bid some $10 million for a spot in East Hampton and, last second, someone else threw $11 million on the table and—bam!—Jerry's looking again. Well, he finally nailed down Billy Joel's old house. It only cost him $40 million!

Can you still find land and build that dream home or summer cottage without busting the bank? Yes. But be prepared to pay premium prices. And get a good real estate agent (see "Real Estate," below). Find one who really knows the East End and one who will take time to sit down with you and figure out what you really want and what you want to pay. If you're seriously considering doing something out here about ownership, I would suggest you rent for a season. Learn the lay of the land. Try things out. Drive around, look, taste, and touch. Stand in empty lots and try on the atmosphere. If it feels like your favorite old sweater, then that's the place you should buy. If renting for a season doesn't work, you can also try a summer share (but don't do it with more than four of your very closest friends!). As a great alternative, rent for a month or two in the early fall, after Labor Day, when prices are lower, the pace is slower, and there's more room for you to maneuver.

Yes, renting for a bit will delay buying something. Should you worry about the market "getting away from you"? Not really. I see too many people throwing money at land and homes just as they do high-definition TVs and the latest stock-du-jour. Buying a place out here is a big decision, I don't care how much money you have. Do it wisely. It has to be the right piece of property or the home that you look forward to racing to on Friday afternoon. If it is, then it doesn't matter. If it's not the right location or the community to match your personality—and all the towns and hamlets differ—you will not be happy. The money you've spent quickly just to "catch the market" will be money ill spent.

The absolute best times to buy something are, believe it or not, in June and November. By June the rental madness and seasonal buying has abated. If it hasn't rented or sold, it's almost too late for owners to "catch the season" and they'll bargain with you. November is also good because this is "post-season" and prices will drop to what the owner will really accept "bottom line." Prices start to climb again in January, since that's when the bonus checks start arriving on Wall Street.

Where are the best values? You will quickly learn that all real estate in The Hamptons has two broad geographic divisions: "North of the Highway" and "South of the Highway." South of the Highway is any land that is south of Montauk Highway. This land is the acreage that borders the Atlantic. It is the most expensive land. It is supposedly the most desirable land. At a Hamptons cocktail party full of strangers where you own land quickly defines who you are and how much money you have. ("Are you North of the Highway or South? You're North? Oh, I see.")

Now, if you're into value, don't give a rat's patoot about who you might meet at one of "those" parties, and are buying something to pine and fuss over, it's OK...go North of the Highway. At least look...Matt Lauer did. He just bought 16 acres in the Deerfield area, north of the highway. Maybe it'll start a whole new trend.

ACCOMMODATIONS

We've put all the different types of accommodations together under one roof, so to speak. Whether you're looking for that cute little B & B or a full service resort, they're all here.

Bed & Breakfasts:

For a community as large and popular as this one, you'd think we'd have many more entries in this category, but we don't since so many people rent homes and then share space. The B&B community is growing, though, and what we do have is excellent. For our Guide, I've also made an arbitrary division between B&B's and Inns. I figure if you're looking for a bed & breakfast you're after small, cute, and personal. If you want something a little larger with a few more amenities, but not a Holiday Inn, you're after a true, old-fashioned Inn. Here are the Guide's award winning B & B's and inns for the fifth edition:

✪✪✪✪ **1708 House**, 126 Main St., Southampton, 287-1708, next to Saks. This is, without question, the premier B&B in The Hamptons. This regal old house was an eyesore until the new owners, Skip and Lorraine Ralph, extensively renovated the place three years ago and turned this property into a real gem. There are four rooms in the 18th Century "original" house, four rooms in the 20th Century east Wing, one room in the South Wing and three very special cottages. Fresh flowers, shiny hardwood floors, wonderful furniture and antiques, and a breakfast to savor. The rooms range from $175 to $275 and the cottages run from $325 to $395 per night, in season with, yes, a three-night minimum. Most of the rooms are already totally booked for the season but call anyway. You might pick up a cancellation. You should also try it in off-season when the rates drop to about half of the in-season rates.

✪✪✪✪ Here's another "golden nugget" right in the heart of Southampton: **The Ivy**, 244 North Main St., 283-3233. This historic building, built in the 1860's, reflects the grand style of The Hamptons in the pre-Victorian era, when the first real country mansions were built. Every room is sumptuous and distinctively decorated. The Ivy is also one of the rare B&B's that has its own pool, so when you're done shopping at all the nearby stores, you can jump in for a quick dip before heading back for an evening on the town. Continental breakfast and afternoon refreshments are served daily. Room rates range from $175 to $295 per night, double occupancy, with a two-night minimum on weekends, three-night minimum on the major holidays. No pets, smoking outdoors only but kids over 12 are welcome. Nice, nice place. Try it!

✪✪✪✪ **The House on Newtown,** 172 Newtown Lane, East Hampton, 324-1858, fax, 329-0762: Lovely, turn-of-the-century bed and breakfast filled with warmth, antiquity, and charm. Walk to restaurants, boutiques, tennis, jitney, theaters, art galleries in the Village; or, bike to the beach. Complimentary breakfasts on a sun-filled porch. Air-conditioned, all rooms with private baths. Special weekly packages available. Daily maid service, beach passes. Featured in *Inn Spots* and *Away for the Weekend*.

✪✪✪ **Mill House Inn,** 33 N. Main St., East Hampton, 324-9766, fax 324-9793, website: www.millhouseinn.com. Loving touches have rebuilt this 1790-era home into a first-rate B&B (despite the "Inn" title). Each guestroom has been individually decorated around a theme: Hampton Classic, Garden Room, Rose Room, etc. A great deal of attention has been spent on hand-painted furniture, antique tubs, fireplaces in some rooms, whirlpools in most rooms, luxurious linens and towels, etc. Full gourmet breakfasts are included along with an afternoon snack! In season rates for '00 will be $235–$425 and off-season rates will be $125–$225.

✪✪✪ **J. Harper Poore Cottage,** 181 Main St., East Hampton, 324-4081. This place is constantly booked. It has just seven rooms. The cottage was featured in *Gourmet* magazine not long ago. Check it out; but, need I tell you it's going to be expensive and will only do two night minimums in season?

✪✪✪ Morning Glory House, Montauk Hwy., Bridgehampton, 537-2324, fax 537-4260. Morning Glory is on the Highway just east of Bridgehampton. It's a Victorian with five suites and king size beds; three suites have private baths. The landscaping is very nice and they have a wrap-around gazebo porch. The Peach Blossom Suite is the largest and can actually accommodate a family of four. Full breakfasts are served daily. Rates in season are from $200 with the usual two night minimums.

✪✪✪ Centennial House, 13 Woods Lane, East Hampton, 324-9414. Just a few steps from Main Street, this turn-of-the-century Colonial has received excellent reviews from *Frommer's*, *Best Places*, etc. There are only five rooms, but they are spectacular. Registration includes an English country parlor, breakfast, and lovely grounds to stroll. Rooms range from $200 to 375 in high season to $150 and up in "quiet season."

✪✪✪ Can't find an old, historic house that suits your idea of a B&B? Then build one! That's exactly what the owners of **A Victorian on the Bay** did. This newly constructed, year round B&B can be reached at 325-1000 or 1-888-449-0620. The Inn is at 57 South Bay Avenue in Eastport (5 minutes before Westhampton). Check out their website at www.victorianonthebay.com. Great views of the water, king-size featherbeds, private decks, fireplaces, afternoon tea, and more! Rates run from $225 to $325 in high season to $157 to $227 in the off season.

✪✪ Greenhedges, 80 Essex St., Montauk, 668-5013. A winner for Montauk. Friends from England stayed here last summer and they were very pleased. Rates are very reasonable, too, from $75 to $175 in season and $65 to $85 in the off season.

Hotels and Motels:

The last chain hotel near us is in Riverhead. It's a Ramada Inn next to Exit 72 off the L.I.E. There are no Marriott's, Hiltons, Four Seasons, or anything of the type east of Route 111. Please note, even though some of these places use Inn in their names, they are hotels. For true Inns scroll down to the next sub-category.

✪✪✪✪ **The American Hotel,** Main Street, Sag Harbor, 725-3535, fax: 725-3573. The hotel dates back to 1846, when Sag Harbor was a whaling town and The American Hotel has the charm reminiscent of those days. Only eight guestrooms but they are lovingly decorated and feature lots of antiques. To the rear of the lobby is a beautiful bar and wood-paneled atrium dining room. Cozy and wonderful best describes this first-rate place. Rooms are booked far in advance, so get on their list now! Rates are $200 (+) per night in season, with two night minimums.

✪✪✪✪ **Enclave Inn,** Main St., Bridgehampton, 537-0197. Owned and operated by our good friends Michael and Suzanne Wudyka. What a wonderful job this terrific couple has done with this location! Sparkling rooms, great decoration, lots of loving touches. Weekend specials are available in Spring and Fall. They have a pool and spacious grounds to lounge about. Ten rooms, ranging in price from $100 to $200 in season. Open year round and they have a website at www.enclaveinn.com.

✪✪✪✪ **The Montauk Yacht Club Resort & Marina,** 32 Star Island Rd., Montauk, 668-3100. Despite the "private" sounding title, this is a public hotel and marina—and a great one! It has over 100 rooms, 3 pools, tennis courts, a 225-slip marina, exercise facilities, sauna, and restaurant (The Lighthouse Grill). In season, rooms start at $300 and go up to $350 with the usual two-night minimum on busy summer weekends. Off-season, it's a great bargain with many rooms dropping below $100. Myra and I had our honeymoon weekend here last November and they couldn't have treated us more graciously!

✪✪✪✪ **The Panoramic View,** 272 Old Montauk Highway, Montauk, 668-3000. Nestled on a thousand feet of prime beachfront, right down Old Montauk Highway (next to Gurney's Inn), you'll find Ellis French's wonderful Panoramic View. And it is panoramic. There are 114 rooms here and three beach houses. Rates unavailable at press time—call and book early!

✪✪✪ **The Beachcomber,** 727 Old Montauk Highway, Montauk, 668-2894. There are 88 rooms here and every one of them has an ocean view. There's also a heated pool if you don't feel like wandering across the highway to wriggle your toes in the surf. Saunas are available and there are kitchens in the rooms. Rates are actually pretty moderate, starting at $115 for a lower deck room, $120-$125 for the upper deck. After June, the rates go up about $50 per room per night.

✪✪✪ **Sunset Beach Hotel,** 35 Shore Rd., Shelter Island, 749-2001. If you want fun, this is it! Plus, it's literally on the beach. There are only twenty rooms here, each with its own private sundeck, so book early. If you do, you'll feel like you're back in the '70's. Remember those canvas chairs with the metal legs? The glass-top coffee tables encased in chrome? The twill bed covers? The slightly musty smell of salt water and sand? Ahh, wonderful! They allow pets (one of the few places that do), and they can arrange horseback riding, tennis, volleyball in the sand, sailing, fishing, and more. Closed in winter.

✪✪ **The Southampton Inn,** 91 Hill St., Southampton, at the end of Job's Lane, next to the movie theatre, 283-6500. This feels and acts like an upscale Hampton Inn (pun intended!), but the rooms are nice and they have conference facilities for business meetings. Its location, in the heart of town, cannot be beat. If you can't find a friend to stay with, this is the place to go. Rates run from $189 to $349 in season and $99 to $139 off-season, with a two-night minimum. Note: Ownership here has just changed. The new owners are promising many upgrades and improvements and intend to turn the property into a first-rate conference center. This would be wonderful for our community.

✪✪ **Gurney's Inn,** 290 Old Montauk Highway, Montauk, 668-2345. It seems as if Gurney's has been around forever (Well, forty-two years this year, anyway). Perched on a set of dunes at one of the finest natural beaches in the world, Gurney's has much to brag about. The views and the amenities are first rate. The restaurant is excellent, the bar is fun, and you can get your own private masseuse or a simple massage in the hotel's spa facilities. Rooms range, in season, from $330 for an ocean view room to $390 for an ocean front room. Sounds steep, but included in that is a dinner allowance ($50 for 2), two American breakfasts, and unlimited use of the spa facilities (massages extra!). Two night minimum on weekends.

✪✪ **The Sag Harbor Inn,** West Water St., Sag Harbor, 725-2949. Forty-two rooms here, most of them with decks overlooking the harbor.

Great heated pool, country pine furniture, and an easy walk to some of the best restaurants around. Rates are pretty reasonable, starting at $85 for a weeknight and $195 on a weekend night. The rooms with better views go up to $295 a night on weekends.

✪✪ **Montauk Manor,** 236 Edgemere St., Montauk, 668-4400. It's the Roaring 20's. Money and booze are flowing freely in Old Montauk, which was a notorious smuggling port for then-illegal "hooch." The man who originally developed most of Miami Beach throws money into a Tudor Castle atop Signal Hill in Montauk and opens the doors to his dream resort in 1927. Two years later his money and most of Montauk Manor are sliding down the black hole known as the Great Crash of '29. The Manor stands lonely and dark for many years until it is carefully restored in the early 90's. It's an interesting project: 140 condo apartments, pools, tennis courts, and conference facilities. Might be worth a try. Pretty good rates, too: $160 to $360 in season and $85 to $185 off-season.

Inns:

OK, we've covered B&B's and Hotels/Motels. Let's tackle the Inns. What's the difference between an Inn and the others? Well, in my view, Inns are "Inn-Between" B&B's and Hotels. That is to say, larger than a B&B, with more amenities, but smaller than what most of us think of when we visualize a hotel. Inns, in my mind, also take you back in time to the days of the carriage trade, when well-heeled travelers expected a fine night's lodging and a sumptuous meal when they stopped for the night. Note: all of these inns, like the B&B's, tend to have 2 or 3 night minimums in season (May through September).

✪✪✪✪**The Maidstone Arms,** 207 Main St., East Hampton, 324-5006. This elegant inn dates from 1740. It has been redecorated and boasts country quilts and easy chairs in all the rooms. This also happens to be the location of one of the East End's finest restaurants. They have a very civilized afternoon tea service in the Wicker Room; or, if you chose to dine here, you may slip out after dinner and sit on the front porch. You'll be overlooking the exquisitely beautiful village green and pond. Watch the swans glide by as you sip an after dinner drink. The Maidstone rates start at $195 and go up to $375.

✪✪✪ Bridgehampton Inn, 2266 Main St., Bridgehampton, 537-3660. This colonial was built in 1795 and has kept to its architectural roots except for big, modernized baths with lots of marble! The whole place is very elegant and is run by Anna Pump, who is locally famous as the author of the very popular cookbook *Loaves & Fishes*. Needless to say, the food's great. Expensive but worth it. Rooms start at $210, with continental breakfast included.

✪✪✪ Hedges Inn, 74 James Ln., East Hampton, 324-7100. The Hedges Inn overlooks the town pond at the head of what has been called the most beautiful Main Street in America and is listed on The National Register of Historic Places. Only eleven rooms, though, with dining at the nearby James Lane Cafe. Rooms start at $165 to $325, breakfast included.

✪✪✪ Huntting Inn, 94 Main St., East Hampton, 324-0410. A beautiful, country elegant sort of place that has the added attraction of well kept lawns and gardens to stroll through. It's also where you'll find one of the best steak places in The Hamptons: The Palm. Rooms start at $195 and go to $325, breakfast included.

ACCOUNTANTS

There are a number of good accounting firms out here, but we want to recommend the best. Now, I admit, I could be accused of a certain loss of objectivity here in that this lovely, talented lady also happens to be my wife! But you should understand that I found this good woman honestly and totally above board. She was exactly the professional that I needed when I was in deep doo-doo, from an accounting standpoint. I've known many accounting professionals over my many years in business and she is, hands down, the most competent I have ever run across. Heck, I would have married her for her accounting skills alone, but she's also beautiful, smart, and very dedicated.

✪✪✪✪✪ **Myra Rosen** (Keith), MBA, CPA, 33 Flying Pt. Rd., Suite 224, Southampton, 287-5559. Myra performs a wide variety of accounting and taxation services for individuals and businesses. She is especially adept in situations vis-a-vis those ever-helpful public "servants" at the IRS. She also has a Manhattan number at 212-447-5958.

AERIAL MESSAGES

Hey! Here's something unique and different—Aerial Banners! Ever want to propose to your fiancée with a real flair? Announce the launch of a new product? Hire an aerial towing company to drag that message across the sky over every beach in the Hamptons!

✪✪✪✪ **Aero-Tag Inc.,** Gabreski Airport, Westhampton Beach, 281-1244.

A.I.D.S.

We are a special community here on the East End, but we are not immune from the challenges of HIV and AIDS. There is a local Hotline for AIDS information at 385-AIDS. The Hotline is staffed Mon–Fri from 8 AM to 8 PM and weekends from 10 AM to 6 PM. You should also talk to the folks at The David E. Rogers, M.D. Center for HIV/AIDS Care, 335 D Meeting House Lane, Southampton, 287-5990 (associated with Southampton Hospital).

The Hamptons is a party place for lots of us...time to make new friends, start new relationships. Let me just say that the worst way to start a relationship is with unprotected sex. OK, OK...I'll stop editorializing.

AIR CONDITIONING

We've already talked about the natural air conditioning we seem to enjoy out here. On even the hottest summer days we are generally blessed with

gentle ocean breezes to cool us. Last summer I think there were—
maybe—a total of 10 days when you actually might have wanted a central
air conditioning system. Makes me wonder why we even have air conditioning at all; but, like everything else, if you don't have it, there will come a
time when you wish you did. If you do want air conditioning or need to get
your current system serviced, try these guys.

✪✪✪✪ **(Gold) Hardy Heating & Air Conditioning, Inc.,** 1654 County
Road 39, Southampton, 287-1674 and fax at 287-1673: They are
the best at responding quickly-even in the middle of a heat wave.
And you should have thought about getting your unit serviced last
Spring when we weren't in the middle of a heat wave! Hardy does
both residential and commercial work on-time and for a fair price.
Courteous staff, expert technicians, and they cover the entire North
and South Forks.

AIRCRAFT CHARTERS

The closest airport to The Hamptons is East Hampton Airport. Operating out
of East Hampton are two charter companies that we would recommend.

✪✪✪✪ **East Hampton Airlines** at 537-3737 or 1-800-FLY TO LI. East
Hampton Airlines operates on-call 24 hours a day and flies jets and
props, multi and single engine. They can arrange helicopters and
seaplanes, too. If you want to extend your weekend until early
Monday morning, hop on a seaplane and glide to a stop on the
East River a few blocks from the office, give these guys a call. They

also fly to over 12,000 airports, big and small, all over the Northeast and operate a semi-scheduled service between East Hampton and LaGuardia. It's actually a shared charter. Call for schedules, but there are a couple of flights a day and more on Fridays and weekends. Cost is currently $129 one-way, which may seem a little steep, but there have been some nights when I was gridlocked on the LIE that I would have gladly paid twice as much.

✪✪✪ Another charter service that comes highly recommended is **T.D. Aviation**. They operate out of Farmingdale's Republic Airport, up island, but they can be out here in a flash. Call 753-5757.

AIRPORTS

There are three airports accessible to the East End (unless you count several grass strips for general aviation). The largest and most commercial, by far, is MacArthur Airport, sometimes referred to as Islip or Long Island-MacArthur Airport. The town of Islip owns and operates the airfield. Islip is about 40 miles from Southampton. You can get to anywhere from Islip.

USAirways Express has the most flights and the most destinations: Albany, Baltimore-Washington, Boston, Ft. Myers (Florida), Philadelphia, Providence, Syracuse, Tampa, and West Palm Beach.

Spirit Airlines flies to Florida, specifically: Ft. Myers, Tampa, and West Palm Beach.

American Airlines has daily service to Chicago

Business Express Airlines (Delta commuter airline) flies to and from Boston

ComAir (another Delta partner) goes to and from Cincinnati

Delta Express Airlines (the low fare version) goes to Orlando and Ft. Lauderdale

Southwest Airlines has landed and is offering about 12 daily flights to hubs such as Nashville, Baltimore-Washington and Chicago (Midway).

Sunjet International (another low fare carrier) flies to Ft. Lauderdale

Islip has just completed a $13 million dollar expansion program. The renovations doubled the size of the terminal, expanded parking by 300 spaces and vastly improved the baggage handling capabilities of the airport. And I have to say that I like going in and out of Islip, even if it means an extra stop along the way to make a connection. It's just so much easier to park, get checked in; and, coming home, it's a breeze to get back out to your car and on the way home. Parking is currently $6.50 per day and the spaces are right in front of the terminal. Try it! Sure beats the mess at LaGuardia and JFK.

The other two local airports are Westhampton Beach Airport and East Hampton Airport and both are dominated by general aviation. Neither has scheduled airline service.

Westhampton is partly an Air National Guard base and has an active Air Force Rescue Squadron. Westhampton also houses a number of aviation training facilities. It is only 15 miles from Southampton, so, if you have your own aircraft and need a place to park, it's a good spot.

East Hampton Airport is certainly convenient to all The Hamptons. Most weekends in summer you will see a dazzling array of personal aircraft parked on the tarmac along with a few corporate jets and a private helicopter or two. There are charter services available to fly you to other major airports (see "Aircraft Charters") and private flying instruction is available. For general airport information, call the Airport Manager's office at 537-1130.

AIRPORT TRANSPORTATION
(see also "Limos" and "Taxis")

There are several airport shuttle services to and from The Hamptons.

Islip (MacArthur Airport) Connections:
Hampton Jitney 283-4600 (but you have to take a short cab ride to the airport from the drop point just off the LIE).

Classic (701-2085) operates shared-ride passenger vans (about $45 one-way)

Standard taxi service (about $70 one-way) is available, too.

LaGuardia Connections:
Other than a limo, the absolute best way is to take Hampton Jitney (283-4600) to the LaGuardia Airport connection stop in Queens. There's a cab connection service (718-279-4444) working with the Jitney that will have a cab waiting to take you the rest of the way to LaGuardia (about $5 extra). The Jitney ride, one way, is $20. It works the same way in reverse. But don't put yourself on a tight schedule. Give yourself plenty of time to make your flight—I'd say leaving The Hamptons 3 hours in advance would do it.

If you go the limo route, call Mollie at Southampton Limo, 287-0001 or Hampton Jitney Limo at 287-4000. The cost isn't that bad.

Kennedy Connections:

The Jitney connection to Kennedy works the same as LaGuardia (see above) it's just a slightly longer cab ride. Other than driving yourself to the airport (which is a pain in the you-know-what) this is your best and "least expensive" choice. I checked with the best-known blue shuttle service and, yes, they'll come to The Hamptons from either LaGuardia or Kennedy, but you have to guarantee the entire bus cost of $125 one-way! Talk about highway robbery! You could also take a limo. Considering the cost of gas, parking, wear-and-tear and so forth, it's not a bad alternative. Call Hampton Jitney Limo (287-4000) or Mollie at Southampton Limo (287-0001). The ride will be a lot more comfortable—and private.

ALARM COMPANIES (see also "Security Companies")

We have an alarm system connected to a central monitoring station. If the alarm goes off, the central station calls us. If we're not home (or can't answer!) they call the police. The alarm company also has a list of contacts that we have given them. After the police are called, the alarm company calls our contact list, trying to track us down. We also have a 'panic button' and a special voice code. The bad news is that the local Police will only give you a couple of "free" mistakes a year. After that they start charging for false alarms. It's $25 a pop in Southampton. We do not have patrol service. Since we live here full time, we didn't think that was necessary. If you don't live here full time, you should give patrol service some consideration. The other thing you must do is keep your alarm notification list updated. When the alarm goes off, and you're not around, the alarm company will start calling your list. If cousin Vinnie is at the top of your list and he moved to Columbus two years ago, the alarm company will have a hard time finding you. If you're off on an extended holiday, fax the alarm company a number where you can be reached or at least give them the name and number of someone who can find you.

Alarm Service (only):
✪✪✪✪ **General Security** (central monitoring—no patrols): 349-8989, and about $300 per year.

Alarm and regular patrol service:
✪✪✪✪ **Bellringer Communications**: 283-3400
✪✪✪ **Holmes Protection**: 283-0569

AMBULANCES

All of the ambulance services on the East End are either operated by the local fire departments or are volunteer and independent services. Not that you much care. When you need an ambulance, you don't give a darn whose ambulance races to the house as long as the people operating it are qualified. On that score, whether the ambulance is Southampton's lime green color scheme or Amagansett's red and blue, you can rest assured that the people in the trucks are EMTs and certified professionals. **SPECIAL NOTE:** 9-1-1 is now effective in all areas of the East End. So, if you need an ambulance in an emergency, call 9-1-1.

If you need an Ambulette (non-emergency service) you might try giving one of these folks a call:

(NR) **All Island Ambulette,** 224-1414
(NR) **Island Wide Ambulette,** 665-0044

If you need an air ambulance, call:

(NR) **Air Ambulance by Air Response** (NYS Certified), 800-631-6565, 24-hour-a-day service.

ANIMALS/ANIMAL CONTROL (see also
"Cats," "Dogs," "Pest Control" and "Wildlife Removal")

Animal control in The Hamptons is more than keeping your hormones in check at a raucous beach party.

I found out first hand that this is a curious and somewhat confusing area of Town and Village government. I had a wild cat problem and the blasted cats were jumping all over the birds at my bird feeder. I called Southampton town and asked them to please come and remove the cats, humanely, of course. "No, can't do that. You'll have to call a professional removal service. Yes, we do have a Dog Warden (as does East Hampton), and we'll come get your wild or stray dogs, if you have any, but, sorry, not the cats." What's the difference? Is this sanctioned animal discrimination by our local governments? Actually, it's more of a budget issue. The Town and Village animal control people have to pretty much deal with the emergencies; that is, wild or stray dogs (dogs are generally bigger than cats), rabid raccoons, deer struck down on the highways, and so forth. By the way, I got rid of the cats by giving up my bird bath type bird feeder and going to tree-only feeders. Now I have squirrels...Oh, well.

ANIMAL HOSPITALS

We don't have any pets at home, so
we have relied on friends who do to select our winners in this category.
Here is a list of the best animal hospitals by location.

East Hampton:

✪✪✪✪ **East Hampton Veterinary Group,** 22 Montauk Highway, 324-0282

✪✪✪✪ **Veterinary Clinic of East Hampton,** 3 Goodfriend, 324-7900
Hampton Bays:

✪✪✪✪ **Shinnecock Animal Hospital,** 2121 East Montauk Hwy., 723-0500 (also provides grooming, boarding & pet health foods).

Southampton:

✪✪✪✪ **Southampton Animal Hospital,** Bishops Ln., 283-1094
Wainscott:

✪✪✪✪ **South Fork Animal Hospital,** Montauk Highway., 537-0035
Westhampton

✪✪✪✪ **Westhampton Beach Animal Hospital,** 126 Montauk Hwy., 288-8535.

ANIMAL SHELTERS

Boy, this is big stuff out here, protecting animals. One of the biggest summer benefit parties is run by the Animal Rescue Fund (otherwise known as ARF!, don't you just love it?!) in Wainscott, 537-0400. You can call ARF for advice on just about any of your animal problems. Other good resources are:

Wildlife Control of Long Island, 722-2666

Southampton Town Dog Warden, 653-5900 (they have a shelter).

ANIMAL RESCUE

No, this is not about bailing your buddy out of the slammer after an inebriated public pee against a storefront window on Jobs Lane. This is about rescuing non-human wildlife that has been injured, orphaned, or otherwise in trouble.

The first rule of thumb is: Wildlife is just that: WILD. It's probably better that you just be an observer and reporter and leave the actual animal handling up to the experts. If you think you have an orphan or abandoned wild animal on your hands, call one of the following organizations.

East Hampton:

Veterinary Clinic of East Hampton, 324-7900
East Hampton Veterinary Group, 324-0282

Shelter Island:

Wild Animal Rehabilitation Center, Inc., Shelter Island, 749-0708

Southampton:

Heart of the Wild Rehabilitation Centre, Inc., Southampton, 287-5428
Olde Towne Animal Hospital, Southampton, 283-0611

ANTIQUES (AND ANTIQUE DEALERS)

You gotta be careful. There are true antique dealers, there are people who deal in "junk" passing it off as "antique," and there are people mixing antiques with "reproductions" and calling themselves antique dealers. How do you know the difference? First, you ask! Every reliable dealer will quickly point out what's truly antique and what's a "repro." How do you know what's of value and what's just, plain "junk"? Now, that's a little harder. I've been in places out here that looked as if someone just cleaned out an attic and a garage and then opened an "antique shop." The true professionals will be able to show you the heritage on any piece that's truly antique. They can do this via any number of reliable printed resources or through documentation on the piece itself. So, how do you know the Century Period tilt table is really one hundred years old? You don't, unless you're an expert. Even if you are an expert, but especially if you're not, ask for a letter or even just a hand written note from the dealer attesting to the age and authenticity of your new prized possession. They could still lie, but the good ones don't.

Are people looking for fine antiques out here? Yes, to some extent. But I think most people are looking for something to put in the beach house. We are, therefore, going to make a distinction between "fine" antiques and "fun" antiques.

The "Fine" Antiques:

✪✪✪✪✪ **Legendary Collections** (at Bull's Head Inn), corner of Ocean Road and Montauk Hwy., Bridgehampton, 537-2211. This is that big, white colonial at the east end of Main Street in Bridgehampton across from The Monument. See Justine Marko, the lovely lady who owns the place. 18th and 19th Century antiques are her specialty. And these are true antiques, beautifully presented, and lovingly displayed. I think this is the best antique store in The Hamptons, and with two floors of space and lots of rooms, there's really a chance to see how a piece looks in a room, not just displayed in a cramped shop. There's an old marble topped bar I'd love to have in our basement, an inlaid table that would look wonderful in our dining room, and...oh, well...I could go on. I also like Justine's sense of fun. There's a large tabletop sign just inside the door as you enter. It says: "Your husband called ahead and said you could buy anything you want!"

✪✪✪✪ **Balasses House,** Main Street, Amagansett, 267-3032.

✪✪✪✪ **Victory Gardens,** 63 Main St., East Hampton, 324-7800.

✪✪✪✪ **Lars Bolander,** 74 Montauk Hwy., East Hampton, 329-3400

✪✪✪✪ **Architrove,** 74 Montauk Hwy., East Hampton, 329-2229

✪✪✪✪ **Donna Parker Habitat,** Montauk Hwy., Water Mill, 726-9311

The "Fun" Antiques:

✪✪✪✪ **English Country Antiques,** Snake Hollow Road, Bridgehampton (behind the Bridgehampton Commons), 537-0606

✪✪✪✪ **Carriage House Antiques,** 12 Main St., Sag Harbor, 725-8004, fax 725-8006

✪✪✪✪ **Nellie's,** 230 Main St., Amagansett, 267-1000

✪✪✪✪ **Ruby Beet's,** 1703 Montauk Hwy., Bridgehampton, 537-2802

✪✪✪ **Chez Morgan**, 53 Jobs Lane, Southampton, 287-3595

✪✪✪ **Fisher's,** corner of Main and Spring Streets, Sag Harbor, 725-0006

✪✪ **Simply French,** Main St., Bridgehampton, 537-7444

APARTMENT RENTAL PROBLEMS
(see "Renters' Problems")

APPLES & APPLE PICKING

✪✪✪✪ **Halsey Farm,** Mecox Road, Water Mill, 537-0175. When the first nippy days of Fall come calling, this is the place to be. John Halsey and his family, who have been planting and harvesting apples here for 20 years, have set up the finest "U-Pick" apple operation on the East End. What could be more exhilarating than walking down row after row of trees bulging with all types of fat, juicy apples, and bagging them yourself, right off the tree? Bring the kids! Show them what country life was like. By the way, when the farm opens, usually in early September (lasting to November) Mr. Halsey has a field next to the orchard overflowing with pumpkins of all sizes. The kiddies can pick their own jack-o'-lanterns for Halloween. Note: The Halsey's also operate The Milk Pail farm stand just down the road (see "Farm Stands").

AREA CODES (phone)

In May of 2000 all Suffolk County switched from the 516 area code to 631. Printing companies are ecstatic. Nassau County gets to keep our old 516 area code. But to make matters even more confusing, Suffolk County cell phones keep the 516 prefix.

ARCHITECTS

Architects are required to hold a license from the state. Licensed architects can "seal" your building plans or major home improvements, which means, in most cases, getting them accepted by the various city, town, and state agencies. If you have any questions about an architect or architectural firm you have employed or are thinking about employing, call the State Education Dept., Board of Architects , 518-474-3930.

✪✪✪✪ **Preston Phillips,** Bridgehampton, 537-1237. Preston has been designing award-winning homes here in The Hamptons for more than 20 years. Some of his designs (including his own home) have graced the pages of *Architectural Digest.*

ART

Ever had the urge to take up the brush? Can't draw a straight line with a ruler? There's hope for you...a place where you can indulge that life-long

wish to become the next Van Gogh (be careful around razors, please!).
Also a fabulous way to augment your summer, taking a few art classes.

✪✪✪✪ There's a local institution called **"The Art Barge."** It opened in
1960, under the auspices of the Museum of Modern Art. It's in
Amagansett, by the water, in Napeague Harbor. They have classes
on all kinds of painting, drawing, photography, printmaking,
collage, work in clay, etc. This is also a great place for the kiddies
to spend some quality time (thereby getting you a reprieve!). To
find out what's happening this summer or to get a schedule of
classes give them a call at 267-3172 or write them at P.O. Box
1266, Amagansett, NY, 11930.

ART GALLERIES AND ART DEALERS

The Hamptons is very much an artist's haven. Some of the world's best
known artists have worked and/or lived here at one time or another
(Jackson Pollock and De Kooning, for example). It's not like The Village, or
Montmarte, mind you, but the same attractions of earth, sea and sky that
all of us love are perfect for practicing artists. To support the local artistic
community we have a number of very interesting and reliable galleries. Our
favorites are listed below.

✪✪✪✪ **Elaine Benson Gallery,** Inc., Montauk Highway, Bridgehampton,
537-3233. Elaine was a fixture on the local scene for many years.
Sadly, she passed away in 1998 after losing her battle with lym-
phoma. Feisty, creative Elaine seemed to be everywhere on the art
scene here in The Hamptons. She penned a weekly column in
Dan's Papers for many years, wrote her own hilarious book *The
History of Underwear*, and ran the best-known art gallery in the
Hamptons. Over the years Elaine helped many a struggling artist to
show his or her works. She was a true patron. The gallery goes on
now under the care of Elaine's daughter, Kimberly Goff. Call for
details on current showings.

✪✪✪ **Chrysalis Gallery,** 92 Main St., Southampton, 287-1883. After all
of Jackson Pollock's "dribbles," DeKooning's "spots and dots" and
Roy Lichtenstein's "pop art," it's nice to have a little dose of "reality." This gallery actual has paintings I can understand without an
interpreter! Wonderful paintings, like local seascapes, farm scenes,
gardens, and so forth. Some pretty clever sculpture, too.

ART MUSEUMS

As mentioned above, there is a strong tradition for art and artists here in The Hamptons. The exhibition of some very important works is upheld well by the following first-rate places.

✪✪✪✪ **The Parrish Art Museum,** 25 Job's Ln., Southampton, 283-2118 ($2 admission fee for non-members, $1 for students and seniors; annual memberships are available starting at $15). There's always something good going on here, for art patrons of all ages. There are Family Fun Days, American Art exhibitions, evening films, lively lectures, and special events, including the Midsummer Gala. There's also a fine Museum Shop in the lobby: jewelry, publications, posters, children's items, and more! The Parrish has a strong program scheduled for this year.

✪✪✪ **Pollack-Krasner House and Study Center,** 830 Fireplace Rd., East Hampton, 324-4929 ($5 admission fee). This is the former home of the world-renowned abstractionist Jackson Pollack and his wife, artist Lee Krasner. Pollack, who has just had a major retrospective at the MoMA in The City, worked here from 1945 until his death in a car crash in 1956. There is still paint from his brushes scattered on the floor. (Lord! I wonder how much the floor would be worth if you could rip it up and frame it?!) There is an appointment-only reference library as well as changing exhibits, lectures, and symposia. Call for current information.

✪✪ **Dan Flavin Art Institute,** Corwith Ave., Bridgehampton, 537-1476. Artists love the light out here, as we have pointed out before, but the late and creative artist Dan Flavin craved a different kind of light: fluorescence. You can see the results of his unique work here, as well as other interesting and changing exhibits.

✪ **Guild Hall,** 158 Main St., East Hampton, 342-0806. A haven for local theater, Guild Hall also houses many fine works from East End artists. You can view the efforts of the 19th Century landscape artist Thomas Moran as well as later styles represented by artists like Dennis Oppenheim, Pat Steir and "bad boy" Julian Schnabel.

ATMs (Locations)

They're all over the place, but here's where you'll find some of them (by town).

Amagansett

Brent's Market, Montauk Hwy.
IGA, Montauk Hwy.
Mobil Station, Montauk Hwy.

Bridgehampton

Bridgehampton Nat'l Bank, Montauk Hwy.*
King Kullen, Bridgehampton Common

East Hampton

Apple Bank, 50 Montauk Hwy.
Bank of New York, 66 Main St.
Bridgehampton Nat'l., 26 Park Pl.
North Fork Bank, 40 Newtown Ln.
Suffolk Cty. National Bank
    351 Pantigo Rd.
    100 Park Pl.

Hampton Bays

North Fork Bank, 93 E. Montauk Hwy.*
Suffolk Cnty. Nat'l, Montauk Hwy.

Montauk

inside **Gurney's Inn**
Bank of New York, at the circle
Suffolk Cty. Nat'l
    744 Montauk Highway
    West Lake Dr.

Sag Harbor

7-11, W. Water St.
Apple Bank, Main St.
North Fork Bank, West Water St.
Suffolk Cnty Nat'l Bank, 17 Main St.

Sagaponack

(none)

Shelter Island

North Fork Bank, 29 West Neck Rd.

Southampton

7-11, Cnty. Rd. 39 & North Sea Rd.
Astoria Federal, 65 Nugent St.
Chase Bank, Main St.
Southampton Hospital, Hampton Rd., Southhampton
Southampton Town Hall, Hampton Rd.
Suffolk Cnty. Nat'l Bank, 295 N. Sea Rd.*
North Fork Bank, 46 Windmill Lane*

Wainscott

(none)

Water Mill

Mobil Station, Montauk Hwy.

Westhampton Beach

Astoria Federal Savings, 71 Sunset Ave.
Bank of New York, 154 Main

*Best ATM's to drive through and not have to get out of your car!!!

AUTOMOBILES

There is a fair scattering of dealerships on the East End. We have (of course) a Mercedes/BMW dealership along with Saturn, Land Rover, Chrysler-Plymouth-Dodge, Jeep/Eagle-Audi-Porsche-Saab, Ford, Pontiac/GMC, and Chevrolet, and that's just Southampton. There's another Ford dealer in Wainscott and another Chevy/Olds/Cadillac dealer in East Hampton. Where are VW, Suzuki, Hyundai, Mazda etc.? Mostly in less-expensive Riverhead.

If you need service on one of these models, it will be more expensive out here than elsewhere, except perhaps Manhattan, but, by and large, we haven't heard any great complaints about the quality or cost of service.

Buying a car, ah, that's another matter. It is definitely going to be more expensive out here. But I guess people do it (I did!) since there are a large number of dealerships on the East End. Like anywhere else, though, it pays to shop around. Call and ask for prices. Here are a couple of possibilities.

✪✪✪✪ As his own radio commercials say, "What kind of name is **Buzz Chew**?!" Sounds like a sneeze, to me, but, whatever. You'll see— and hear—Buzz's name everywhere out here when it comes to cars. He owns the Chevy/Olds/Cadillac franchise in East Hampton and the Chrysler/Plymouth/Dodge dealership in Southampton. His radio spots are, indeed, humorous, but, more importantly for us, he runs a good dealership and two excellent service departments. I am a customer of his Southampton dealership and can attest to their good works. Call Chevy/Olds/Cadillac at 324-0100 and Chrysler at 283-5300.

✪✪✪✪ **Land Rover of Southampton,** 345 Hampton Road, Southampton, 287-4141. As their ads say, "Vehicles fit for a King." Which explains why there's been a Land Rover in the Royal Family since 1948. Be King of your own road, or beach, or whatever. Go see these nice folks at Land Rover of Southampton and get into the SUV generation!

AUTO BODY & REPAIR SHOPS

"Shall we 'dents'?" Here are a couple of excellent suggestions based on our experiences as well as the experiences of some folks we know.

✪✪✪✪ If it involves body work or painting your "classic," be it a BMW, Mercedes, Jag, or other expensive toy, the best place we know is **VAV Classics,** 21 Plant St., Southampton, 283-9409. They do excellent work. They also cooperate with another Gold level winner, Ultimate Motor Werks (see next).

✪✪✪✪ A great place to go—**Ultimate Motor Werks** in Southampton, 87 Powell Ave., near the train station, 287-2187, ask for Steve. Mercedes, BMW, Porsche and Land Rover are their specialties, but they will take care of their best customers no matter what kind of car you drive. Started originally by a couple of guys who left the local Mercedes dealer. These guys are really good, fast, efficient, and—surprise!—reasonably priced. Note: they also do "Ultimate Car Cleaning" (see also "Auto Detailing") and they can also winterize your car if you're going to leave it out here until next Summer.

✪✪✪✪ **Kalbacher's,** 33 Fort Pond Blvd., East Hampton, 324-4244. These folks have been around a long time and have a well deserved reputation for service. They also have a selection of used cars and will even search for that classic car you might want to get your driving gloves on! They do superb restorations, mostly Mercedes, Volvo, Jaguar and Jeep.

✪✪✪ Another shop that will handle any auto body repair needed, a shop that has a good reputation, is **Corwith's Auto Body,** 40 Willow Rd., Water Mill, 726-2776. They have been around awhile. They are located just off Montauk Highway, just after Baywoods and just before the Mobil Station.

✪✪✪ For repairs to brakes, mufflers, and shocks, go to the **Meineke Muffler Shop** in Southampton, County Rd. 39 just after the Burger

King, 283-9142. No, you probably won't see "George," but you will get fair prices and good service—most of the time you'll be able to wait for the car.

AUTO DETAILING

✪✪✪✪ **VAV Classics,** 21 Plant St., Southampton, 283-9409, just down the street from the Southampton LIRR Depot (see also "Auto Body Shops," above). Doesn't matter if it's your treasured Gull-Wing Coupe or your '68 Nash Rambler, Vernon and his crew will give it their best TLC. In fact, I've seen some real junkyard cases come out looking more like Gull Wing Coupes after they're done.

✪✪✪ **Ultimate Car Cleaning,** part of Ultimate Motor Werks, 87 Powell Ave., Southampton, 287-2187. The folks at Ultimate are known for the quality of their auto care (see also "Auto Repair," below). You can also rely on them to keep your chariot shined up for the Games and free of dust from your sandals. Oh, they also winterize Cherished Investments if you're going to be leaving them here while you're in Palm Beach for the winter (see "Winterizing").

✪✪✪ **Southampton Car Wash,** County Rd. 39, Southampton, 283-8990. In addition to the best car wash in the Hamptons, there is a facility here that does some pretty decent detailing. Call for an appointment. Even the $99 special will make your iron horse look like a thoroughbred.

AUTO INSURANCE (see "Insurance Agents")

AUTO RENTAL (see "Car Rental")

BACKFLOW VALVES (Testing)

If you're on city water, especially if you have a sprinkler system, you should have a "backflow test" every year. The local authorities will send you a notice. Backflow testing is done so that the water authority is confident that your household water system isn't "back-flowing" what it shouldn't back-flow into the city's water system. This back flow could be household waste-water, sprinkler water that has run through your lawn and is therefore potentially contaminated with chemicals, etc. The test can only be done via certified testers and there are fines if you don't comply. The average cost is about $75. Here are some reliable folks who can do the testing for you.

D&F Plumbing & Heating Services, 30 Miller Rd., Southampton, 283-3138

Essay Plumbing, 247 Major's Path, Southampton, 283-0956

BAD CHECKS

Let's suppose you're unfortunate enough to be in receipt of a "bad check." We're also going to presume it's from someone who lives out here and your bank has done what it can to collect on the check, sent the proper notices and so forth; and, you've contacted the writer of the check and tried to collect and you've gotten nowhere. What do you do? You've got two choices. First, call the local police. The police can contact the bad check writer and cite them for writing a bad check. The amount of the check does not matter. They'll likely do this in person and that will likely get the attention of your check bouncer and they will probably pay up. If they still don't or can't pay, you've got a legal claim and you may, in the long run, get your money.

The other choice you have is taking the check writer to small claims court. This is a pretty fair means of getting redress, especially if the check is for $3,000 or less—that's the new and current limit on small claims matters (See also "Small Claims Court").

BAGELS

✪✪✪✪ **The Golden Pear**—all locations—Southampton (97 Main, 283-8900), East Hampton (34 Newtown Ln., 329-1600), Main Street in Bridgehampton (537-1100) and now in Westhampton Beach, on Main Street (closed Oct.–March). "The Pears" are so wonderful for everything, why wouldn't their bagels be great, too? And the bagels are great!

✪✪✪✪ **Twice Upon A Bagel,** Montauk Hwy., Wainscott, 537-5553. Every kind of bagel imaginable with every kind of spread or filling imaginable! Lines out the door.

✪✪✪✪ **Bagel Buoy,** Bay St., Sag Harbor, 725-7690. Could get my vote for the freshest bagels…certainly among the largest and tastiest. Delectable fillings, including a superb whitefish…friendly staff.

✪✪✪ **Village Cheese Shop,** 11 Main St., Southampton, 283-6949—located near the south end of Main Street just before the Library. The bagels are excellent here, too, and this is a great little shop for other stuff. You can pick up some exotic cheese, or a tin of English marmalade, or a jar of weird looking mushrooms from some place I can't pronounce, or....

✪✪✪ **The Beach Bakery,** 112 Main St., Westhampton Beach, 288-6552. Lots of homemade goodies plus great coffee, bagels, and *The New York Times*.

BAIT & TACKLE SHOPS

Somethin' "fishy" going on in your life? Then here's where to get all your supplies:

✪✪✪✪ **Altenkirch Precision Outfitters,** 243 East Montauk Hwy., Hampton Bays, right at the Shinnecock Canal, 728-4110. These guys can do it all: precision build your tackle, supply you with everything you'll need for both fresh-and salt-water fishing, and charter you a boat if you need one. If you happen to catch something, they can officially weigh it for you and even get it stuffed and mounted!

✪✪✪ **Johnny's Tackle Shop,** Montauk Hwy., Montauk, 668-2940

✪✪ **The Tackle Shop,** 575 Montauk Hwy., Amagansett, 324-7770

BAKERIES (see also "Bread")

[Where the heck is the usual Platinum Level Winner here—Kathleen's Bakery? Well, sad to say, as we go to press, it's a mess. Please read our comments in the "Farewell" section toward the end of the Guide.]

✪✪✪✪ **Georgica Bakers,** 622 Montauk Hwy., Amagansett, 267-6773. Fabulous specialty cakes for your wedding, important event, or make-or-break party. They decorate to please!

✪✪✪✪✪ **Plain & Fancy Catering,** 85 Springs Fireplace Rd., East Hampton, 324-7853. My East Hampton "Chief Spy" tells me that everyone she knows (and—boy!—does she know! This lady is more connected than Bell Atlantic!) has used Plain & Fancy at one time or another.

✪✪✪ **The Beach Bakery,** 112 Main St., Westhampton Beach, 288-6552. Mmmmm! Fresh breads, pizza, cannolis, and lots of other home-made goodies. Plus great coffee, *The New York Times*, and a place to park your buns while you nosh on their buns!

BANKS

If you're a visitor, it's not likely that you're going to have much to do with our local banks except maybe use their ATMs (see "ATMs" for locations). If you're settling down here or if you find you do need a local bank, we have some recommendations.

✪✪✪✪ My wife Myra has had excellent experiences with **Chase Bank,** Main Street in Southampton, 935-9935. It even looks like a bank is supposed to look: tall, gray, cold, and impersonal. But the folks inside are warmer than the place looks. The tellers smile! The branch has all the services of a major bank, including on site investment help, large safe deposit facilities, funds transfer, notary service, traveler's checks, etc.

✪✪✪ **Bridgehampton National Bank,** headquartered in, no surprise, Bridgehampton, along Montauk Highway. Business must be good! The brand new headquarters building looks pretty snazzy! Bridgehampton National has offices scattered about The Hamptons (see below). They are a true hometown, home-owned operation. They have a pretty good reputation among some of our friends for service and also for their home loans. Give them a try at one of these locations:

> Main Office in Bridgehampton 537-1000
> 26 Park Place, East Hampton 324-8480
> 1 The Plaza, Montauk 668-6400

BARBER SHOPS

✪✪✪✪ **Ralph's Barber Shop,** 71 Main St., Southampton, 283-6918. Ralph also wins a "Gold" for best pricing scheme: the price chart in Ralph's shop is simple but eloquent: "PRICES ARE CHARGED IN ACCORDANCE WITH CUSTOMER'S ATTITUDE." If Ralph likes your attitude, a haircut is $13. Well, Ralph also wins the "Gold" because he gives a darn good haircut, too! And not only does he get mentioned in the Guide year after year, he got the nod from *New York Magazine* last year as the Hamptons best barber. That means he's got to get some better jokes…next stop the Leno show!

BARS

These are the best bars to hang out in—if you like to hang out in bars, that is.

✪✪✪✪ **The Cigar Bar**, 2 Main St., Sag Harbor, 725-2575. Ooh, I like this place! It's really small and it sure is cozy. Don't go here if you can't stand smoke, but if you like a perfectly chilled Cosmopolitan and a good cigar after dinner, this is The Place! There are, maybe, half a dozen seats at the bar itself, but there are some comfy stuffed chairs and a few tables, too. There's also a walk-in humidor from which you can select a stogie then wander back to your cocktail and light up. Best little bar in The Hamptons.

✪✪✪✪ **(the) Laundry,** 31 Race Ln., East Hampton, 324-3199. You've got to really look for this place but if you do, you will be more than pleasantly surprised. It's a gracious bar, not old and smoky, like the Oak Bar at the Plaza, but surprisingly similar in its feel and comfort. It's not a "Generation-X"-place, either, which those of us over (way over) 29 will like.

✪✪✪✪ The bar at the **American Hotel,** Main St., Sag Harbor, 725-3535.

One of the grand ol' bars around. Top-notch bartenders, excellent selection of rare cognacs, etc., and a great place to smoke that cigar you've carried around in your briefcase all week. Always crowded, though.

✪✪✪✪ **Bobby Van's,** Main St., Bridgehampton, 537-0590. For many years this has been one of the better places in The Hamptons to occupy a barstool. In addition to a great atmosphere, you'll never know who'll walk in here and plop down next to you: Billy Joel, Kurt Vonnegut, Linda Evalgelista, or me! Believe me, Linda's cuter.

✪✪✪✪ **Savanna's,** 268 Elm St., Southampton, 283-0202. Another one of my very favorite bars. (Jeez…I have a lot of favorite bars, don't I?) I love the atmosphere here, too. The folks are friendly, it's not too cramped, they serve decent champagne by the glass, and they know how to mix my favorite cocktail perfectly: Dewars on the rocks. Tough, eh?

✪✪✪✪ **World Pie**, Main Street, Bridgehampton, across from Bobby Van's, 537-7999. This is a real man's bar…Sorry, ladies. I don't mean it that way. It's for you gals, too, but, you know what I mean: lots of glass and real wood and atmosphere. Truly comfortable and the bartenders are first rate. "Big Mack" works here and he's the best. Wonder if he's still making my favorite Sambuca shakes.

✪✪✪ **The Driver's Seat:** The word that best describes the Driver's Seat (62 Job's Lane, Southampton, 283-6606) is "quintessential." It's probably the best-known bar in The Hamptons. It's open year round and has decent food, too: burgers, sandwiches, and lots of blue-plate specials. The front bar offers you a view of all the folks strolling down Jobs Lane but the back bar, which is only open in warm weather, is where the real fun is. Many people don't consider the season really started until they open the back bar at The Driver's Seat.

✪✪✪ **The Southampton Publick House,** Bowden Square, Southampton, 283-2800, fax 283-2801. The new owners of the Publick House have returned this place to what it was many years ago: a cozy bar where you can enjoy a favorite cocktail in a relaxed atmosphere. You must try some of their local brews. They are making some mighty fine beer, here (see "Beer," below).

✪✪✪ The bar at **Fellingham's,** 17 Cameron St., Southampton (behind
the Chase Bank building off Main Street), 283-9674. This bar is
very small, but it is very friendly. Kind of a "locals" place, but all
are welcome. They even have a "Breakfast Club"—for those of you
who up and out the door at 2 AM and done with work at 8 AM (like
some of our local fisherman) and need a "warm libation."

✪✪ **Cyril's Fish House,** Montauk Hwy., Montauk, 267-7993. On any
given night this summer, you'll find dozens of folks just off the
beach and looking for a "cold one" at Cyril's. The crowd often spills
outside. It's a fun spot and if you want the best frozen drinks in the
Hamptons, go here…ask for your favorite concoction with a rum
floater.

✪✪ **The Wild Rose,** Bridgehampton Turnpike, Bridgehampton, 537-
5050. Located in an old two-story home on the Turnpike between
Bridgehampton and Sag Harbor, this is an eclectic place, mostly for
the younger crowd. Good drinks, dancing, and an impromptu ses-
sion of something or other is likely to break out any moment.

BATHROOMS (Public)

There's nothing more annoying than not knowing where the local "potties"
are—especially if you're jumping up and down on one foot in the middle of
Main Street. The second most annoying thing is those inhospitable signs
some of our local merchants display prominently: "Bathrooms for Patrons
ONLY!" I mean, how rude! Don't these folks understand that the name of
the game is getting people inside your door, no matter how you get them
in? And where do these enlightened "service providers" go to the bathroom
when they're out of town, I wonder?

Public Bathrooms in The Hamptons:

Amagansett: Behind Joan & David's, at the shopping square.
Bridgehampton: Inside King Kullen.
East Hampton: There are new public restrooms on the far side of the
main parking lot behind Coach and all the other stores on Main Street.
The restrooms are right on the edge of the baseball field.
Montauk: Right behind the Montauk Police Station, in the middle of
town.
Sag Harbor: Tough, but try the Bay Street Theatre Building if it's open or

the Corner Restaurant across the street. B. Smith's Restaurant on the wharf has also been very accommodating.

Southampton: The Chamber of Commerce Building in Main Street—please replace the key, thanks!

Water Mill: Not much here, but you might try going through the back door at Meghan's Saloon, next to the Post Office. Then go buy a beer.

Westhampton: The Golden Pear on Main when it's open (closed in winter) or the Post Stop Restaurant at the east end of Main Street.

If you're straining not to bust a gut while stranded on the L.I.E., listed herewith, for your ultimate relief, are a number of (whew!) convenient "johns." (Hopefully, you'll read these notes well in advance.)

Rest Stops along the LIE:

Exit 40: Howard Johnson's
Exit 46: Howard Johnson's and Holiday Inn
Exit 49: Marriott (north service road)
   Hilton (Rte 110 southbound)
Exit 52 (eastbound): Hampton Inn
Exit 53 (westbound): Hampton Inn
Exit 57: Hampton Inn (south of the expressway)
Exit 58: Radisson Hotel
Exit 63 (Bathroom Heaven!): Best Western, McDonald's, Burger King
Exit 70: Mobil (a really nice Mobil!), Grace's Restaurant

Rest Stops on the Southern State:

Uniondale: the Marriott just off the Meadowbrook State Parkway, going west on the Hempstead Turnpike
Route 110: McDonald's, just south of the parkway
Seaford-Oyster Bay Expressway: McDonald's at Old Country Road

Best Rest Stop coming into The Hamptons:

Hampton Bays Diner, Exit 64 (east) off the Sunrise

BEACHES

Folks who are new to The Hamptons are always amazed by the quality of our beaches. I see reactions like, "Wow! Nobody told me you had beaches like this!" As I have said many times, if we had a more temperate climate year round, you'd swear you were in the Caribbean. We are blessed with beautiful, white sand beaches up and down most of the Atlantic-facing coast from Westhampton to Montauk. On the Peconic Bay side, it's a little different, but there are some wonderful beaches there, too. Sometimes Mother Nature can get a little testy with us, though. Big Atlantic storms, especially in the hurricane season and winter can sometimes wipe away big stretches of pristine beach. Just be patient. What Mother Nature takes away, she eventually gives back. Here are the Guide's recommendations on the best beaches in The Hamptons.

Best Family Fun Beach:

✪✪✪✪ For a lovely beach with wide expanses, pretty good wave action, lifeguards, rest rooms, and, generally, uncrowded sand, you can't beat Flying Point Beach in Southampton (guard shack, 726-9686). There are plenty of dunes to wander and you can even walk around to Mecox Bay, in back of the beach. The Bay makes a safe and fun place for the kiddies to get wet if they're fearful of some of the big breakers or the surf. From atop the dunes you can see some of the most expensive ocean front homes on the East End—and you can walk for miles in either direction. Carefully controlled fires and grilling are allowed after dark (with a permit from Town Hall costing $5). To reach Flying Point Beach it's best to locate the Cobb Rd. turnoff from Montauk Highway just before Water Mill (if you see

the actual mill you've gone too far). Go down Cobb Road all the way to the end. You'll come to a "T" intersection. Turn left. That'll be Flying Point Road. Take Flying Point all the way to the end. You'll run into the beach parking lot. With the expansion, in '97, of the beach's parking lot, there are a lot more parking spots; but, to get one, you have to have a town parking permit ($10 annually for residents, $100 annually for non-residents, sold on site or call Town Hall 283-6011). Unfortunately, there are no daily parking spaces. There are a few spots a half mile down the road that are free (take a left before the parking lot), but you've got to get there early. If that doesn't work, find a friend with a house nearby! You could also take a taxi to the beach. Why not? Get sand in the taxi instead of your van…

✪✪✪✪ **Sagg Main Beach,** Sagaponack, located at the end of Sagg Main Rd. 1,500 feet on the ocean, seasonal permit $10 for residents, $100 for non-residents, $10 daily use pass, lifeguards, showers, restrooms, overlook platform, food stand, volleyball courts. Lots of wide open expanse here, good sized parking lot, too. Even on very crowded summer days you'll likely be able to find an unpopulated patch of sand. Delightful. Myra's favorite.

✪✪✪ Another family favorite is **Hither Hills State Park** in Montauk. Again, the beaches are lovely and wide with miles of walking space in either direction. Hither Hills is a campground, too, if that's your aim. The park has a bathhouse, general store, picnic sites with tables, grills, and athletic fields. Fishing is also available. We took a group of friends there for brunch at the beach early one Sunday morning. We grabbed a picnic spot at the top of a dune overlooking the ocean, whipped out the handy Coleman stove, cooked up eggs and bacon, and buttered some croissants we had picked up on the way. We brewed up some coffee and topped off breakfast with some fresh fruit. Truth is, we snuck a little champagne in, too, and mixed it with our orange juice…doesn't get much better. To get to Hither Hills (668-2461) take Montauk Highway almost all the way to Montauk. Where Montauk Highway and Old Montauk Highway diverge, take Old Montauk Highway (the right fork), go about 3 miles and you'll run into the Park. Fees are $4.00 per car, lifeguards on duty Memorial Day through Labor Day.

Beaches for Solitude:

If it's an escape you're looking for, I have three possibilities for you: Each has the right mix of sun, sand, surf, and quietude. Each spot is far away from the usual crowds.

✪✪✪✪ The first idyll is **Shelter Island** and you're going to have to take a ferry to get there, but it's well worth the trip (see "Ferries—South Ferry"). All of Shelter Island's beaches are secluded and peaceful. Note: beach parking on Shelter Island is restricted to residents, renters and hotel guests. All vehicles parked at the beaches must display a parking sticker. Stickers are available at Town Hall, and are free to residents and $25 to renters and hotel guests. No lifeguards until mid-June, when the town stickers actually go into effect.

　　Crescent Beach, on Shore Road off West Neck Rd., 600 feet on Southold Bay, and a great beach for July 4th fireworks! Lifeguards and food concession.

　　Shell Beach, at the intersection of East Brander Parkway and Peconic Ave., 600 feet on Shelter Island Sound and West Neck Harbor (very picturesque).

　　Wades Beach, off South Midway Rd. on the south side of the island, 500 yards on Shelter Island Sound. Lifeguards and restrooms.

✪✪✪ Our second recommendation is **Cedar Point County Park** in East Hampton. Located on a point that juts into Gardiner's Bay, the park is usually fairly quiet. There are picnic facilities and some camp-sites (tents and trailers only). The park is full during the busiest times of the season so plan ahead. You can have a very blissful day along the water's edge if you hike out along the strip toward the end of Cedar Point. Best way to get to the park is to go to Rte. 114 (the main connector road between Sag Harbor and East Hampton) and turn north on Stephen Hands Path. You'll see a sign there for the park. Take Stephen Hands Path to Old Northwest Rd. (left) and follow this road all the way to the park entrance.

✪✪ Third choice: the **Morton National Wildlife Refuge** in Noyack. In addition to having quiet beaches all along Little Peconic Bay it has the additional advantage of offering you a chance to see some of the local wildlife (other than the kind you find in our local bars). You have to park quite a ways from the beach and hike in, but that's part of the fun. There is a small admission fee. Bring a backpack with a sandwich and some bottled water. Enjoy the solitude and pack out what you pack in. Find Noyack Rd. (convenient from Southampton via North Sea Rd.) and follow it to the refuge, which is well marked and opposite the Noyack Country Club. The park only operates during daylight hours, by the way.

In addition to our favorite beaches, here's a list of all the other beaches, by town.

Amagansett:

East Hampton Town parking rules apply. Permits required and available at the Town Clerk's Office in East Hampton or the Montauk Annex. Resident seasonal permits are free, nonresidents pay $125 but many hotels and motels offer guests free permits.

Atlantic Avenue Beach, at the end of Amagansett Ave., 700 foot beachfront, parking permit required but you can get a day permit here (free for residents, $10 for non-residents), lifeguards, food stand, surfing.

Big Albert's Landing Beach, located at Big Albert's Landing, off Old Stone Hwy., 300 feet on Napeague Bay, seasonal parking permit required. Lifeguards, picnic area, restrooms.

Indian Wells, end of Indian Wells Hwy., for East Hampton town residents only, 700 feet on the ocean, lifeguards, food stand, surfing, restrooms.

Bridgehampton:

Southampton Town beach parking rules apply: Beachgoers need permits, available only at the Town's beaches. Seasonal fee $10 for residents (you need an ID with a local address), $5 for residents over 60, $100 for nonresidents. Non-resident daily parking is $10. Some beaches are "resident only" (as noted below). For all Southampton beach information call 283-6011.

Mecox Beach, at the end of Job's Lane, 250 feet on the ocean, parking permit required or $10 daily use pass, lifeguards, showers, restrooms, sundeck, food stand, volleyball courts.

W. Scott Cameron Beach, at the end of Dune Road, for Southampton Town residents only, 300 feet on the ocean, lifeguards, food concession, picnic tables, outdoor showers, volleyball courts, restrooms.

East Hampton:

East Hampton Town beach parking rules apply: Permits required and available at the Town Clerk's Office in East Hampton or the Montauk Annex. Resident seasonal permits are free, non-residents pay $125 but many hotels and motels offer guests free permits.

Georgica Beach, 324-4150, located at the end of Apequogue Rd. and Lily Pond, 300 feet of oceanfront, limited parking.

Egypt Close, Old Beach Ln., 300 foot beach, no lifeguard, limited parking.

Two-Mile Hollow, Two-Mile Hollow Rd., 300 foot beach, no lifeguard, limited parking.

Maidstone Park, end of Flaggy Hole Rd., off Three Mile Harbor Rd. and Hog Creek Hwy., 400 feet on Gardiner's Bay, seasonal parking permit only, lifeguards, picnic areas, ballfield, pavilion, restrooms.

Hampton Bays:

Meschutt Beach County Park, Sunrise Hwy. Just east of Shinnecock Canal to Canal Rd., north to Bishop Place, north to Dunes Rd., 852-8205. 1,000 feet of protected beach on Peconic Bay. Picnics, snack area, volleyball court, restrooms, fishing. $3 per car per day with Suffolk County Parks Green Key, all others $8 per car per day.

Ponquoge Beach, located on Dune Rd., 600 feet on the ocean, seasonal permit $10 for residents, $100 for non-residents, $10 daily use pass, lifeguards, showers, restrooms, volleyball courts, picnic tables.

Sears-Bellows County Park, off Rte. 24, 852-8290. 693 acre park on the ocean. Horseback riding, fishing, swimming, hunting, rowboat rentals, camping, picnic tables, showers, restrooms, bicycle hostel. $3 per car per day with Suffolk County Parks Green Key, all others $8 per car per day.

Montauk:

East Hampton Town beach parking rules apply: Permits required and available at the Town Clerk's Office in East Hampton or the Montauk Annex. Resident seasonal permits are free, non-residents pay $125 but many hotels and motels offer guests free permits.

Ditch Plains Beach, off Ditch Plains Rd., great surfing beach, 500 feet on the ocean, seasonal parking permit only. Lifeguards, food stand, restrooms.

East Lake Drive Beach, off Rte. 27 at the end of East lake Drive, 300 feet on Block Island Sound, seasonal parking permit only. Lifeguards, food stand, restrooms.

Kirk Park Beach, off Rte. 27, just west of the village, 500 feet on the ocean, daily parking for $10 or seasonal parking permit. Lifeguards, picnic area adjacent, restrooms.

Napeague State Park, off Montauk Highway, west of Montauk Village. Open year round, sunrise to sunset. Limited parking.

Sagaponack:

(See "A Best Family Fun Beach" Gold Award for Flying Point Beach, above.)

Shelter Island:

Award winning! See "Beaches for Solitude," above.

Southampton:

Beachgoers need permits, available only at the Town's beaches. Seasonal fee $10 for residents (you need an ID with a local address), $5 for residents over 60, $100 for non-residents. Non-resident daily parking is $10. Some beaches are "resident only" (as noted below). For all Southampton beach information call 283-6011.

Emma Rose Elliston Park, North Sea, Millstone Brook Rd. off of North Sea Rd., Town residents only, 150 feet on Big Fresh Pond, lifeguards, picnic tables, and restrooms.

Foster Memorial Beach (Long Beach), Noyac, on Long Beach Rd., 1 mile on Peconic Bay, one of the largest beaches in The Hamptons. Great for kids and water sport enthusiasts. Lifeguards, showers, restrooms, food stand, water-ski and sailing areas, sailing, and wind surfing.

Tiana Beach, East Quogue, off Dune Rd., 1000 feet on the ocean, lifeguards, showers, restrooms, food stand, picnic tables, volleyball courts.

Water Mill:

(See "Best Family Fun Beach" Gold Award for Flying Point Beach, above.)

Westhampton:

Cupsogue Beach County Park, west end of Dune Rd., 852-8111, 296 acre park on the ocean, surf casting, diving, camping, restrooms, concession stand, showers, pavilion, changing rooms. $5 per car for county residents, $8 for non-residents.

BEACH CLUBS (private and membership)

✪✪✪✪ **Bridgehampton Tennis and Surf Club,** 747 Mid Ocean Rd., Bridgehampton, 537-1180 (see also "Tennis"). An excellent members-only spot that is right on the beach. Seasonal memberships, full restaurant facilities, and an Olympic size pool (if you don't want sand between your toes...). This is one of the prettiest beach spots in The Hamptons. These are very nice, service oriented folks. A family membership (parents, all children under 21 and the "Nanny") for tennis, beach and pool facilities runs about $8000 for the season (May 29–Labor Day). Full single memberships are also available for about $3500. Private cabanas are extra and range from $1650 to $3300 (but can be shared with up to two families).

BEAUTY

OK, ladies and gentlemen, here's everything you need to know about beauty in one, compact category. By the time you get done with these folks, you'll be ready to do the cover of *Elle* or *GQ*.

Hair:

✪✪✪✪ **Salon East,** 2 E. Montauk Hwy., Hampton Bays, 728-5212, JoAnn Gustafson. JoAnn, by the way, is an American Board Certified Master Hair Colorist—the only one on the East End.

✪✪✪✪ **Echo,** 52 Park Place, East Hampton, 329-0044. My East Hampton Spy goes here, and she says they are great for cuts for both men and women.

✪✪✪ **Fay Teller Salon,** Corwith Ave., Bridgehampton, 537-3393: been around a long time, but now under new management.

✪✪✪ **Water's Edge,** Main St., Amagansett, 267-7766: a full service salon, cuts and coloring for both men and women.

✪✪✪✪ **"KM" (Kevin Maple Salon),** 46 Jobs Lane, Southampton, 283-8230: A reputation firmly established in The City has lead to a branch of KM in The Hamptons. A "famous" place, to be sure, but also one of the best. Prepare to spend serious dollars, but you get serious service, too. Flash! Great News for some of you who are customers of the Minardi Salon in Manhattan (29 E. 61st St.). Beth and Carmine Minardi (and some of their senior staff) have struck a deal with Kevin Maple to spend every other Monday in the Hamptons this summer at the Kevin Maple Salon. The Minardis will also be available for house calls, by appointment. Just call "KM" for Hamptons appointments.

Manicures:

✪✪✪✪ **Nails by Joann** at the Oak Street Salon, 10 Oak Street, Southampton, 287-2763. Ask for Joann. Joann also does pedicures and waxing. It has been our observation that Joann really cares about her clients. Her clients trust her and love her casual and "homey" atmosphere. She'll even let you call her at home (727-4097), and she makes house calls!

✪✪✪ **Beauty Clinic,** Inc., 66 Newtown Ln., East Hampton, 324-1204.

✪✪✪ **Fay Teller Salon,** Corwith Ave., Bridgehampton, 537-3393.

✪✪✪ **Water's Edge,** Main St., Amagansett, 267-7766.

Facials, Waxing, etc.:

✪✪✪✪✪ **Naturopathica,** in the Red Horse Plaza, Montauk Highway, East Hampton, 329-2525. "Traditional and natural therapies (from the world over) to assist in your health and well being...." So says their brochure and we believe it! Facials of all types including deep pore cleansings, peels, aromatherapy and paraffin treatments. One visit here and that tired ol' face you stared at this morning in the mirror will look like a new woman...or man. All treatments are available for both men and women. You really should try them.

✪✪✪✪ **Susan Ciminelli,** 34 Pantigo Rd., East Hampton, 267-6300. Again, the East Hampton Spy, who hangs around EH like crazy, says Susan is one of the best!

✪✪✪ **Beauty Clinic,** Inc., 66 Newtown Ln., East Hampton, 324-1204.

✪✪✪ **Water's Edge,** Main St., Amagansett, 267-7766.

Beauty Products

✪✪✪✪ **Naturopathica,** in the Red Horse Plaza, Montauk Highway, East Hampton, 329-2525.

✪✪✪✪ **Susan Ciminelli,** 34 Pantigo Rd., East Hampton, 267-6300.

✪✪✪ **Water's Edge,** Main St., Amagansett, 267-7766.

✪✪✪ **White's Pharmacy,** 81 Main St., East Hampton, 324-0082.

BED, BATH, & LINENS

✪✪✪✪ **Portico Bed & Bath**, Bridgehampton Commons, Bridgehampton, 537-1449. Really elegant. Same finesse as the Soho store in The City. Lots of fine linens and accessories for the bedroom and bath.

✪✪✪✪ **Hildreth's Bedding & Bath Shop,** Main St., Southampton, 283-2300. A truly well-stocked bed and bath shop can be found here. Order your mattress, pick out an armful of those big, fluffy towels, grab a bunch of pillows and you'll be "livin' it large"—and comfortably. Oh, don't forget the soap!

✪✪✪ **Elegant John,** 74 Montauk Hwy., East Hampton, 324-2636: they have all the basics and the selection is very complete.

✪✪ **Roberta East,** 62 The Circle, East Hampton, 324-2518, fax 329-5167. Our shoppers rated this yet another wonderful stop for bed and bath needs.

BED & BREAKFAST PLACES
(see "Accommodations" for recommendations)

Just in case you were thinking of cashing in your portfolio and chucking the frantic pace of Wall Street to open a B & B, I do want you to know there are rules for operating a B & B—and the rules are different between the various Villages and Towns. The basic rules for any area can be obtained from the town Building Inspector's Office. Here are some hints: Generally, your B & B must be your primary residence. You can only offer breakfast. Most local rules will limit you to a maximum number of guests as well as a maximum number of sleeping rooms (in Southampton its no more than 10 guests and no more than 5 rooms). In the Village of Southampton only "historic buildings" can be converted to B & B usage. In any case, if the "country life" is tugging at your heartstrings, and you are thinking of opening a B & B, check with the local building department. Both the Town of Southampton and the Village of Southampton are encouraging the conversion of homes to B & B use. Neither the Town nor the Village wants more hotel or motel rooms, so this is a good compromise.

BEER

Where to get it at a great price.

✪✪✪✪ **Peconic Beverage:** Great selection, a lot of it already cold; kegs, soda, snacks, etc. And this is a discount store, so the prices are the best I've found out here. You can also recycle your cans and bottles here. Three locations in The Hamptons:

74 County Rd. 39, Southampton, 283-0602, just before the intersection of Rte. 39 and North Sea and across the street from Burger King.

East Hampton on Pantigo Rd., 324-0602 .

Bridgehampton Beverage, Montauk Highway and Lumber Ln., 537-1644.

Where to have fun drinking beer:

✪✪✪✪ **Southampton Publick House,** Bowden Square, Southampton, 283-2800. The Publick House is a genuine microbrewery, making and serving some really interesting beers. In fact, the Publick House has won two Silver Medals for their brews: one medal was for Southampton Saison, awarded by the very prestigious Great American Beer Festival in Denver. Southampton Secret Ale captured a second silver medal for the Publick House at the 1998 World Beer Cup in (of all places) Rio de Janeiro. OK, so they make great beer! It still has to be a fun place to drink beer if its gonna get in the Guide, right? Well, it is! The atmosphere is cozy and pub-style.

"BENEFITS"
(A BIG thing out here...see also "Events")

As you might well guess, the East End is saturated with "benefits." Some of us are beginning to think there are too many. It seems that just about every summer weekend some group is trying to fish $500 or more out of your pocket for "dinner under the stars" or cold-poached salmon in some huge tent-by-the-sea. There are some good benefits, though, and we herewith list our favorites. These events are open to the public. These are the soirees where you don't need to "know someone" to get invited. Each event supports a truly worthy cause and therefore merits your participation.

✪✪✪✪ Share Our Strength, Taste of the Nations—East End Restaurant & Ball: "SOS" has a rousing event in The City every year to raise money for a worthy cause: hunger. This is the East End version. Look for announcements in April and May. The '00 outing is scheduled for May 21st at NV Tsunami in East Hampton. It's a great way to get a preview of the Hamptons summer scene. Last year's festivities were very well attended and seemed to us to be the kickoff event of last summer's wonderful season. Some of the Hamptons finest restaurants participate along with some eager newcomers who want to show you what they can do. At about $75 per person it's well worth the price. Call 267-2411 for details.

✪✪✪✪ For a little mid-winter fun, especially for those of you sticking around during the winter, go to next year's **Have-A-Heart Ball**. It's held somewhere on or near Valentine's Day and benefits the East End Food Pantry. Funds raised go to providing food and other essential services for those in need out here. I know, hard to imagine hunger and desperation in The Hamptons, but, hey, life is full of all kinds of challenges and surprises. Last year's gala was at the Atlantica in Westhampton Beach. When you see the announcements, beginning in January, give them a call (about $100 per person). Try 329-5480.

✪✪✪ Group for the South Fork. The Group is concerned with protecting the "character and quality of life on the South Fork through public advocacy and community education" That means preserving the farms, ecosystems, wetlands, and resources of the coastal zones. A worthy cause. Last year's benefit was at an Ambassadorial estate in Sagaponack. Delightful dinner, dancing, plus live and silent auctions. This event is usually one of the first of the big summer benefits and is held in late May or early June. Terrific way to kick off the summer season! Information at 537-1400.

✪✪✪ Southampton Hospital Benefit, south lawn of the Hospital's grounds on Wickapogue Rd., Southampton, usually in August. Call the hospital for details at 726-8200. This is the one benefit out here where you can really meet some of your year-round neighbors and where you'll find the folks who are really entrenched in the local scene. It's not a "locals only" event, don't get me wrong, it's just the one benefit that you won't want to miss if you're a long-timer, local politician, or want to get politically connected with the power structure of the East End. The Hospital has been raising money at this benefit for many years. And they really need it. Not to get too political, but the hospital suffered a major financial setback two years ago amid great controversy over the stewardship of the hospital's former director. No malfeasance, just poor financial decision making, apparently. This is one of the finest hospitals around with a lot of talented health care providers. They are worthy of your support through this benefit evening.

✪✪✪ **The Bay Street Theatre Festival Benefit Bash,** The BSTF Bash is usually held in July in Sag Harbor, near the theatre itself. The Bash consists of a wonderful cocktail hour, catered dinner, celebrity auction, and—later—dancing under the stars (and sometimes with the stars!). You'll see many of the notables who are associated with the theater. Rosie O'Donnell hosted last year and she was a huge success! Call the BSTF Development office for ticket information at 725-0818.

BETTER BUSINESS BUREAU

The local office is actually in Farmingdale ("up Island") and can be reached at 420-0500. The BBB will advise you on "pre-purchase inquiries." If you're about to spend a lot of dough on a product, service, contractor, or what not, they will tell you if there have been any complaints or cases filed against that service provider or establishment. They can't, of course, give you opinions or forecast the future; but, before spending a bundle, it wouldn't hurt to check.

BICYCLES

My first bike cost $25, brand new. I won't tell you how long ago that was but by the price tag you can probably make a good guess. My most recent bike cost $300 and that was for a fairly modest combo street and off road bike with shifters for 7 gears. I have now seen bikes that cost more than my first new car! Unbelievable. But biking is big out here (see "Biking," below) and there are a couple of places where you can get great service, good advice, and excellent equipment.

✪✪✪✪ **Rotations Bicycle Center,** 32 Windmill Lane, Southampton, 283-2890. They offer a dazzling array of bikes and equipment, hel-

mets, and roller blades. I also like their service and repair department. For a really cool look at some suggested bike treks, check
out the web site for Rotations Bicycles: www.rotationsbicyclecen-
ter.com.

✪✪✪✪ **CyclePath Bikes,** Montauk Hwy., Wainscott, 537-1144. Great
service and repairs, great knowledge of local biking excursions,
great selection of bikes!

✪✪✪✪ **Bermuda Bikes,** 36 Gingerbread Ln., East Hampton, 324-6688.
Bermuda Bikes has a full line of bikes and accessories for both
adult and juvenile enthusiasts. The owners are graduates of the
Barnett Bicycle Institute "Mechanics Certification" program. That
means they can really fix that busted rim or get that piece of pant-
leg cloth out of your gears.

BICYCLE RENTAL

All of the folks in the previous listing will gladly rent bikes. You can also
rent bikes on Block Island, if you take that trip (see "10 Most Fun Things to
do in the Hamptons.")

BIKING

This could be one of the greatest natural
biking environments in the world—could be, but
isn't—yet. With the 35 miles of relatively flat surface between Southampton and Montauk
Lighthouse we could have a cyclist's dream ride,
what with all the scenic beauty we have. The
problem is, you have to cycle down Route 27, the
Montauk Highway, to access most of it. And that
means jostling with lots of cars. All drivers on 27
are doing the swivel-head routine, gawking at the
scenery, just like you are. You've got to be careful.

There are some bike lanes in some of our terri-
tory, but they aren't
universally connected from town to town. There is
a move afoot, though,
to create a bike path along the roadbed of the Long Island Railroad. That
would take a lot of bike traffic off the highways, but then you'd have to look
out for trains.

Whether you take one of our suggested rides or just get on a bike and start pedaling, there are lots of side roads and long, flat winding streets for casual cyclists. Just try and stay off the main streets unless you're an experienced rider and have full body armor. Enjoy, keep to the right, and always wear your helmet, no matter how stupid it looks or what it does to your hair. Helmets are REQUIRED for anyone under the age of 14 (a State law).

The East Hampton Town Clerk's Office has some good maps of bike trails in the area, available for a nominal fee.

Here are two established bike routes that you will enjoy, one moderately easy, the other a little more challenging.

✪✪✪✪ **Shelter Island** (see "Ferries"). This 25-mile double loop is well marked and moderately easy. It begins as soon as you get off the ferry (either one). The west loop swings around Southold Bay along Nostrand Parkway. The east loop goes around Rams Island and passes near the Mashomack Preserve (see "Hiking"). This is a Gold level ride because the traffic on the island is relatively low and the scenery along the way is spectacular.

✪✪✪ A longer ride with glimpses of all the East End has to offer begins in Riverhead, swings through Hubbard County Park, where it passes interesting salt marshes and two freshwater ponds. It then skims along Peconic Bay to Sag Harbor, runs along State Rte. 114 to East Hampton then onto Montauk Highway. Once you're to this point, you'll wheel through Amagansett and Napeague (a long stretch of about 5 miles). As soon as you see Old Montauk Highway, bear right. Go past Hither Hills State Park. This is where the road is most challenging with a couple dozen up and down hills. You'll rejoin Montauk Highway, cycle through Montauk, and on out to the Montauk Lighthouse. Total mileage: about 60 miles. Whew! Have someone pick you up at the other end!

BIRDS/BIRDING

We got 'em. By the flock. "Birding" is another big hobby out here. On the opposite side of the spectrum, there are still places where you can hunt several types of birds: goose, duck, pheasant, and grouse are the most sought after. Hunting takes place primarily in the early winter months.

A couple of birds that you should definitely NOT hunt are the piping plover and the osprey. The plover is extremely endangered, having been reduced to a very small population living along the dunes, mostly in

Southampton and East Hampton. The Nature Conservancy is trying very hard to separate the beach goers from the plovers—they don't really go together. (Last summer I spotted a bumper sticker on the back of a pickup truck, you know, the kind with the gun rack in the window? It said "Piping Plover tastes Like Chicken." Man, there's a real environmentalist.)

The osprey is a large, fish-eating eagle and builds its huge nests atop old, dead trees, or sometimes on top of poles that have been erected for them. They are magnificent birds to watch, swooping and snaring fish from the waters of the bays and ponds all around the East End. But they are protected, so just watch.

The Canada goose has started to show up here on the East End in large numbers. At first, they were a novelty, honking their way over the fields, cleaning up loose corn after the harvest. Now they are viewed by many as noisy, messy pests. The pickings are so good here that some of these birds have simply stopped migrating South and have moved in permanently! They are now eligible targets for the annual hunt.

If you want to see more of the wild birds, visit the Mashomack Preserve (see "Hikes" on Shelter Island) or the Morton Wildlife Refuge in Noyac (see "Beaches"). Little sparrows and chickadees will eat right out of your hand. If you want to see them up close and personal, put a bird feeder in your yard. You'll get all types of sparrows, plus cardinals, wrens, chickadees, blue jays, grackles, starlings, red-winged blackbirds, flickers, etc. Bird feeders are, by the way, an environmentally friendly way to reduce the insect population around your property. The birds will certainly eat the seeds you put out, but they will also eat many of the bugs around your yard. One word of caution: If you go to the trouble of providing a feeder for your feathery friends, you're sort of duty-bound to keep restocking it. After a few weeks, the local population of birds will become more or less reliant on this food source; so, as tempting as it might be to set out some seed for just a while, you're actually doing more harm than good if you abandon your efforts after a few weeks. Another note of caution: birds attract cats!

If you're a "birder" and want to know what sorts of birds have been sighted out here, you can call the Rare Bird Alert Hotline (bet you didn't know there was such a thing!) in The City at 212-979-3070. Some of the rare birds you can see out here: common eider and red-breasted merganser, razor-billed and black legged kittiwake, bluebirds (rare to Long Island), leasterns, upland sandpiper, migrating warbler, wild turkey, skimmers, roseate terns, nesting kingbirds, and nesting marsh wrens.

BIRD FEEDING SUPPLIES

✪✪✪✪ **Wild Bird Crossing,** Bridgehampton Commons, Bridgehampton, 537-SEED. OK, so now you've decided you want to befriend the chickadees flitting around your yard. This is the place to go. Food, feeders, and bird watching paraphernalia of all sorts can be found here. They even have "Common Bird Songs" cassettes. I dare you to play that in the office next week.

✪✪✪✪ The **Agway** in Bridgehampton on Snake Hollow Road, 537-0007, is also an excellent source for all kinds of seeds and feeds. Local farmers go here.

BIRTH CONTROL (see "Family Planning")

BOATING (see also "Fishing" and "Sailing")

Eastern Long Island has one of the finest boating environments anywhere. Whether it's open ocean boating, sailing, wind surfing, fishing, jet skis, or cruising along the waterways of the Great Peconic Bay, this is a boater's nirvana.

Suffolk County operates a marina at Shinnecock Canal in Southampton, 854-4952. The marina has about 35 acres with 35 transient berths available on a first-come, first-served basis. Transient boaters may stay up to two weeks, including three weekends. The berths have hookups, showers, and sanitary facilities. Visitors may also use the Meschutt Beach County Park adjacent to the Marina at no charge.

The East End's premier boating center, however, has to be Montauk. There are some 20 marinas and over 400 charter boats. That is to say nothing of the restaurants, salt air, fabulous views...well, let's take this one step at a time. And we'll start with motor craft. To "real" sailors these vessels are known as "stinkpots."

If you want to look at **BUYING** a boat, take a look at:

✪✪✪✪ **Dave Bofill Marine, Inc.**, right on County Rd. 39, North Highway, Southampton. 283-6736. Talk about "big-boys toys!" What a great showroom and selection of boats!

✪✪✪ **Bruce Tait & Associates,** Sag Harbor, 725-4222 (right by the American Fitness Factory). Experienced and reliable, excellent local coverage for both sales and chartering.

If you want to **RENT** a power or sail boat:

✪✪✪✪ **Uihlein Marina & Boat Rental** in Montauk Harbor is the place to go. They are at West Lake Dr., 668-3799. They have cabin cruisers, ski boats, skiffs, jet skis, scuba equipment and they all rent by the hour, half day, or day.

If you want to go **canoeing:** (see "Canoeing")

If you want to go **row-boating:**

Cedar Point County Park in East Hampton (see "Beaches") and Sears Bellows County Park in Hampton Bays both offer a concession with rowboat rentals.

If you want a fun little boat trip:

✪✪✪✪ Get aboard the **"American Beauty,"** docked at Long Wharf in Sag Harbor. This little cruiser has ninety-minute nature cruises around Sag Harbor, two and three-hour romantic sunset cruises, a ninety-minute wake-up cruise, and they do charters for private parties. Prices vary for each type of cruise. Call Capt. Don Heckman at 725-0397.

BOAT REGISTRATION & TITLE

As with vehicles, you should register your boat with the State. The DMV will handle this for you (if your boat dealer hasn't done so already). (see "DMV")

BOOKSTORES

✪✪✪✪ **Book Hampton**—two locations— 93 Main St. in Southampton (283-0270) and 20 Main St. in East Hampton (324-4939). Both stores carry all the latest titles plus a very nice selection of specialty books. The staffs at both stores are very helpful in locating special editions and ordering whatever they might not have in stock. The East Hampton store is roomier. Both stores feature a nice selection of coffee table books to decorate your Hamptons home. Check out the section on Hamptons books (like this Guide!) Flash! Soon to be three locations: Hal Zwick, the creative new owner of BookHampton, is adding another store to his growing empire. He's bought the old Paradise Café in Sag Harbor and is turning it into a combination bookstore and restaurant. Thus: "BookHampton in Paradise," which I think is pretty cute! One-third of the old downstairs and all the upstairs area will be devoted to books. Hal's adding an outdoor patio on the back for dining in the fresh and wonderful Sag Harbor air.

✪✪✪ **The Book Shoppe,** on the Plaza, Montauk, 668-4599. A handy, well-stocked bookshop. Call ahead and order—Jeff will have it there waiting for you when you arrive. Lots of books of local interest and lots of local authors (like me!).

✪✪ **Canio's Books,** two locations: the original store on Main Street in Sag Harbor, 725-4926 and also on Long Wharf in Sag Harbor, 725-4462. Canio Pavone, long a fixture on the local book scene, retired last year. The operation has been purchased by two local writers who have pledged to keep the atmosphere, ambience, and selection in the Canio tradition.

BOREDOM

What to do when you're bored: Pick up this Guide and read it!

BOWLING

You can't be serious! Bowling?! In The Hamptons? Yup. And why not? Too "blue collar" for you? Naaaah! It's great fun! Try:

✪✪✪✪ **East Hampton Bowl**, 71 Montauk Highway., East Hampton, 324-1950, right across the street from the Red Horse Market, 16 lanes.

✪✪✪ **Westhampton Lanes,** 87 Sunset Ave., Westhampton Beach, 288-4244, 24 lanes.

BREAD (see also "Bakeries")

The essential "staff of life," as they say. Here are the best stops for fresh bread (Note: all of these winners have been reviewed elsewhere in the Guide, mostly under "Bakeries," some under "Delis" and "Restaurants"):

✪✪✪✪ **Breadzilla,** Northwest Rd., Wainscott, 537-0955: My East Hampton Spy says these folks have the best bread in the Hamptons. I tend to agree. I've seen—and tasted—some of their wonderful, hot, fresh, clever and twisted breads at several different benefits and events.

✪✪✪✪ **Razzano's,** in the back of the Bridgehampton Commons Shopping Center, Bridgehampton, 537-7288. Wow! Great Italian breads. My favorite is the olive loaf—if you can ever beat the crowds to get one!

✪✪✪ **Schmidt's Produce Co.,** 120 North Sea Rd., Southampton, 283-5777. Schmidt's trucks their bread in from the City, but it's from the same places there that you like best (like Eli's).

✪✪✪ **King Kullen,** Bridgehampton Commons, 537-8103. Surprise! A giant supermarket with a really good on-premises bakery!

✪✪✪ **Barefoot Contessa,** 46 Newtown Ln., East Hampton, 324-0240. Their country rolls are the big winners here—and you can get great health breads by the pound.

✪✪✪ **The Beach Bakery,** 112 Main St., Westhampton Beach, 288-6552.

BROKERS (see "Stockbrokers")

BRUNCH

The best places for brunch in The Hamptons are listed below. Each of these spots is also listed in our section on the very best restaurants in The Hamptons, so go to the "Restaurant" section for complete descriptions.

✪✪✪✪ **Belle's Café,** at the Westhampton Airport, Gabreski Field, 288-3927.

✪✪✪✪ **East Hampton Point,** 295 Three Mile Harbor Rd., East Hampton, 3292800.

✪✪✪✪ **Hampton Maid,** Montauk Highway, Hampton Bays, 728-4166

✪✪✪✪ **Savanna's,** 268 Elm St., Southampton, 283-0202, fax 283-6034.

✪✪✪✪ **The Maidstone Arms,** 207 Main, East Hampton, 324-5006.

✪✪✪ **B. Smith's**, 1 Bay Sr., Sag Harbor, 725-5858.

✪✪✪ **The Post Stop Café,** 144 main St., Westhampton Beach, 288-9777.

BUILDING PERMITS

Woe to those of you who want to build that little dream house—or the addition for junior—and run afoul of the local Planning Board because you didn't get the proper permit or variance. Things have gotten a little better in the past couple of years, but it wasn't that long ago that the planning boards of Southampton and East Hampton were known far and wide for their "Puritan Ethic" when it came to planning decisions. These folks often took it as their God given mandate to protect the East End forever from any sort of modernization or further encroachment on open space or architectural "aberrations." Before proceeding with the add-on and absolutely, positively before breaking ground, always, always work with your builder or contractor to secure the proper permits in advance. If you plow ahead without the necessary permits and then the permit is denied, they WILL make you tear down or dig up what you've done. The Southampton Board can be reached at 283-6000 and the East Hampton Board at 324-2696.

BURGLARY
(see also "Alarm Companies" and "Security Companies")

We made some comments up front in this Guide about crime on the East End. It's not a huge problem, and burglary is not a big problem, but some common sense is in order. We also said that some folks wander off and leave their doors unlocked, and that's true, but not terribly wise.

If you are renting for the season, do you really need your mink and the jewels out here? Aren't they better off locked in your home or safe deposit box in the City? If you must bring the gold Rolex with the diamond bezel and the emeralds, or the 4-carat engagement ring, there are banks here that offer safe deposit services. You might even get your own small safe. Stick it in your closet and bolt it to the floor. Burglary is usually a crime of immediate opportunity. The objective is to get in, rip stuff off, and get out quickly. A safe bolted to the floor will discourage burglars.

If you're in a share situation, know your partners, and see if there's a lockable space in the rental for each of you. Make extra keys to the place and hide a key where all of you can find it in case you're away and a partner gets locked out. If there's an alarm system in place, use it—especially as you leave on Sunday. When you take off for the beach, lock the doors, if not the windows, too. I've seen a couple of situations where the group has gone off to the beach or a party and have come back to find everything of value gone.

BUSINESSES—STARTING YOUR OWN
(see also "Assumed Names" for permit information)

I've seen a lot of folks come out here, fall in love with The Hamptons, and decide they're going to move out here and "go into business." I've seen considerable fortunes invested in dreams. I've seen life savings blown and dreams turn into nightmares. Let me give you some of the best advice you're ever going to get if you decide to go into business here in The Hamptons: Don't. Not unless you are willing and able to do the market research necessary to prove your hypothesis. Your new company must be exactly what The Hamptons needs in order for you to compete successfully. Whether you hire a professional to test the market or do it yourself, please, for your own financial well being, "do the math." Talk to people. Visit the Chambers of Commerce. Talk with professional business brokers and, by all means, take time to visit with the people who will be your competitors (you don't have to tell them you're going to be a competitor, for Heaven's sake, just buy them a cup of coffee and ask them, "How's business?") If things still look good to you, consider the people who will be buying from you. The full-time residents (like me) are fussy, picky and bargain minded (how else can we afford to live here?!). The summer residents may have lots of money, but, remember, they "get it wholesale"—and have been used to buying in the City or elsewhere. Why do they need you?

Here's something else to think about if you are going into the service business: do we need (a) another restaurant? (b) another antique store? (c) another clothing store? (d) another shoe store? (e) another art gallery? (f) another trendy jewelry store? (g) another faux furniture store? (h) another bookstore? (i) another gift shop? The answer to these questions is: NO! NO! and NO! Not unless you are willing and able to make it the best damn store of its type. What are some good examples of how to do this? Jewelry: London Jewelers in East Hampton. This is not, by any stretch, "just another jewelry store." It's a showplace. Men's clothing store: Sak's new Men's Department on Main Street in Southampton. Restaurant: Alison on Dominick branches out, with the same winning formula, to Alison's By The Beach.

Is there any good news? Yes. If you are the best, you can be the best here, too, no matter what you do. More good news: it's a great environment for the entrepreneur who can work from here and tele-commute or cyber-commute to "the real world." If you need help doing that, hire a truly professional business service.

BUSINESS SERVICES

So, you're out here relaxing, and your assistant is in Manhattan and you need some work done FAST and you need some work done WELL? Who do you call?

✪✪✪✪ **East Hampton Business Services,** near the railroad station in East Hampton, 324-0405. Full-service word processing, general business services, faxing, copying, collating, and otherwise getting your fanny out of the sling you've gotten it into.

✪✪✪ **Letter Perfect,** 93 Main St., Sag harbor, 725-1942, fax 725-1944. Resumes, faxing, copies, ad design & layout, newsletters, mail-list maintenance, letters of all kinds. If you're computer shy, they can ever teach you how to boot up that new machine of yours and get started.

BUSES

✪✪✪✪ **Hampton Jitney**—hereabouts known as "The Jitney" (283-4600 for reservations and information or 1-800-936-0440 from The City and beyond), main office located at The Omni, County Rd. 39 in Southampton. The Jitney is the most reliable, on-time and comfortable service between anywhere in The Hamptons and The City. The peak fare, $40 round-trip, is less than parking your car in the City for a day, the wear and tear on your car, and gas. The buses are always clean and roomy, even with someone next to you. You get complimentary reading material, free coffee or juice, and a muffin or snacks. The Jitney makes a number of convenient stops going into The City and has several well-placed pickup spots for the outbound traveler. There is also an airport connection service (Islip, LaGuardia, and Kennedy) that is very convenient, both coming and going. They also do special trips and charters.

BUTCHERS (see "Meats")

C

CABINETS

✪✪✪✪ The folks at **E.T. Raffel** have been doing their magic with cabinets and such for a long time. Now, they have a new showroom in Southampton and you should stop and take a look! It's at 73 County Road 39A, 283-4433. I was very impressed with the quality of the craftsmanship as well as their selection. They've done a lot of the work in many of the finest homes out here. They can show you the pictures, too.

Custom Woodworking

Monday through Friday, 10:00 - 4:30
Saturday, 9:00 - 5:30

73 Country Road 39-A
Southampton, NY 11968
(631) 283-4433
Fax (631) 283-3281

CABLE TV

There's only one choice out here and it's **Cablevision.** And Cablevision is becoming one of the giant companies in this business. They also own the Knicks, The Garden, and the Rangers. I have to say that their service has been pretty good the last couple of years—better than it used to be, especially in the customer service area. They have also been engaged in a major upgrade of their infrastructure here on the East End. Their cable trucks have been everywhere of late, with service people scrambling up poles or digging up turf. It's called "Optimum TV" and what used to be 60 channels of availability is now like, 85 channels. I do admit: the reception seems to be better and there are, indeed, more and better channels. Naturally, rates have gone up. There was a small increase at the beginning of last year. The very basic, minimal package of channels is going to cost about $14 per month, the so-called "Optimum Channels" (most everything else you'd probably want to have) adds another $25 per month. "Premium" channels" (HBO and the like) add another $20 per month, so, after it's all said and done a pretty decent average package is about $58 per month. Call them in Riverhead at 727-6300 or Amagansett at 267-6900 for both service and repair. You can also visit their website at www.cablevision.com.

CAKES (see "bakeries")

CAMPING

At this end of the island, you have three excellent choices for camping. These spots run from grounds with lots of amenities to "wild and wooly."

✪✪✪✪ **Hither Hills State Park,** Old Montauk Highway, Montauk (668-2461). Hither Hills is right on the beach, has tent sites as well as trailer sites, and offers showers, a general store, playing fields, picnic sites and fishing—and miles of gorgeous beach. Reserve well in advance, this campground is frequently full.

✪✪✪ **Cedar Point County Park,** East Hampton (852-7620). 608 acres, mostly on the water, with a number of tent and trailer sites. Water and sanitary facilities are next to the campsites, but there are no hookups. The park juts out into Gardiner's Bay and its furthest point is a stones throw (well, maybe a Schwartzenegger throw) from Shelter Island.

✪✪ **Shinnecock County Park**—East, across the Ponquogue Bridge, Southampton, 854-4949. This is the wide open, no facilities, wind in your face, open beach camping, test me, I'm tough spot. Good luck...and don't call me up at 2 am to come get you.

CANCER

Two comments need to be made about cancer and the East End. The first applies to women and should be taken very seriously. Over the past few years the incidence of breast cancer has been higher here on Long Island, especially on the South Fork (Yikes! The Hamptons!) than most any other place in New York state. A new report in late 1999 indicated that the breast cancer incidence rate here has been much higher than normal. That's quite alarming. There have been comments about "cancer blooms" and "pockets of cancer," etc. There are other studies still ongoing and nothing definitive has been uncovered—yet. The search goes on. I suspect that if you summer here you're in no more danger of breast cancer than anywhere else. If you live out here, there's nothing to panic about—you should just take all the precautions. You should be doing self-exams and, if you're over 40, follow your doctor's advice on mammograms. If you've not yet felt the need to do these helpful and preventive things, and you spend a lot of time out here, you should reconsider your approach to the potentiality of this disease. And I know you've heard it before, but, for heaven's sake remember: the cure and remission rates are so much higher with early detection.

If you'd like more information on breast cancer, or if you have concerns, suspicions, etc., there is a very special group you can call: the Breast Cancer Hotline and Support Program, Garden City (800-877-8077). "The program offers information and emotional support by trained personnel, among whom are women who themselves have had breast cancer. The service is also available to concerned family members and friends. Support groups are in continuous formation. All services are free of charge."

The other cancer comment is relative to sun worshipers of all ages: the sunlight out here, as we have said before, is very special and beguiling. It doesn't mean the UV rays are any less intense because the light is "softer" and the atmosphere is more alluring. If you're prone to burning, have fair, Northern European skin, skin cancer in your family, etc., be careful. Slap on the "30" and get in the shade once in a while.

If you're interested in more information on the subject of cancer, cancer treatments, programs, etc., the American Cancer Society has an office on Long Island in Hauppauge and they can be reached at 800-ACS-2345 or 436-7070.

CANDY

Here are some shops where you can indulge your sweet tooth to the ultimate delight of your dentist's retirement plan:

✪✪✪✪ **Lindt Chocolate Shop,** Tanger Mall II, 369-6005.
✪✪✪✪ **Nuts About Chocolate,** 52 Main St., East Hampton, 329-5202.

✪✪✪ **Going Nuts,** 28 Hill St., Southampton, 283-3901

✪✪✪ **The Penny Candy Store,** Montauk Hwy., Water Mill

✪✪ **A Little of What You Fancy,** 19 Newtown Ln., East Hampton, 324-3113.

✪ **S & L Sweet Shop,** 37 Newtown Ln., East Hampton, 267-3099

✪ **Fudge Company,** 67 Main, Southampton, 283-8108 and 66 Jobs Lane, Southampton, 283-8108.

✪ **Fudge & Stuff,** The Plaza, Montauk, 668-4724

CANOEING (and Kayaking)

Not since the Shinnecock Indians peacefully paddled the laconic waters of Peconic Bay some 300 years ago, have we seen so many canoes on East End waters! It's a canoe revival, and it's fun.

✪✪✪✪ **The Peconic Paddler,** 89 Peconic Av., Riverhead (OK, OK!! I know Riverhead is not the Hamptons, but you can paddle to the Hamptons from there. Good enough?!), 727-9895. You can rent one of the over 400 canoes, kayaks, or shells on display. The shop is located where it is for a very good reason: it's right next to the easiest access to the Peconic River. The waters here are flat and gently flowing, but if you're more ambitious you can paddle down the river a little further, past Indian Island County Park and right out into Flanders Bay.

✪✪✪✪ **Ultimate Kayak Fishing,** Montauk, 668-2929: My Montauk spy, who knows all, says these folks are the best for getting some fun out of kayak fishing. They supply everything.

✪✪✪✪ My Montauk spy has more: **Montauk Kayak & Outfitting**, 668-3899, should also be considered. They are grand for beginners, apparently. Lost of lessons as well as kayak excursions.

✪✪✪ **East End Kayak,** at Main Beach Surf & Sport, Montauk Hwy., Wainscott, 537-2716. Lots of canoes, kayaks, for sale or rent, and they also offer expert guides for East End kayaking either by your-self or with a group!

✪✪ **The Group for the South Fork** sponsors weekly canoe safaris lead by a local nature historian. There is a charge for canoe rentals. Call 537-1400 for schedules, prices, and information.

CARPETS

As their commercial says, "If you don't know carpet, know your Carpetman."

✪✪✪✪ **The Carpetman,** 633 County Rd. 39A, Southampton, 283-0885.
A full warehouse of all kinds of carpet as well as services for cleaning, stain removal, and restoration of your favorite carpets.

CAR POOLING

There's not a lot of this going on out here on the East End. Either we drive the Mercedes or the BMW with defiance or we take an alternative form of transportation—the LIRR, the Jitney, etc.; but, if you are interested in ride sharing or car pooling call the Suffolk County Transportation Information line at 852-5200, weekdays, 8:00 AM to 4:30 PM.

CAR RENTALS

Most of the major companies have offices here although they are more active in the spring and summer than fall and winter. For those of you in The City that have checked out car rental rates in Manhattan and then fainted, a smart alternative is to get on the Jitney and rent out here. If you're flying in, you can rent much more easily and cheaply at Long Island-MacArthur or East Hampton Airport.

✪✪✪✪ **Enterprise,** 395 County Road 39A, Southampton (inside the Jitney stop at the Omni), 283-0055. Reasonable rates plus, like the ads on TV say, they'll come and pick you up—which is a great convenience out here. Their personal service, as well as the convenience of being at the jitney stop, gets them the Gold. Oh, by the way, they're open year 'round.

✪✪✪ **Hertz's** location in Bridgehampton, on Montauk Highway, next to Hayground Farmstand, 537-3843, looks like its was mistakenly placed in the middle of a used car lot. Well, I don't know about a mistake, but it is, indeed, in the middle of a used car lot. Why does this innocuous and somewhat cluttered location get an award? Easy pick up and drop off, excellent service, and nice folks. You can reserve well in advance using the Hertz national 800 number, and the car will be in Bridgehampton when you need it to be.

✪✪ If you just need wheels—cheap wheels, call **Rent-A-Wreck** in Hampton Bays at 728-1536.

CAR WASH

✪✪✪✪ **Southampton Car Wash,** 404 County Rd. 39, Southampton, 283-8990. These guys are good and the prices are pretty reasonable. If you pick up one of their repeat customer cards, you can get a free wash after every ten trips. They're open seven days a week (even in the middle of January) weather permitting, and if you get rained on within a week of your wash, bring 'er on back and they'll do it again and give you a dollar off. There's also a detailing facility on site (see also "Auto Detailing").

CATERERS & CATERING

There are an enormous number of folks out here willing to cater your dinner party, wedding, or other special event. The offerings run from the exquisite (caviar and quail eggs) to the sublime (sandwiches for the game). Many of the better restaurants offer catering services, too. Here are some suggestions.

For the Exquisite:

✪✪✪✪ **Loaves & Fishes,** Main St., Sagaponack, 537-0555. Superb food, and they somehow manage to do it even if they re serving 500. Loaves & Fishes does many of the prominent local benefit parties.

✪✪✪✪ **Art of Eating,** P.O. Box 3232, East Hampton, 267-2411, fax 267-2435. Another one of the companies that seem to get many of the "hot parties." They serve great food, that I can tell you—and they do event planning, too.

✪✪✪ **Food & Co.,** Pantigo Rd., East Hampton, 329-1000.

✪✪✪ **The Barefoot Contessa,** 46 Newtown Lane, East Hampton, 324-0240.

✪✪✪ **Brent Newsom,** Caterer, 85 Sherrill Rd., East Hampton, 329-7365.

✪✪ **Sydney's "Taylor" Made Cuisine,** Westhampton Beach, 288-4722.

✪✪ **Cynthia Battaglia,** Sag Harbor, 329-5878.

For the "Fun Stuff":

✪✪✪✪ **La Parmigiana,** Hampton Rd., Southampton, 283-8030. The very same superb Italian entrees that you can scarf up at your table at "La Parm" can be catered to your party. Call Patty.

✪✪✪✪ **The Golden Pears,** 283-8900 in Southampton, 329-1600 in East Hampton, 537-1100 in Bridgehampton, and 288-3600 in Westhampton Beach. The same wonderful and hearty fare prepared at their local cafes can be picked up or brought to your party.

✪✪✪✪ **Razzano's,** Bridgehampton Commons, 537-7288. Get a couple of big plates of sandwiches for the Game, complete with salads, etc.

✪✪✪✪ **Village Cheese Shop,** 11 Main St., Southampton, 283-6949.

CATS-WILD

No, we don't have a puhling population of pumas. What we do have, and it's a problem, are the so-called feral cats: these "kitties" were once house cats that have been cast out or otherwise abandoned by un-caring former owners. They live out here in the hundreds. With the abundant bird population and numerous small mammals in the fields, there is plenty for them to eat. And the feral cats are multiplying. The situation has spawned radio commercials about spaying and neutering as well as pleas to keep your house cats at home and not set them loose. If you put up a bird feeder, expect feral cats to come a-calling. Amazingly, local Animal Control won't deal with them. Animal Control is under-staffed and poorly funded. In these times of fiscal austerity, they deal with other, bigger issues (like dogs and deer). If you have a cat problem around your property you're going to have to call a commercial animal removal service or a local pest control company. They'll set out traps for the cats (see "Pest Control" and "Animal Rescue"). Or I guess you could buy a BIG dog.

CERAMICS

✪✪✪✪ **O*Suzanna,** 108 Main Street, Westhampton Beach, 288-2202. Boy, is this a great place! One of the best stores in the Hamptons. Everything, and I mean everything, you could possible want in ceramic bowls, dishes, vases, etc. They even have ceramic tables, for heaven's sakes! I'd be nervous as a cat working in this place, afraid to turn around and break something exquisite. Need an over-sized platter for that 25-pound turkey? Unique glassware to match the country set of dishes? A ceramic centerpiece for the table? They're all here—and much more.

CESSPOOLS (and septic tanks)

Many of the homes out here are not on city sewer and have cesspools or septic tanks instead. If you've never owned a home with a septic tank, you should consider getting the tank pumped at least every other year. Some people (mostly the cesspool companies) say you should do it every year. Unless you're having an entire Roman Legion showering and going to the bathroom at your place every weekend, it's probably unnecessary. If you ignore this dirty but essential task, believe me, one day you'll know it. You'll awaken to a truly interesting aroma wafting from your shower or "john." For cleaning and service here's the best.

✪✪✪✪ **Norsic & Son,** Henry Rd., Southampton, 283-0604. They roam the entire East End and do a very credible job. Excellent service and really helpful information. Here's an example: I was tele-marketed recently by a company touting their "sooper-duper" enzyme enriched, scum-busting, clog-dissolving septic tank elixir. It sounded so good you almost wanted to take it as a vitamin supplement! I called a very helpful gentleman at Norsic, Rene, who, with great forbearance, informed me that, sure, I could buy their "gunk" if I had money to throw down the toilet. Well, I don't, so he politely advised me to tell the telemarketing company to put their stuff where the sun don't shine—and definitely not in my septic tank. Rene tells us that if we have the tank serviced regularly, none of that stuff—although it's harmless—is really necessary. He also sent me an informative brochure on septic tanks and their maintenance. Whew! Read it the next time your insomnia kicks in. Anyway, these are good folks. Call 'em.

CHAMBERS OF COMMERCE

We are fortunate to have three very fine local Chambers of Commerce. And I've been lucky enough to get to know the Directors that run each of these Chambers. They have been very supportive and helpful to me in publishing this Guide but more importantly they are stalwart champions of the various businesses that are members of their respective Chambers.

The East Hampton Chamber is lead by Executive Director Marina Van. The offices are located just off Main Street and can be reached at 324-0362, fax 329-1642, and www.easthamptonchamber.com.

The Montauk Chamber's Executive Director is Laurie Costello. The office is right on Montauk Highway just as you get to the circle in the center of Town. Call her at 668-2428 or visit their website at www.montaukchamber.com.

The Southampton Chamber of Commerce is located on Main Street in Southampton. They can be reached at 283-0402, www.southampton.com/chamber. Talk to Executive Director Millie Fellingham. Millie hangs a restroom key on the front door for anyone to use (and return!).

CHILD CARE (see "Day Care")

CHILDREN'S WEAR

Oh baby, oh baby, oh baby!—and kids, too! Here are the best spots for all the tots.

✪✪✪✪ **Punch,** 55 Newtown Ln., East Hampton, 329-3897. This is the place for all the best in clothes and accessories for the kids. This wonderful shop will keep any parent—and grandparent—occupied for hours!

✪✪✪✪ **Gap Kids,** at Bridgehampton Commons, 537-2428. Would we be complete without a Gap Kids? Wonderful, cute, and cuddly clothes for kiddies!

✪✪✪✪ **Hildreth's,** Main St., Southampton, 283-2300. As cute as your kid is he or she will be even cuter if you shop for their clothes at Hildreth's. Great selection and excellent prices.

✪✪✪✪ **Rumrunner Kid,** 41 Main St., East Hampton, 329-5870. Beautifully laid out store with a splendid selection of children's duds and superb baby furniture.

✪✪✪ **Aunt Suzie's,** Hampton Rd., Southampton, 287-4645. Another fun shop for clothes (preemies to age 14), accessories, toys for your "little angels."

✪✪ **Tanger Mall** (while you're there) check out:
OshKosh B'Gosh, 727-7657.
The Gap Outlet Store, for Baby Gap and Gap Kids clothes: 369-1454
J. Crew, Kid's fashions: 369-9474.
Old Navy, lots of T-shirts, pants, etc., for kids: 369-5831.

✪✪ **Laura Ashley,** 87 Main St., Southampton, 287-2104. Wonderful clothes for little girls that are very reasonably priced. They also have bedding for kids and grown-ups. Open 7 days, 12 months, and they have two great sales a year.

✪ **Breezin' Up,** 21 Main St., East Hampton, 329-9370, and 54 Jobs
Lane, Southampton, 283-5680. Cute "Hamptons" signature products for babies and Kids.

CHIMNEY CLEANING

If your cozy little cabin has a fireplace, and even if you use it only occasionally, you should have your chimney swept at least every other year.
Two reasons: (1) For safety. Even a few uses each season will build up
residual carbon and ash inside your chimney. If the conditions are right,
and you have gone a while without a cleaning, these partially burned leftovers can ignite and cause chimney fires. Just a tiny crack in your chimney
can set the second floor or the roof afire. And that'll ruin your day. (2) For
getting rid of unwanted "critters." Chimneys, especially those that are used
only once in a while, are tempting nesting sites for squirrels, some birds,
bats, and other forms of wildlife. A good chimney screen will take care of
this problem, but when was the last time you dragged out that heavy extension ladder and went up on the roof to look? Let a professional do the job.

✪✪✪✪ **Meadowgrass Company,** 14 Meadow Grass Ln., Southampton,
283-6929.

✪✪✪✪ **Bonac Brushers** in Southampton at 283-5333 and East
Hampton at 324-4963. Excellent service, fully insured and they do
inspections, too.

CHINA & GLASSWARE

✪✪✪✪ **Fishs Eddy,** 50 Jobs Lane, Southampton, 287-2993. I love this
place. I found old ceramic teapots from the Harvard Club of New
York City, plates from a couple of the Navy Officers' Clubs I've
eaten in over the last three decades, and great tulip glasses for
those perfect ice cream sundaes! You can furnish your entire country kitchen for very little cost at this eclectic but wonderful store.
By the way, do you know what a "fishs eddy" is? And, no, it's not a
typo. A fishs eddy is that little place in a rushing stream where the
roiling waters curl and pool in a quiet spot. That "eddy" is where
the fish are, so say the smart fishermen. Now, what that has to do
with this store, I haven't a clue. (See also
www.fishseddy.com).

✪✪✪✪ **Hildreth's,** Main Street, Southampton, 283-2300. Good stuff. Solid stuff. Dependable stuff. It's all here at Hildreth's. Platters for the giant roast turkey, all sorts of designer glasses, tableware for just about any Holiday.

✪✪✪ **Villeroy & Boch,** 35 Main St., Southampton, 283-7172. If you want up-scale china and glassware for your country kitchen, you stroll around the corner from Jobs Lane to Main Street and walk into Villeroy & Boch. This store has wonderful collections of first-rate glass and china and it's a Villeroy & Boch Outlet store, so the prices are really good.

✪✪ **Dansk Designs,** 5 Main St., Southampton, 287-2093. OK, OK, you want solid, dependable, moderately priced china and glassware. Somewhere between Fishs Eddy and Villeroy & Boch. This is where you stop. And it happens to be between the two stores, right on Main Street. This is an outlet store, too.

✪ At the **Tanger Mall,** check out these great stores for china and glassware:

Lenox Outlet, 369-6955. It's a Lenox outlet. What more is there to say!

Mikasa Outlet, 369-7245. You know their china. Here it is at great prices!

✪✪ **Home James**, 55 Main St., East Hampton, 324-2307. An excellent shop in East Hampton for china and glassware, but also check them out as a gift shop (see "Gift Shops").

✪✪ **O*Suzanna,** 108 Main St., Westhampton Beach, 288-2202. We've given them a "Gold" in the "Ceramics" category, so see that section, too. They're mentioned here so that you check them out for your needs in plates, etc., even though they're ceramic, not china. Am I making sense?

CHIROPRACTORS

Oh my aching back. Well, if you have a backache or something else out of alignment, here are some people to call. Have you seen any other professionals we should put in the "Guide"? If you have, give us your feedback ("feed-BACK," get it?). We'd like to rate more of these folks for our next issue.

✪✪✪✪ **Dr. Ron Brack,** 10 Pantigo Rd., East Hampton, 329-3523. Dr. Brack has been practicing in East Hampton since 1980. He received his BA from Stony Brook and his Doctorate from NY

Chiropractic College. He has treated literally thousands of East Enders since 1980 and "If you've twisted your back go see Dr. Brack." Well, a poet I'm not, but a good chiropractor he is, so ignore my poor attempts at rhyming and call the good doctor.

✪✪✪✪ **Dr. Robert Merrihew,** 728 Montauk Highway, Water Mill, 726-4580. I got a glowing referral to Dr. Merrihew this past year: "well informed, supportive, and pleasant in every area of chiropractic care." Sounds good to me!

CHRISTMAS & CHRISTMAS TREES

Christmas Trees: There are a number of places here where you can buy cut Christmas trees or go cut-your-own. You can also get living trees to plant in the yard after the Holidays. The idea of "saving a tree" by buying a living tree appeals to my sense of ecological guilt but an 8-foot tree weighs 500 pounds, root ball and all, and costs anywhere from $250–$500! Do you want to scratch the floor and break your back in the process of hauling that sucker into the living room? Then after Christmas you're going to have to wait until Spring to dig a hole big enough to plant a tree that's been sitting on the deck for three months. The average price for an 8-foot cut tree: somewhere between $50 and $80 bucks. You decide how guilty you feel. Here is where to get the best cut trees:

✪✪✪✪ **Eastlands Nursery and Farms,** 1260 Montauk Hwy., Water Mill, 726-1961. An 8-footer, fresh and fragrant, about $50. Eastlands also has a nice selection of wreaths, roping, extra boughs, and branches for decoration, etc.

Christmas Shops

✪✪✪✪ **Christmas Southampton,** 20 Main Street, Southampton, 287-8787. Great selection of ornaments and lights. And if you're a smart shopper, go there the day after Christmas to stock up for next Christmas.

✪✪✪ **Christmas East Hampton,** 70 Park Place, East Hampton, 324-5577. Same idea as Southampton and very well stocked.

CHUCKHOLES (see "Potholes")

CHURCHES (see also "Synagogues")

I think the best church in the Hamptons is the Beach. Any beach. Get up early, for once, and drive, walk, or bike to the beach before sunrise. Sit in the sand and watch the sun come up. Pray. It's as close to God as you'll ever feel.

CIGARS

.".."and a good cigar is a SMOKE!" How true, but where can you go to get a good "cee-gar"? Better yet, where can you go to actually smoke your stogie? Well, since cigars are going through a political rehabilitation, there are a couple of spots where you are welcome to buy a good cigar and puff away.

To sit and have a smoke:

✪✪✪✪ **The Cigar Bar,** 2 Main St., Sag Harbor, 725-2575. One of my favorite spots in The Hamptons. Just a nice place to sit and have a smoke and a cool and delicious cocktail of your own personal choosing.

✪✪✪✪ **The American Hotel,** Main St., Sag Harbor, 725-3535. In addition to this being one of the most picturesque spots in The Hamptons, The American Hotel is a headquarters for cigar lovers. The hotel's gift shop sells a grand variety of smokes. The hotel has special dinners or evenings centered around smokers or special wines. Stop by for a puff, relax on the front porch. Call for details on special dinners.

To buy your stogies:

✪✪✪✪ **London Jewelers,** 2 Main St., East Hampton, 329-3939. What!? Cigars in a jewelry store?! Yup. Wonderful walk-in humidor and a great selection of the best; or, at least the best you can get without smuggling them in from Cuba or St. Barth's.

✪✪✪✪ **The American Hotel,** Main St., Sag Harbor, 725-3535. There's a wonderful cigar and "necessary provisions" store adjacent to the hotel. In addition to your Davidoff's and such, you'll find Petrossian caviar, foie gras, smoked salmon, Limoges, Fragonard perfumes and long stemmed roses!

✪✪✪✪ **Doug & Besim's,** 46 Jobs Lane, 287-9230. Doug Osvath &

Besim Cukaj have partnered to create a first-rate tobacconist's shop here on Jobs Lane. Best selection of cigars in the Hamptons. They just recently moved from down the block to this new location. Lighters, humidors, local papers, and magazines. Cappuccino, Espresso, and fresh, hot coffee and teas. And there may be more. This new location has a lot of interesting possibilities. Go check it out! Good guys and they deserve your business.

✪✪ **Shinnecock Smoke Shop,** Rte 27-A, Southampton, across from LIU (Southampton College), 283-0666.

CLAMBAKES

The clambake on the beach, with fire pits, steamed lobsters, mussels and clams, corn on the cob dripping in butter, etc., is, for the most part, a lost art. Plus, there are fewer and fewer beaches where you are allowed to have a clambake. Southampton will allow them after dusk at Flying Point Beach, with a permit from Town Hall. But no alcohol. If you want a real, professional clambake, have someone cater it and have it in your back yard. Less sand in the food, too.

✪✪✪✪ **The Clamman,** North Sea Rd., Southampton, 283-6437 (see also "Fish Markets"). The Clamman will stuff a clambake in a bucket for you, (about $25 per person), which you can take away and "bake" yourself, either on a beach or in your back yard. They will cater to groups as small as 10, up to several hundred. They'll supply everything including the food, bartenders, tables, fire pits, and so forth.

✪✪✪ **East End Clambakes,** 131 Upper 7 Ponds Rd., Water Mill, 726-6351. Capt. Phil Gay has been a Bayman for over 20 years. Let him show you his "mussels"—as well as his clams, lobsters, barbecued chicken, fresh local corn, etc.

✪✪ **East End Catering & Tent Rental,** 40 Old West Lake Dr., Montauk, 668-4483. These guys can do it all, too: clambakes, luaus, bands, belly dancers, Elvis impersonators, etc. Their beach or yours?

CLOTHING STORES (see the "Men's Clothing," "Women's Clothing," "Children's Wear," and "Malls" sections)

CLUBS & THE "CLUB SCENE"

We're talking about The Places to be seen. The Club Scene in The Hamptons can be very exciting, but it's also very unstable. There have been mega-hits and major disasters. If a club survives for more than two years it's actually a minor miracle. Here's the scoop on what you might expect this season.

✪✪✪✪ **Jet East,** North Sea Rd., Southampton: Hands down, the hottest club in The Hamptons. If you're a "celeb," you're in (and a ton of them turn up here). If you're unaccompanied and beautiful (male or female), you're in. If you're not in one of those two categories, you're at the mercy of the maniac who works the rope line. And he has his own set of convoluted rules on who's going to get in and who's going to be behind the ropes all night. I'm told that "old guys" (over 30) get in if they have a woman on each arm and the women have the least possible clothes on that are legal in public. Giggling gum-chewers don't get in. Anybody with a tie on doesn't get in. Middle-aged couples don't get in unless their name is Perleman or Spielberg or Kennedy or something like that. This is definitely not democracy in action. Of course, the "concierge" is trying to get the hippest, coolest, most beautiful people in the club, but I, for one, would rather be at the Cigar Bar in Sag Harbor sipping a scotch. Anyway, as Groucho Marx once said, "I wouldn't go to a club that would let me in…"

✪✪✪✪ **NV Tsunami,** 44 Three Mile Harbor Rd., East Hampton: Same owner (Frank Cilione) as the NV in The City, and Frank has successfully transplanted his tres chic ideas to East Hampton. This is a very attractive club and it's my bet that it'll be one of the Hot Spots in The Hamptons this summer. NV has also added a restaurant and I hear it's pretty darn good.

✪✪✪✪ **Tavern,** 125 Tuckahoe Lane, Southampton, 287-2125. Tavern is the veteran of the Clubs out here. Doesn't seem possible, but Tavern is going into its 7th season. Gordon Van Broock and his partners have been doing well in this converted potato barn and were among the first to successfully bring "nightlife" to The Hamptons.

✪✪✪ **Canoe Place Inn,** Montauk Hwy., Hampton Bays, right at the Shinnecock Canal, 728-4121. This venerable spot is simply known as "C-P-I." It's rockin' on all Friday and Saturday nights from May through September. CPI books a lot of acts. Been around a long time, and its lots of fun.

✪✪✪ **The Wild Rose,** Bridgehampton-Sag Harbor Turnpike, Bridgehampton, 537-5050. This is a favorite for "locals." In fact, one of my good local friends asked me if I was putting The Wild Rose in the Guide and I said, yes. "Oh, no!," was his reply, "Now everyone will know about it. Do you have to?" "Yes," was my reply, if I want to do the right thing with the "Guide." Fun place. Good spot to fuzz out on a weekend night. Light menu. And this spot is open all week April through October, otherwise Wednesday through Sunday, and it is CASH ONLY!

CLUBS & ORGANIZATIONS (Fraternal and Social)

The following is a list of the more popular and recognized Clubs and Organizations that you'll find out here. They are listed with their local numbers. Since you belong to or know something about these clubs, we haven't provided in-depth discussions of each—you probably know all that stuff already, but at least you'll know your favorite group is here and you can give them a call:

Business:

AARP Meets 4th Monday, 1 PM, 1st Presbyterian Church, South Main St., Southampton
American Assoc. of University Women 324-7534
Rotary Club: Southampton 283-0700; Hampton Bays 728-3261
SCORE, 454-0771.
Zonta Int'l (Eastern Suffolk Club), 726-2767

Environmental (see also "Environmental" for local groups):

Group for the South Fork, 537-1400
Nature Conservancy, 329-7689

Fraternal:

D.A.R., 283-3366
Elks-Southampton: Men 283-1574/Ladies 283-1574
Friends of Erin (Montauk), 668-3575
Kiwanis (Southampton), 728-1479
Knights of Columbus (Southampton), 283-3326
Columbiettes, 283-3326
Masons (Southampton), 283-8419
Moose (Riverhead), 727-6667
Women of the Moose, 727-6667

Political:

Democrats (East Hampton), 324-8778
League of Women Voters, 537-0120
Liberal Party, 271-6920
NOW-Southampton, 725-3577
Republicans (East Hampton), 668-2411

Service:

American Cancer Society, 436-7070
American Heart Assc., 567-7900
American Red Cross, 283-8336
Emergencies, 924-6911
Big Brothers & Sisters, 360-8908
Catholic Charities, 733-7000
Chabad Crisis Intervention, 938-1177
Coop Extension (4H), 727-7850
Hadassah, 325-1525
Human Resources of Sacred Hearts, 283-6415
La Leche League, 267-7613
Lion's Club, call John Ducks', 283-0311
MADD, 547-MADD
Parents Without Partners, 283-0762
Rotary, call John Duck's, 283-0311
St. Vincent de Paul Society, 277-9600
Salvation Army, 363-6100

Veterans:

American Legion:
    Bridgehampton, 537-0601
    East Hampton, 267-8728
    Sag Harbor, 725-9759
D.A.V., 727-2027
V.F.W., 499-7651
Vietnam Vets of America, 473-2253

Youth:

B'nai B'rith Youth (BBYO), 499-4384
Boy Scouts (Suffolk Council), 924-7000
Girl Scouts (Suffolk Council), 543-6622
Little League:
    Hampton Bays, 728-0066
    Montauk, 668-3398
    Southampton, 283-8085

COFFEE SHOPS & DINERS

"Whaddya have to do to get a good cuppa coffee around here?"! Well, get to one of these spots. Some of them are also known for some pretty decent, food, too.

✪✪✪✪ **Bridgehampton Candy Kitchen,** at the first stoplight on Main Street in Bridgehampton, 537-9885. Spotless little place where you can grab a sandwich, the papers, a good cuppa coffee, and, if you have the time and the calories to waist, er, I mean "waste," you can dive into a really good, sloppy, gooey sundae.

✪✪✪✪ **Planet Java,** 107 W. Montauk Hwy., Hampton Bays, 723-3238. A Bohemian little place. It's in the Hamlet Green Shopping Complex next to the 7-11. New Age music plays in the background while you select and sip a delicious brew. Sit on the couch with your coffee and relax while tackling a fat muffin or a homemade donut.

✪✪✪✪ **Java Nation,** just off Main Street, Sag Harbor, 725-0500: Just like Paul Simon said: "Duck down the alley way with the roly-poly little fat-faced girl...." Well, your girl (or guy) doesn't have to be chubby, but you will have to duck down the alley off of Main Street and bound up the steps to find Java Nation. If you do, you'll get great, home-brewed coffee and some mighty fine pastries, too.

✪✪✪✪ **Sip 'n Soda,** 40 Hampton Rd., down the block from Saks, 283-9752. There is no better place for that first cup of coffee in the morning to get you rolling—or to get you back to level after one of those nights! Pitch into one of their hearty breakfasts, too, especially if you need some extra "carbs."

✪✪✪ **McDonald's,** North Sea Rd., Southampton, 283-6777. Even though the Golden Arches are missing (the town wouldn't grant a variance to erect them!), the best chain-prepared cup of coffee is not. I don't know how McDonald's manages to prepare such good coffee so consistently from store to store, but they do. Just don't spill it in your lap.

✪✪✪ **Starbucks,** Main St., Bridgehampton. We finally have a Starbuck's! Now, you may feel the Hamptons have officially "arrived" or that we're on our way to "LA-LA Land." In either case, you'll find all the Starbuck's signature brews at this new store.

✪✪✪ **Hampton Bays Diner,** Montauk Hwy. And Rte. 24, Hampton Bays, 728-0840. This convenient spot is just off the Sunrise Highway at exit 64 (east) just as you come into The Hamptons. Great omelets, good burgers, and a bathroom stop, which you're probably in need of since leaving the City two hours ago!

✪✪ **Southampton Princess Diner,** at the stoplight in Southampton, where Route 39-A turns left and becomes Montauk Highway, 283-4255. They say you can always tell a good diner—and a safe one!—by all the police cars parked in front of it. If that's true, then this must be a great place. They feature many specials and the desserts are mostly home made.

COLLEGES & UNIVERSITIES

We have only two college campuses in or near The Hamptons.
The first is a branch of Suffolk Community College in Riverhead and the second is the campus of Long Island University (LIU) in Southampton.

The Suffolk Community College branch is actually the college's Eastern Campus, located in Riverhead on Speonk-Riverhead Rd., 548-2500. The school offers a number of the same two-year college courses given by the main campus in Selden; but, to finish a full, two-year degree it may be necessary for you to attend some additional courses "up island," depending on your major.

The LIU campus in Southampton is a four-year school granting bachelor's degrees in a number of areas. The school is actually very well regarded for many of its courses but is perhaps best known for its excellent program in marine science. There are a limited number of graduate programs, principally in education (the M.A.T., for example) and a new Master in Fine Arts in Writing Program. This campus is also affiliated with C.W. Post, as part of the LIU system, so students can also take courses at Post. LIU Southampton is very lovely and offers a quiet, laid-back lifestyle for its students. The grounds border Shinnecock Hills (and the world famous Shinnecock Golf Club) on one side and stretch nearly to the shores of Shinnecock Bay on the other side. The college's main information number is 283-4000.

COMPUTERS (purchasing and repair)

With more and more people using computers and surfing the Internet out here, a business niche is slowly developing for the computer professional on the East End. Several companies have come and gone in the past couple of years but the business is building. Here are some good folks you can rely on for sales, service, software, upgrades, etc..

✪✪✪✪ **East End Computer Company,** 30 Long Island Ave., Sag Harbor, 725-4000. When I'm not writing books, I spend a lot of my time in the service industry. Here are people who understand service. When I had a printer unexpectedly blow up on me, I called around to several companies for help. Noone seemed really enthused about messing around with my rather low-end printer. Except for East End Computer. Even though my immediate business would be marginal, at best, they treated me like Bill Gates (a good thing to do if you're in the computer business!). They found answers to my questions, got the info I needed, and made me feel like someone cared about my problem. Net result is that my poor ol' printer really belonged in Printer Heaven. So, I buried it quietly and bought a new machine from East End Computer. They'll be getting my future business because they believe in service!

✪✪✪ **Charde Computer Service,** 350 Montauk Hwy., Wainscott, 324-2064. PC specialists that make house calls.

✪✪ **Computers Unlimited,** 2228 Montauk Hwy and Butter Lane Corner, Bridgehampton, 537-2210.

CONCIERGE SERVICES

I don't feel comfortable rating the very best Concierge service in the Hamptons, the "Hamptons Concierge" because, well, I own it! But I don't run it. That important job has been taken over by two very capable and wonderful ladies, Barbara Stone and Christina Redding. Please call them (726-7565) for anything you might need in the line of Concierge services. Better yet, go on line and check out www.hamptonsconcierge.com. Then tell me what you think. You can rate me for a change!

CONTRACTORS

Although this category is primarily for homebuilders, or "general contractors," I want to start out with a special note on contractors of all types. Sometimes, it seems to me, that there's an undeclared war going on between homeowners and our local contractors: plumbers, painters, electricians, you name it. I hear too many complaints from homeowners about the snail-like pace at which their contractors seem to work. I hear just as many complaints from contractors about the totally unreasonable demands that many homeowners place upon them. Here's the deal, and this should not be "rocket science": When Ron Perleman, who has more money than God, bought his estate in East Hampton, he had 30 (+) trucks packed with contractors sitting outside the gates of The Creeks on the morning of the closing. As soon as the documents were signed, a signal was sent via cell phone to "Go." Ron wanted to completely gut the place and have everything done so that he could enjoy the upcoming summer season, just six weeks away. So, Lesson Number One, if you have a bank account similar to Ron Perleman's, you'll get all the help you can stand and the work will be done quickly.

If you have less money than Ron Perleman (and that's 99.9999999% of the rest of us), be patient. The best contractors (like those listed in this Guide) will have full work schedules all the time, especially "in season." There are times, though, when the schedules are lighter, that is to say, in the Fall and Winter. If you can possibly do it, it's always better to schedule your work during the months of October through February. You'll get better prices, too!

And speaking of prices, make sure you get complete, written estimates on the work to be performed. There's a wonderful tradition out here, among even some of the best service providers, to tell a homeowner, "Well, it'll cost about 'X' and I'll have it done in three weeks." Suddenly, 'X' will be spent in one week and then there will be unanticipated add-on costs because of 'Y'. "And, oh, because of 'Y', I can't get the work done in two more weeks. It'll take six more weeks, unless you want to add 'Z' to the cost, then I can get it done quicker." If a contractor is not willing or able to give you a complete, written estimate up front, call someone else. Call someone else anyway, even if they do. Second opinions are good. Don't be afraid to compare and contrast, and tell the contractors about the competing estimates.

But, dear homeowners, don't make unreasonable demands. This is where I see the biggest arguments erupt. The pace of life out here is, indeed, less frantic than in The City. Ripping out your old deck and putting in a new one so you can have that client cocktail party in two weeks is just not as important to some of our contractors as it is to you. And don't use "the attitude" on them, either. If you do, you will experience the Great Hamptons Construction Corollary: "The pace of completion of any project is inversely proportional to the negativity of the client."

Now, if you're building a home or doing any extensive remodeling, an honest, reliable contractor is essential. You're going to be involved in a very intimate relationship with this person, so chose carefully! Here are the best.

Home Builders:

✪✪✪✪✪ **Tedaldi Construction,** 653-5588. Although Ken Tedaldi is located in Quogue, he's been doing a lot of construction in The Hamptons over the past few years. Ken is a perfectionist—and that's what you want! He has built some of the most beautiful homes out here. His style is mostly quasi-contemporary, with lots of columns and pillars, angles and windows.

Here are some other excellent contractors:
✪✪✪✪ **Andreassen & Bulgin,** 88 Mariner Dr., Southampton, 283-9670
✪✪✪✪ **Ben Krupinski,** 15 Toylsome Ln., East Hampton, 324-3656
✪✪✪✪ **Pat Trunzo,** Buckskill Rd., East Hampton, 324-5025
✪✪✪✪ **C. S. Hildreth,** General Contractor, Bridgehampton, 537-1972
✪✪ **KMI,** Ltd., 34 Tanager Lane, Water Mill, 726-3066

Major Remodeling:

✪✪✪✪ **Gaeton Berube,** 399-2274. Gaeton does a lot of work with Ken Tedaldi (above). He is a master craftsman and does impeccable work.

COOKIES

✪✪✪✪ **Hampton Chutney Co.,** 74 Montauk Hwy., Amagansett, 267-3131. The East Hampton spy says that "Their peanut butter cookies are the best in the universe!"

✪✪✪✪ **Round Swamp Farm,** 184 Three Mile Harbor Rd., East Hampton, 324-4438. A family operation turning out some of the most delicious cookies you've ever had!

✪✪✪ **Beach Bakery,** 112 Main St., Westhampton Beach, 288-6552. Lots of great cookies to sample at one of the great general bakeries in The Hamptons!

✪✪ Another favorite cookie hangout of ours is **David's Cookies,** 30 Main St., East Hampton, 329-2738.

COPIES (and Copying)

Here's where to get those quick copies done by folks who are really helpful.

Bridgehampton:

✪✪✪✪ **Ocean Copies** in Bridgehampton, Snake Hollow Rd., backside of Bridgehampton Commons Shopping Center, 537-1220.

East Hampton:

✪✪✪✪ For full service copies and duplicating, **East Hampton Business Service,** 19 Railroad Ave., East Hampton, 324-0405 (see also "Business Services").

Southampton

✪✪✪✪ **Southampton Stationery,** 18 Hampton Rd., Southampton, 283-1964.
✪✪✪ **Rite-Aid Pharmacy,** Hampton Rd., Southampton, 283-2604.

CORPORATE FUNCTIONS

Well, we're in trouble here. There just aren't many places where you can have a corporate meeting—at least not one of any size. If you need a small meeting, check out our "Accommodations" category for Bed & Breakfasts, Hotels, and Inns. If you need a quiet, private dinner (always difficult at most of the restaurants) try calling one of the B & B's listed and just have them cater a private meal. I know of several companies and groups who have found this to be a very acceptable alternative. The biggest corporate retreat centers out here are probably Gurney's, the Montauk Yacht Club, and Montauk Manor, all in Montauk (see "Accommodations—Hotels"). Plus, call the Southampton Inn. They've just remodeled and have added some decent meeting room facilities.

COSMETICS

Here are two truly unique and wonderful stores that feature cosmetics.

✪✪✪✪ **The Cosmetics Company Store,** Tanger Mall II, Riverhead, 208-1765. This is an outlet store with great prices on all the major brands of cosmetics. If you can't find it here at a great price, you're not going to find it.

✪✪✪✪ **Naturopathica,** Red Horse Plaza, 74 Montauk Hwy., East Hampton, 329-2525. Everything to go with the fabulous facials, massages, and spa treatments they offer.

COSTUMES

You can walk around Main Street in Southampton or Main Street in East Hampton any given Saturday night in summer and swear that there must be a costume party going on somewhere! Truth is that most of these people are, well, shall we say, "fashion challenged?" If you really do need a costume, there aren't many choices out here, but here are the good ones.

✪✪✪✪ **The Party Shoppe,** 82 Park Pl., East Hampton, 324-9547.

✪✪✪ **The Whalebone General Store,** 3495 Noyac Rd., Noyac, 725-2277.

CULTURAL ACTIVITIES

The Cultural and Civic Center of Southampton, Pond Lane (across the street from Agawam Park), 287-4300, offers a wide range of year round activities in music, dance, drama, and the arts. Just give them a call to see what's going on.

You might also try the **East End Arts Council** in East Hampton, 133 East Main St., 727-0900. These folks present jazz festivals, performing-arts series, children's theater, gospel concerts, arts and education projects, and so forth. Again, give them a call.

Other "cultural activities" are represented throughout these listings. Check out, among others, "Museums," "Theaters," "Clubs and Organizations," "Nature," the "Environment," "History," etc.

Its' also a good idea to pick up the weekend edition of the *Times*, Long Island section, to get the latest cultural "doings."

DAY CAMPS (see "Kids, Kids, Kids!")

DAY CARE

What more important decision can you make than whom to watch over your children while you're doing other things? There are a number of day care providers and baby-sitters, many of whom advertise in the local papers. It's always best to get a referral. We've done a bit of digging for this category and we feel comfortable, very comfortable, giving you the following recommendations, by area. But first, a word of advice: most day care centers are set up for continuous, affordable day care for working parents in the Hamptons. Not all of them are equipped for nor do all of them accept children for "occasional days." It's best to call ahead and ask.

Bridgehampton:
    Hampton Day School, 739 Butter Lane, 537-1240
East Hampton:
    East Hampton Day Care, Gingerbread Lane, 324-5560
    Camp Karol, 44 Woods Lane, 324-3510

Montauk:
Pathfinder Country Day Camp, Second House Rd., 668-2080
Southampton:
Once Upon A Day Care, Inc., 502 North Sea Rd., 283-6265
Fountain of Youth Day Care, David White's Lane, 287-8734
Westhampton:
Raynor Country Day School, 145 Montauk Hwy., 288-4652

DEER

They are abundant out here. It may be wonderful and exciting to see these little bambis strolling through your backyard, but be careful. First, believe it or not, deer can be aggressive when they are threatened, especially the males and especially during mating season. Those antlers can be dangerous! Secondly, all the deer out here have deer ticks. Deer ticks carry Lyme disease. Check out our notes on Lyme disease, below, to see what a nasty situation that can be. Thirdly, although it might be thrilling to have a half-dozen deer standing outside your back deck waiting for your leftovers (they eat darn near anything), if you feed them once, they'll come back to drive you nuts. They are very territorial, and once your yard gets imprinted in their pea brains, they will circle by your place every day. Everything in your yard of an edible nature becomes a target: your prized vegetables, to be sure. They will also eat your tulips, dig for your newly planted bulbs, ravage your blossoming flowers, nibble your bushes, raid your flower boxes, and on and on. Once you have deer, it's a real challenge to get rid of them. You might not even know you have deer until it's too late. They are mostly nocturnal, raiding in the wee hours of the morning. A sure sign that you have deer, other than the disgusting little round droppings they leave in piles everywhere, is the evidence they leave on your plants. Deer don't nibble leaves. They tear them. So, if your leaves and stems look torn, you probably have deer. Deer out here have no natural enemies—except during the very short and very limited hunting season. And they will go anywhere. Once you have them, how do you get rid of them? It's not easy. The secret lies in getting your place off of their trek list—break their habit of wandering into your yard. You could put up fencing, but a deer can leap an 8-foot fence with no effort whatsoever. And most deer fences are ugly. John Halsey had to fence his beautiful commercial apple orchards last year (see "Apple Picking"). The fence must be ten feet high and it's tasteful, as deer fencing goes, but now his acreage looks like Stalag 13. You might try two things: I was fairly successful last year with—are you ready for this?—coyote urine! Yes, they make a synthetic coyote urine, sold at most garden centers. Coyotes, even though we don't have any out here, are natural enemies of the deer, and the smell of coyote piss is imprinted somewhere deep in those deer brains. They smell it, they turn tail and run. I sprinkled it on strips of rags that I put on 3-foot stakes around my vegetable garden. It worked OK until it rained, then you have to reapply it. Oh, and don't spill it on yourself. You'll smell like a bowl full of coyote pee and your mate won't let you in the house for a week. Another thing you can try is putting up some stout wooden stakes or thin, metal rods around your garden. Get them 6–8-feet tall and place them about every six feet or so. Get some monofilament fishing line (cheap stuff) and string it around the poles at the 3- and 5-foot levels. Tie a few old aluminum pie pans to the fishing line. Deer can't see the line at night and will run into it. They won't go where they can't see or where they get blocked. The pie pans will rattle when the line is touched or even when the wind blows. Deer don't like noise, either, and they will flee. You could also get a big dog, but the dog will be up and barking all night.

DEER TICKS (see "Insects" and "Lyme Disease")

DELIS

There's a deli on every corner! Which are the best? I'll pick some for you by location, but I think the best three are Razzano's, the Village Cheese Shop, and La Parmigiana.

Amagansett:

✪✪✪✪ **Brent's,** Montauk Hwy., 267-3113: A local institution. Go for the sandwiches, for sure, but also pick up some wonderful homemade salads and some of the best fried chicken in the Hamptons.

Bridgehampton:

✪✪✪✪✪ **Razzano's,** in the back of the Bridgehampton Commons Shopping Center, Bridgehampton, 537-7288. If there's a Zabar's or a Bari's out here, this is it. Anything you might want to grab to complement your table in the line of meats, cheeses, prepared Italian dishes, salads, and sandwiches can be found at Razzano's. They also have a fine line of packaged specialty foods, pastas, and breads. There's a small restaurant area where you can sit down and order some of the goodies staring at you from behind the enticing glass cases. Nice friendly folks, too.

East Hampton:

✪✪✪✪ **Villa Italian,** 7 Railroad Ave., 324-5110. Owned by the same family for over 20 years. They make a lot of what they sell—and you will absolutely LOVE the homemade sausages. Man, are they great on the barbecue! Humongous and delectable heros, too.

Hampton Bays:

✪✪✪ **Scotto's,** 25 W. Montauk Hwy., 728-5677, fax 728-7743: Finally! A real Italian Pork Store comes to The Hamptons! Breads and cookies from Brooklyn, homemade sausage, pasta, fresh mozzarella, Boar's Head meat products, and an on-site butcher. Open 7 days, 9 AM to 8 PM and they accept major credit cards.

Sagaponack:

✪✪✪✪ **Sagg Main Store,** 542 Sagg Main Road, 537-6036 (it's attached to the Post Office!): Fresh bagels, all sorts of condiments, salads, meats, cheeses, and much more. You might try one of the delicious looking shepherd's pies, or maybe a chicken pot pie. Just bring it home, pop it in the oven and you're a hero!

Southampton:

✪✪✪✪ **La Parmigiana,** 48 Hampton Rd., 283-8030. Known for its superb Italian food served in a casual atmosphere, "La Parm" also dishes up wonderful take-home items. Great deli meats as well as olives, cheeses, cookies and salads. Freshest mozzarella in The Hamptons!

✪✪✪✪ **Village Cheese Shop,** 11 Main St., Southampton, 283-6949: You can pick up some exotic cheese, or a tin or English marmalade, or a jar of weird looking mushrooms from some place I can't pronounce, or....

✪✪✪ Another place I've discovered that I like is the **Jobs Lane Deli,** 76 Jobs Lane in Southampton, 283-0909.

Wainscott:

✪✪✪✪ **Ceriello Fine Foods,** 352 Montauk Hwy., 537-8157. This "fine" store, in the Wainscott Village, has a grand selection of Italian specialty foods including home made mozzarella, sausage, pastas, and sauces. They also have their own butcher and do catering.

DELIVERY COMPANIES

All the major companies have service to The Hamptons and the coverage is good. Here's the scoop.

✪✪✪✪ **FedEx,** 1-800-238-5355. Most drop boxes, most trucks, friendliest drivers, most reliable delivery schedules. Best place to catch them at the last moment: just before 5 PM at the office complex on the corner of Hampton and Flying Point Rds., behind Southampton Buick Cadillac. There's usually a truck and driver parked there. Our local driver is Tony, and he's terrific!

✪✪✪ **UPS,** 1-800-742-5877. Reliable delivery throughout The Hamptons, and the drivers seem to go the extra few steps to make sure packages are safely delivered or tucked out of the weather if you're not at home.

✪✪ **Airborne,** 1-800-247-2676. Just a little more complicated to get them to pick up and irritatingly few drop-boxes, but they are catching up. And their delivery service is excellent.

✪ **Rite-Aid Pharmacy,** Hampton Rd. and Windmill Ln., Southampton, 283-2604, has UPS and Airborne pick-up spots. They can also help you wrap the package!

✪ **Dial-a-Delivery,** 537-3621, beeper: 831-2314. Call Michael. "Anything, Anywhere, Anytime," delivered door-to-door. Anything legal, that is.

DENTAL CARE & DENTISTS

Finding a good dentist can be like, well, "pulling teeth." I know. Starting with a football injury that knocked out a front tooth many years ago and a jaw that was partly smashed while I was in Vietnam, I have been personally supporting the lifestyles of many dental professionals for a long time now. Here are some really, really good people:

General Dentistry:

✪✪✪✪ **Dr. Eugene Greco, DDS,** 64 N. Main St., Southampton, 283-1040. Gene knows all the best dental specialists in the area and is an excellent dentist himself. Gene's approach is one of keeping you totally informed, I appreciate that a great deal, and he has all the latest state-of-the-art equipment for diagnosis and teaching his patients about dental health (and ask to play with his "virtual reality" equipment while you're in the chair!). He's done great things for me, even teaching me a trick or two about my back swing. (Do not challenge this guy for a buck a hole unless you feeling really generous.)

✪✪✪ **Dr. Richard Nesi,** 67 Hampton Rd., Southampton, 287-1472. I have not personally been to Dr. Nesi (Gene Greco is my dentist), but he comes highly recommended by someone I trust. Dr. Nesi is also the dentist for our local PBA (Police Benevolent Association).

✪✪✪ **Dr. Peter McGuinn, DDS,** Hampton Dental Group, PC, 339 Meeting House Ln., Southampton, 283-0352. Some very good friends of ours recommended Dr. McGuinn.

Orthodontia:

✪✪✪✪ **Dr. Leo J. "Bud" O'Callaghan,** DDS, PC, 339 Meeting House Ln., Southampton, 283-0222. Imagine someone my age going to an orthodontist! Well, I did and the experience was positive and pleasant (after the first set of braces!) thanks to Bud O'Callaghan. I was right there in a chair alongside the 8th and 9th graders. I never had the nerve to pick any other color than plain, dull gray for my rubber bands, though...

Endodontics:

✪✪✪✪ **Dr. Alan Nevins,** DDS, 339 Meetinghouse Ln., Southampton, 287-4824. I have had to go for root canal surgery three times in the past three years and Dr. Nevins handled it expertly. Even the dreaded novocaine needles were relatively painless! Each time I had to undergo this procedure I was in and out quickly and I never had any after-surgery pain or problems. And I have to say a couple more things about Alan, even though he'll be characteristically modest about all this. When Myra and I got married last November it was at the lovely Rams Head Inn on Shelter Island. We hired a professional photographer (Debbie Kalas—see "Photographers") and she was wonderful, but after Debbie was done, Alan graciously stepped in with his marvelous amateur's eye and produced many marvelous candid shots that made superb wedding memories for us. And then there was, of all things, last New Year's Eve. Gene Greco was finishing a new bridge for me, but I bit down hard on something and part of the bridge fell out. Of course, it had to be the front tooth! I mean, for Pete's sake, it's New Year's Eve of the new millennium, Myra and I are going out to dinner at Serafina, and I look like I've gone three rounds with Mike Tyson or substituted in-goal for Mike Richter. I call Gene. He's in Vail. In desperation, I call Alan. He's literally pulling out of his driveway headed for New Year's Eve with friends in Boston. Service? You want to know about professional service? Alan drives to his office, changes into his scrubs and pieces me back together. Now that's a great dentist—and a good friend.

Oral Surgery:

✪✪✪✪ **Dr. Jack Nelson,** DDS, 240 West Montauk Hwy., Hampton Bays, 728-1300. Dr. Nelson extracted a friend's wisdom teeth and made it as positive an experience as yanking out four severely impacted teeth could be. Dr. Nelson even followed up by phone to check on him (how many health professionals are still doing that?!). Dr. Nelson can also treat TMJ.

Pediatric Dentistry:

✪✪✪✪ **Hampton Pediatric Associates,** 97 N. Main St., Southampton, 287-TOTS. Dr. Nancy Cosenza and her associates specialize in making kids (and fretful parents) comfortable with the sometimes frightening and bewildering world of pediatric dentistry. The office is designed to be "kid friendly" and they keep all kinds of weird hours to accommodate the most bizarre schedules. Orthodontics for kids, here, too.

Periodontics:

✪✪✪✪ **Dr. Gary Brenner, DMD,** 97 North Main St., Southampton, 283-6362. If you need some periodontal work done, implants, or have an unfortunate breath disorder, Dr. Brenner is the one to see.

DEPARTMENT STORES

✪✪✪✪✪ The number one department store in The Hamptons is **Hildreth's Department Store,** 51 Main St., Southampton, 283-2300. If there is one store that defines the link between the "good ol' days" and the dawn of the New Millennium, it's Hildreth's. Hildreth's is, no kidding, America's oldest department store, having been founded in 1842; and, even more amazingly, still run by members of the Hildreth family. I think Hildreth's was the very first store I first stepped into when I first came to Southampton almost ten years ago. And I have crossed that transom many times since. I doubt there is much for the home that you couldn't find somewhere in the 35,000 square feet that Hildreth's manages between this store, the Clearance Center in back of this store, and their House and Garden Store (see "Outdoor Furniture") in Bridgehampton. Yes, the floors are old, wooden and they creak appreciatively even if you're a 90-pound waif. BUT! Everything inside is thoroughly up-to-date and the selection can't be beat. And last year Hildreth's put up an exciting new addition to its main store! Check it out!

✪✪ **K-Mart,** Bridgehampton Commons, Bridgehampton: 537-6449: This "Big K" version of K-Mart took over the spot vacated last year by the now defunct Caldor. And it's been a pleasant surprise. The store is well stocked, well lit, clean, and attractive. And great prices! The service end of the business leaves a little to be desired (slowness, lack of general product knowledge, in particular) but I'm sure they'll work on it. What I want to see, however, is if Martha Stewart will really come by and shop here.

DINERS (see "Coffee Shops & Diners")

DMV (Dept. of Motor Vehicles)
(see also "Licenses" and "Motor Vehicles")

The closest DMV office is in Riverhead, right off Route 58. It's next door to a McDonald's and close to the Cablevision office. Best way to get there is to go to Riverhead, go all the way east down Main Street to the end. You'll come to Route 58. The DMV is to your left, but you can't turn left just there. You'll have to go right then do a quick U-turn at the next intersection. As opposed to going to the DMV up island or, worse, in The City, this is a pleasure. It's never very crowded, especially if you avoid lunchtime hours. You can take care of driver's licenses, car registrations, personal plates, ID's, boat registration, etc. The information number is 800-342-5368, but that is not the Riverhead office. It's the main DMV number in Hauppauge and I've never found it very helpful. Just go to the DMV in Riverhead, no appointment necessary, hours generally 9-to-4, and they'll take care of you.

DOGS

The towns out here have very strict ordinances about dogs and dog droppings on public property: Dogs must be on a leash, and you're obligated to clean up after your pet, just like in The City.

For dog problems, especially with strays or suspected wild or rabid dogs, call the local Dog Warden:

East Hampton: Betsy Bambrick, Warden, 324-0085
Southampton: Donald Bambrick, Warden, 653-5900
(Hmmm...Do I detect a family empire here?!)

DOMESTIC HELP (see "Housekeepers")

DONUTS

The absolute best donuts in The Hamptons can be scarfed up here.

✪✪✪✪ **Dreesen's Market,** 33 Newtown Lane, East Hampton, 324-0465
✪✪✪ **The Milk Pail,** Montauk Highway at Mecox Rd., Water Mill, 537-2565 (home made cider donuts in this case!), seasonal: call ahead.

DRUG STORES (see "Pharmacies")

DRY CLEANERS

It surprises me we don't have more dry cleaners out here, given the fastidiousness of this crowd; but, here's what we do have and some of them quite good.

✪✪✪✪ **Water Mill Cleaners,** Water Mill Sq., 726-6400: I've been "taken to the cleaners," so to speak, with dry cleaners out here over the past 10 years. I think I've finally found a "keeper." These folks are fast, efficient, and very, very good. For all your most pressing needs, these folks will iron everything out for you!

If Water Mill is not convenient for you, here are some other good spots.

✪✪✪✪ **Hampton Arrow,** 84 Main St., Southampton, 283-0059.
✪✪✪ **Village Cleaners,** 56 Jagger Lane, Southampton, 283-2299.
✪✪ **East Hampton Cleaners,** 104 Newtown Ln., East Hampton, 324-0036.
✪✪ **Whaler's Cleaners,** 7 Main St., Sag Harbor, 725-0342.

DUMPS & DUMPING
(see also "Garbage & Trash" and "Rubbish Removal")

Recycling has become a major issue on the East End, and rightly so. To aid in that effort, the Towns and Villages are cooperating in a massive effort to recycle as well as provide adequate disposal sites. Southampton abandoned a yearly fee system in favor of a "pay by the bag" system. Anyone can use the dump for free and deposit all their recyclables for free but standard, non-recyclable trash must be placed in approved green disposal bags. The bags are available at the dump as well as many retail and grocery sites. Cost: $2 for a 30-gallon bag. I guess it's fair. The more trash you create the more you'll pay. But it's amazing to see how much trash some people try to stuff in a $2 bag. Sixty gallons of trash will not fit, folks, in a 30-gallon bag.

Southampton Town Dump, Majors Path, Southampton, 283-5210, hours are from 8 AM to 4 PM, seven days, except for a few major holidays.

Sag Harbor Recycling and Trash Station, Bridgehampton/Sag Harbor Turnpike, 725-3097.

East Hampton Recycling and Trash Station, 260 Springs Fireplace Rd., 324-2199.

Montauk Recycling and Trash Station, Montauk Highway, 668-5813.

ELECTRICIANS

Shouldn't come as a "shock" to you, that there are some good folks in this category! One guy (who will remain nameless) has one of the all time best bumper stickers plastered on his truck: We want to get into your shorts!.

✪✪✪✪ **Celi Electric,** 211 Riverhead Rd., Westhampton Beach (but doing work throughout the Hamptons), 288-2227.
✪✪✪ **Thomas A. Guldi Electric, Ltd.,** Southampton, 283-0005 or 537-1777.

ELECTRICITY

To get your electrical service set up, turned on, turned off, or transferred or to get billing information call: 755-6000.

Some history: The venerable butt of all complaints about the cost of electricity, the infamous Long Island Lighting Company ("LILCO") is no more. "LIPA," or, the Long Island Power Agency, now serves us. Just to give you a bit of the story, LILCO was a publicly owned company and provided all the power for most of Nassau and Suffolk Counties. Service was pretty good, really, but the rates were astronomical. They were, in fact, the highest utility rates in the continental U.S. Plus, LILCO was the company that brought us the infamous Shoreham Nuclear Power Plant. This monstrosity, which no one but the Directors of LILCO seemed to want, cost billions and never pumped out a kilowatt. The plant had engineering and other difficulties, but its main foes were the environmentalists who successfully shut this white elephant down before it ever had a chance to open. The costs for this disaster ended up being borne, of course, by the ratepayers and the local governments. Shoreham is the single biggest reason why our sales tax is still at 8.5% out here. Anyway, the State, Governor Pataki in particular, had finally had enough and LILCO became a big political issue. In 1998 the state took LILCO over and it became LIPA. Much of the debt was reduced through the issuance of billions in state backed municipal bonds. LIPA was also joined, via merger, with Brooklyn Union Gas. The whole operation is now called Keyspan Energy.

Utility rates have, indeed, gone down by 20% in one of those rare instances where a politician's promise has actually come true. We are getting natural gas service here on the East End for the first time ever (see "Gas"), through Keyspan. All of us living here got $101 rebate checks as a "gift" after the takeover of LILCO. Life is good! What's the catch? We hope there isn't any, but it'll take another year, I think, to shake it all out. I'm particularly worried about customer service. When costs are cut and rates are lowered, something has to give somewhere. We'll see.

Oh, just in case you wanted to know, basic electrical service costs about 18 cents a day plus about 14 cents per kilowatt hour on top of that. How many hours will you use? Depends on you, of course, the size of your house, and whether you keep the lights on all night. One nice thing LIPA can do for you, though, is put you on a level pay or budget-billing plan at your request. This means that your monthly bill is the same every month. If there is an overage or underage at the end of the calendar year they will adjust your bill.

EMERGENCIES

The entire East End is now covered by the 9-1-1 emergency dialing system. Now, when you dial 9-1-1 you'll get a dispatcher in the police office closest to you who will be able to send the police or the nearest ambulance as appropriate. Please! Use 9-1-1 for real emergencies only. Running out of Veuve Cliquot just after midnight is not considered a real emergency, just a social crisis and a faux pas of the worst sort.

EMPLOYMENT

Looking for work? Well, the employment environment has changed for the better here on the East End in the last couple of years, but you had best be looking for work in the service industry if you're looking for work. Jobs are plentiful in the restaurant trade, especially for experienced wait service and cooks. Construction is great, too. Landscaping is also pretty good. Beyond that, if you're looking to make a "fortune" you've probably already done it so you can live out here. If you haven't quite made the first "mil," you're probably best off setting up your own company and providing some unique product or service that would appeal to the folks who live here or flock here during the summers. And what is that, pray tell? Well, I'm hoping writing Guides pans out, but beyond that, you'll have to look around and try to come up with something appealing. Ask yourself the following: "What does this place really need it doesn't have?" Once you decide that, make sure "it" appeals to the type of patron that frequents the Hamptons (see "People of the Hamptons"). In any case, best wishes, and if you have good luck, maybe you'll be in the Guide next year!

On a more practical basis, the State Employment Development Dept. in Riverhead actually maintains a pretty fair (electronic) listing of all kinds of jobs and opportunities. Call them at 366-0092.

You could also try a new service here in the Hamptons: eastendjobs.com. A division of Manley Associates, eastendjobs.com is an Internet posting website and placement service serving all the East End. You can also call them at 287-4455.

ENTERTAINMENT
(also see "Events," "Bars," "Clubs," for Theater (live) see "Theater" and for Movies see "Theaters," too)

ENVIRONMENTAL

Concern for the environment, all aspects of the environment, is a very hot topic out here. As well it should be. We have a very fragile ecosystem, one that is being tasked with supporting the natural elements as well as numerous quality of life demands. Preserving what we have and coexisting with this beautiful spot should be a major concern for anyone who appreciates the East End. Some of the most active groups are:

The Peconic Land Trust, Southampton, 283-3195, is the most dedicated organization for the preservation of land on the East End. They also operate a cooperative organic farm in Amagansett, where members can pick fresh, seasonal, organic produce throughout the growing season.

The Nature Conservancy operates the Mashomack Preserve on Shelter Island (749-1001) as well as a South Fork Branch in East Hampton (329-7689). If there's any controversy relative to environmental preservation out here, the Conservancy is probably going to be in the middle of it. The Conservancy is a national organization, but its activities here are all for preservation of the East End. The Conservancy has been active in buying up open land for long-term preservation. The Preserve on Shelter Island is perhaps the best known of its local successes. A visit here is well worth the trip.

The Group for the South Fork, Main St., Bridgehampton, 537-1400. The

Group for the South Fork has a very strong concern for the "preservation of the quality of life" on the East End. This means dealing more with the "people issues" in environmental preservation. They are aggressive. The Group has many social activities during the course of the year including an annual benefit fund-raiser (see "Benefits"). They also sponsor a number of walks, talks, hikes, lectures, clean-up days, and so forth. Well worth joining the Group if you are local and/or want to help preserve our special lifestyle. Call the office in Bridgehampton for details.

EVENTS

We have lots of events out here, as you might well imagine. Some of them are for show and some of them are for real. Many—too many!—events are simply vehicles for those who want to "see or be seen." I've been to a few of those "plastic" affairs and I don't care to go to another. Here are a few of the best events out here that are worth your time and money. They aren't just "for show."

✪✪✪✪ **Hampton Classic Horse Show**—and you don't have to be "into horses." This is just a lot of fun and it's a rolling, continuous party. It usually takes place in late August, in Bridgehampton. For the last few years Calvin Klein (an East End resident) as well as Louis Vuitton and Crown Royal have lavishly supported this event, but there are many other sponsors. Companies rent private, catered tents. Posh vendors have booths with everything from T-shirts to crystal. The Classic attracts the very best riders and horses from around the world. Even if you haven't ever been to a show like this, I promise that just an hour in the general admission seats ($10) on a warm, pleasant August afternoon will make you a convert. The Classic runs for about a week and you can get general information, sponsor packets, etc., by calling their offices at 537-3177. The Classic usually occurs the week just before Labor Day.

✪✪✪✪ **The Hamptons International Film Festival**—now in its sixth year and held in October in East Hampton. The Film Festival certainly extends the summer season into the golden months of Fall; and, the Fall season is still spectacular out here. The thrust of the Festival is showcasing boutique productions—films that, though not necessarily low budget are certainly not major releases. The purpose is to introduce new talent, promote innovative film ideas, showcase leading edge filmmakers, and so forth. A couple of the entries have even garnered Oscar consideration. Many star-studded gatherings and private parties accompany the premieres and showings. Many of the "Hollywood Crowd" can be found in attendance at both the public and private events. The local theaters take turns showing the featured works but most of the screenings take place at the East Hampton Cinema. The Festival lasts a week. The best ticket is a Founder's Pass that entitles you to all the events and gets you an invite to a number (but not all) of the better parties. Costs about a $1,000 per pass, though. If that price gives you "agita," there are lower priced options like: a Film Buff Pass, for all the showings at $400; an Opening or Closing Night Pass for $100; etc. The Festival office can be reached at 324-4600. Dates for 2000: October 11th through the 15th.

✪✪✪ **Montauk's annual Shakespeare Festival,** this year during August at Theodore Roosevelt County Park. This year it's *Much Ado About Nothing*—sort of like this year's elections. Anyway, call the Montauk Chamber for a full schedule of days, times, etc.: 668-2355.

EXERCISE & FITNESS (see also "Health Clubs")

Exercising and keeping in shape are two hot topics here in The Hamptons. Along about May each year, the roads start to fill up with runners, joggers, and cyclists. The local health and fitness clubs start to overflow and every-one's looking for ways to work off their excess energy—and a few pounds. Here are some of the best ways to keep fit in The Hamptons.

Outdoor Exercise
(see "Canoeing," "Biking," "Hiking," "Sailing," and "Tennis")

Health Clubs

These award winners will have all the exercise equipment, machines, tread-mills, Stairmasters, and weight sets you could possibly want. Membership fees are generally the same for year round members (about $400) and there are special summer and six-month memberships at some clubs, too.

✪✪✪✪ **World Gym,** 250 West Montauk Hwy., in the King Kullen Shopping Center, Hampton Bays, 723-3174.

✪✪✪✪ **Omnihealth & Racquet Club,** County Road 39A (Montauk Highway), Southampton (283-4770).

Alternative Exercise:

✪✪✪✪✪ **Symmetry Studio,** 395 County Road 39-A, Southampton, in the Omni Atrium, 204-0122. Our friend Jeanette Davis runs Symmetry which is a registered Pilates® Method of Body Conditioning studio. Pilates is a full-body workout that strengthens upper and lower body muscles (especially the "abs," the lower back and your all-important buttocks!) Improve your posture and help restore your muscular balance. Pilates will challenge people of all ages and physical conditions, from beginners to advanced fitness levels. Try it! These classes will leave you with a wonderful sense of physical and mental well-being. All instructors are Pilates certified. Call for an appointment. Semi-private and private sessions are available.

EYEWEAR

If you're ready for something better than those $10 specs you've been buying off the rack at the drugstore, these are the places to go to.

✪✪✪✪ **Gruen Optika,** 10 Main St., East Hampton, 324-5441. A full line of really cool sunglasses, eyewear, and the type of "shades" you really want to be seen in when you're strolling about the East End trying so hard to be recognized, but "not."

✪✪✪✪ **Southampton Optiks,** 414 County Rd. 39 in Southampton (across the street from the Omni and Jitney) 283-6226. The Doctors (yes, plural) T. J. Calabrese, father and son Optometrists, run a very fine vision center here with exams, of course, but a really terrific line of lenses, glasses, frames, and sunglasses.

FACIALS (see "Beauty")

FALL COLORS

We get a good bit of Fall color out here. Maybe not like northern Vermont in early October, but not bad. One of the prettiest spots is actually right at the gateway to the Hamptons: Exit 70 off the L.I.E. Going down Highway 111 toward Route 27, there are several stands of oak, elm, and maple that can be wildly colorful in late October and early November. Some other spots with good colors are:

Cedar Point County Park in East Hampton

Main Street in East Hampton (the "prettiest Main Street in America")

The Maidstone area of East Hampton

all of Shelter Island, especially the Mashomack Preserve.

FARM STANDS

You can find farm stands, large and small, on virtually every roadside throughout the East End, especially in the Fall months. You'll find everything from "honor farms," where you drop your money in a coffee can as you take your flowers or tomatoes with you, to very large and bountiful places.

✪✪✪✪ **The Milk Pail,** just east of Water Mill on Montauk Highway, 537-2565. This is a specialized farm stand. The principal products relate to fruit, especially apples and peaches, which are grown on the John Halsey acreage just across the highway and down the road (see also "Apples"). Why the "Milk Pail"? Well, actually Mr. Halsey, who owns and runs the stand with his family, opened the stand in the '70s when he owned dairy cows and was selling milk by the side of the road. All that changed when the dairy business became less profitable. Mr. Halsey switched to apples but didn't change the name. John's fruit is simply wonderful. So is the apple cider he presses from the fruit; even better are the cider donuts that are made fresh daily! The stand also sells dried flower arrangements made by Amy Halsey. The stand is not open all year, generally shutting down from June to August and reopening when the peaches and apples start to come in.

✪✪✪✪ **Hayground Farm Stand,** Montauk Highway just east of Water Mill and just before Bridgehampton Commons Shopping Center, 537-1676. This somewhat ramshackle and rambling affair has everything you'll need, scattered across displays made from upturned wooden baskets plus big, rickety wooden farm tables overflowing with all manner of fresh produce. In the Fall, the fields behind the Hayground are ablaze with colorful zinnias and other flowers, which you can pick for yourself. The prices are a little better here than some other places, especially on the vegetables that are currently in season. The stand is open most of the year, usually from April to November.

✪✪✪✪ **Round Swamp Farm,** 184 Three Mile Harbor Rd., East Hampton, 324-4438. Family owned for more than 20 years and a local standout for home-grown produce, homemade baked goods, and fresh, local fish. Beautifully maintained.

✪✪✪ **The Green Thumb,** Montauk Highway, just east of the actual mill in Water Mill, 726-1900. I like the Green Thumb for two particular reasons: (1) they have more organically grown produce than just about anyone else and (2) there has been a farm stand on this site since the 1640s. These folks have inherited great ground! In the summer there are pony rides for the wee ones. In the fall, there's a pumpkin patch for the kiddies as well as a great selection of Halloween and Thanksgiving decorative gourds, squashes, pumpkins, etc. The stand closes in late November and re-opens in early May.

FAMILY PLANNING (see "Maternal & Child Care")

FEDERAL GOVERNMENT

Who wants to think about the "Feds" when we've got The Hamptons on our minds? Besides, we're just about as far from D.C. here, mentally and physically, as we are from the yak herders in Outer Mongolia. But, if you're interested, the Federal listings for the services that are most accessible to the East End are at the end of this Guide. Oh, by the way, The President's number in the White House is 202-456-1414. Just in case you have something you want to chat about.

FENCES & FENCING

A couple of things you'll want to know about fences: (1) If you have a pool, you must have a fence around it, and I mean completely around it. (see "Pools—Construction" for more detail.) (2) You can't just throw up any ol' kind of fence or wall around your property. Here's where you need to check the CCR's (see "Deed Restrictions") to see what you're allowed. Generally, unless you have one of the oldest houses or oldest land grants, you're not going to be able to put up any kind of enclosed fencing, i.e., the kind of fence that can't be seen through. Why do you think so many homes use privet (hedge) type fencing? Because the owners are all environmentally conscious? Nah…hedges, even though some people grow them thirty feet tall and as thick as a set of IRS regulations, can still—technically—be "seen through" (especially in winter).

Question: what's the most rapidly growing type of fence out here in terms of popularity? "Invisible fencing"—the kind that keeps your dog in the yard by blasting the poor mutt with a high frequency radio signal when he or she gets too close to it.

Another newly popular type of fencing, which I call faux fencing, has sprung up. It consists of plastic fence pieces that try and simulate wood fencing. I know they won't rot like wood fencing, but, jeez, don't we live in a "plastic" enough world already?

FERRY SERVICE

Ferries are one of the fun things you can do out here that doesn't cost an arm and a leg. You must take at least one ferry if you ever want to see Shelter Island—unless, of course, you are an exceptional swimmer.

The big daddy of the ferry services is Cross Sound Ferry, which, as its name implies, carries passengers as well as vehicles across Long Island Sound to New London, Connecticut. If you're going to New England from anywhere on the East End, taking Cross Sound Ferry sure as heck beats driving back up island, through Queens, over the Triboro, etc. The trip takes about an hour and a half. On a calm, sunny day, it's the poor man's cruise.

The Ferries are large and quite stable in all but the worst weather. (You can call ahead for sea conditions. If they say anything other than "calm,"

bring a barf bag!) The ferries offer food service (but it's more fun to bring a picnic or delicacies from one of our favorite delis) and have full bars. Cross Sound Ferry Leaves from Orient Point almost every day of the year and operates almost hourly (both ways) from 6 AM to 9 PM. The cost is $9 per adult passenger (one way), $4.50 for kids 2 to 11, free for kids under 2. To take your car—and the driver—it's $32.00, one way. Cross Sound has also started a high-speed (passenger only) ferry service (Orient Point to New London and back, $14 round-trip). It's a great ride on a stable hydrofoil and cuts the crossing time nearly in half. The schedule for this service is seasonal, though, so it's best to call ahead. Cross Sound offers a "gambler's special" package for those going to Foxwoods Casino.

There is another cross-sound ferry from Port Jefferson (LIE Exit 64) to Bridgeport, Connecticut. Different operating company, but the costs are about the same.

In summer there is a passenger-only ferry from Montauk to Block Island. This is an exceptional day trip on a sunny summer day. You can leave at 9 am, take the ride to Block Island, hike and swim, have lunch, and board for the return trip at 4:30. You'll be back in Montauk in time for clam chowder and a fresh fish dinner. No reservations needed—just show up by 8:00 am. Ferries run daily from Memorial Day to Columbus Day, fares are $32 for adults, round trip, $16 for kids 5 to 12, under 5 free.

There are two other ferry services we must mention. The Shelter Island Ferry or South Ferry operates from a tiny pier just north of Sag Harbor off Rte. 24 (follow the signs). This anachronism operates early to late and takes you across the narrows between North Haven and Shelter Island's southern shore. On a good day, with the wind at his back and a trusty "Big Bertha," John Daly could probably hit a golf ball as far as this ferry actually travels. The five minute ride for you and your car costs $8, same day, round trip, $2 for each extra passenger, and gets you to another slice of the Hamptons' life: the quiet and undiscovered Shelter Island.

Across Shelter Island is the Greenport or North Ferry. Surprise, surprise, it takes cars and passengers from the north side of Shelter Island to Greenport. This ride might take ten minutes, so you only need a short beer and not a six-pack. Cost is $8 for car and driver, round trip, same day.

Passengers only, $2 each. Under 12 free.

If you are going to New England from the East End and don't want to take the drive to Orient Point via the North Fork and Route 25, the best thing to do is get on the South Ferry to Shelter Island and drive across the island (ten minutes on a bad day). Next, take the North Ferry to Greenport and then it's only 12 miles to Cross Sound Ferry at Orient Point. Takes about an hour to go from Southampton to Orient Point, but DON'T press the ferries into a tight schedule. These modes of transportation are for leisure travel, not making a time-certain lunch meeting in Boston.

Phone Numbers

Cross Sound Ferry: 323-2525 (schedules and rates only!)
(Orient Point)860-443-5281 (reservations & schedules)
Port Jefferson-Bridgeport Ferry: 473-0286.
Shelter Island: 749-1200 (South Ferry to North Haven);
        749-0139 (North Ferry to Greenport).
Block Island: 668-5700 (Montauk).

FIREWOOD

Ahhh…Nothing like sitting around a roaring fire with a good book and a cup of hot cocoa. So, let's have a fire tonight! Oops! We're out of firewood! Well, I suppose you could buy a bundle of wood from the local market, or from one of the guys that sits along Montauk Highway selling wood from the back of a truck. That'll get you through one fire. Smarter thing to do is to order a big pile of wood when you don't need it. Try and order your wood in the Spring. Even though most wood sold to you is dry, it's still a god idea to let it sit for a few months before you really use it. Where should it sit? The garage is good, on a protected part of your deck is OK, but somewhere out of the elements (or covered with a waterproof tarp) is where the pile should be. Also, put the woodpile in a spot convenient to your fireplace. You don't want to be schlepping an armload of wood half way across your acre in the middle of a January blizzard. If you can place your woodpile in the garage, mud room, or on the deck, make sure it is stacked on an elevated rack. Six inches off the ground will do. If you don't do this, you will have mice in your woodpile for sure. How much wood should we get? Well, depends on how many fires you're going to have dur-ing the cold months. If you have a fire every weekend during the winter you can get by on a half-cord of wood. If you're going to be using the fireplace more frequently than that or keep a fire going all day every weekend, you'll need a full cord. The folks from whom you order your wood should deliver it and stack it where you want it. You can get logs in all "hardwoods," which means you'll have slower burning and hotter fires needing less wood, but hard woods are expensive. We get a mix of woods. It's actually fun to smell the varying aromas of the different woods. Especially apple. Sometimes the folks delivering your wood will ask for a stacking fee of $25 or so. That's OK, especially if your pile is to be located somewhere far from the delivery truck. Cords of wood are running about $200 per cord and half-cords are about $100 to $125. Here's where to get the wood laid to you, so to speak.

✪✪✪✪ **Scott's Firewood,** 725-2066. Scott just delivered a half-cord, pretty much all oak, stacked it neatly (at no cost!), and charged us $100. He even swept the garage afterwards! Pretty good deal. Full cord would have been $195.

✪✪✪ **John Leuthardt,** 878-1387. John is our top landscaper, but he also has a business in firewood.

FIREWORKS

Prohibited at all times and in all forms—even sparklers. There are, however, any number of spectacular Fourth of July displays out here, all open to the public. Now, don't expect something like the East River displays. We're just poor country folks out here. But you'll have fun.

✪✪✪✪ **Gosman's Dock,** Montauk: We were just out driving, enjoying the balmy evening air when we decided to stop by Gosman's for dinner. Had an excellent meal, then wandered out to the patio for a coffee. Gosh, it sure seemed like a lot of people were waiting for dinner…Hundreds! Then we noticed they were all sitting there facing out to sea, not anxiously checking their reservations. Lo and behold, the annual Montauk Fourth of July Fireworks Display was being held just across the inlet from Gosman's. We grabbed just about the last two available chairs, sat back with coffee, and enjoyed the show!

✪✪✪✪ **East Hampton Main Beach**—call the Chamber of Commerce for details, 324-0362.

FISH, FRESH (see "Fish Markets")

FISHING

Remember that monster shark in the movie *Jaws*? Well, its twin was captured right off of Montauk—and gave Peter Benchley the idea for the story. If you don't believe me, go to Gosman's Dock in Montauk. A replica of that very shark is hanging there.

The fishing out here, both commercial and recreational, is world class, whether in fresh water ponds or on the open ocean of the Sound. If you're over the age of 16 you must have a New York State fishing license. Licenses are available at just about every bait shop and boatyard where charters are available. Regulations change frequently on how much fish you can take, by type. Check the rules before you go out, either with your charter boat skipper, the Local Park office or the Harbormaster.

We have fish for all seasons. In the early spring its cod, followed by flounder, striped bass, weakfish, and bluefish. Summer fishermen go after fluke, tuna, and the trophy fish: marlin, swordfish, and those big ol' sharks. In the autumn, the striped bass return along with a jazzy new sport fish everyone's talking about, the so-called "false albacore" or "albie." Winter? Well, if you're crazy enough to be pitching around off of Montauk in a January gale, more power to you. Read *The Perfect Storm* by Sebastian Junger before you go out.

✪✪✪✪ **Montauk Point.** Montauk is only 50 miles from the Continental Shelf, so even day charters can get you out to where the real monsters bite: those marlin, shark, swordfish, and tuna we talked about. Forget Hawaii...records have been set on Montauk boats including the world record striped bass: 76 pounds!

✪✪✪ **Shinnecock Canal.** You don't even have to get on a boat. Just drop a hook off the Shinnecock Bay entrance. But wait for the canal gates to close. When the gates are open, flounders, fluke, and weakfish course through the canal at great speed. When the locks are closed, they tend to gather at the gates, along with the smart fishermen.

✪✪ **Peconic Bay.** Whether fishing from the shoreline around the bay or aboard a boat, you'll get porgies, weakfish, and flounder.

✪ **Three Mile Harbor.** Much of the harbor is quite shallow, but there are lots of fish, especially flounder, along the channel on the western side of the inlet.

✪ **Gardiner's Island.** Right between the forks of the East End sits Gardiner's Island. There are Atlantic conditions on the eastern side and calmer conditions on the west side. Lots of flounder and good striped bass.

FISHING BOATS & CHARTERS

There's an ocean of possibilities here. There are dozens and dozens of charters and party boats available from Montauk alone. And fishing has been "hot" in recent years! Charter boats are booked well in advance and some of them are already booked for this season. Chartering an entire boat for you and your friends can cost $300 to $700 a day and $1,000 or more for a two-day trip. Party boats are generally available even in season and they charge $20–$45 per day, per fisherman. The Long Island Recreational Fishing Guide, a free, 50-page booklet published by the New York Fishing Tackle and Trade Association, offers a comprehensive list of Long Island party and charter boats. You can get a copy by writing to the Association at 265 West Main St., Patchogue, NY, 11772.

Oh, one more note: "seasickness." Despite what you may have heard, there is no cure—except not to go out. Even Admiral Nelson, England's all-time greatest naval hero, got seasick repeatedly. The waters around Montauk are teeming with fish, yes, but they can also be very turbulent, even on bright sunny days. Fifty-foot charter boats will wallow and pitch like the devil, so be prepared. Take any seasickness remedy before you get on the boat. It won't do you any good if you wait until you feel queasy. Dramamine has been around a long time. It works, but it makes me sleepy. Bonine is better, at least I can stay awake with it. Some people swear by the behind-the-ears patch, some people are equally fanatic about the wristbands. See what works for you. Personally, I think the best cure for seasickness is tossing your cookies. Once it's done, it's done, and then you can eat a ham and cheese sandwich and get on with the fishing.

To get advice on available boats in Montauk call Capt. Joe McBride of the Montauk Boatman and Captains Association at 329-0973. Capt. McBride is widely recognized and respected for his knowledge of what's going on in charters and fishing. You can also call the Sportfishing Charter service in Montauk at 668-2707. These services are free and can lead interested fishermen to boats with available slots instead of having to call around to each boat.

If you want to try some individual boats here are some of the best (they are all out of Montauk).

✪✪✪✪ *Joy Sea,* with Capt. Chuck Mallinson, 668-5829.

✪✪✪✪ *Lazy Bones,* 668-5671. I love their new slogan: "Bring your lunch and catch your dinner."

✪✪✪ *King Wayne,* 668-5843.

✪✪✪ *Blue Fin IV,* 668-9323.

✪✪✪ *Marlin V,* 668-2818.

✪ For something different, as well as a lot less expensive, take the **Viking Fishing Fleet Charter** (they operate the Block Island-New London ferries from Montauk)—advertised as "The World's Largest Passenger Fishing Vessel." Montauk, 668-5700. You can fish from the decks of a large (and more stable) passenger ferry on certain cruises (seasonal).

FISH MARKETS

✪✪✪✪ **The Clamman Seafood Market,** 235A North Sea Rd., Southampton, 283-6437. This market is just down the block from McDonald's. If you aren't looking for it, you might drive by it unless you happen to catch the somewhat psychedelic, hand-painted sign out front that advertises the daily specials. But once inside you would see Paul (who unfortunately just passed away), "the Clamman," himself, filet knife in hand, slicing into a yellow fin tuna that was swimming blissfully off Montauk Point just three hours ago. Needless to say, the seafood is fresh—pricey, but fresh. You'll find whatever is "running," in season, and available in our local waters: live lobster, mussels, clams, crabs, weakfish, tuna, sea bass, halibut, sole, squid, and so on. The staff will scale, de-bone, wrap, give advice on how to cook your catch and even tell you how to eat it. The Clamman also caters parties and clambakes. Another wonderful feature is his "clambake in a bucket." For about $25 The Clamman will pack a tin bucket with steamers or mussels, a small lobster, fresh corn and so forth. All you have to do is take it to the beach (or your backyard) and cook it. NOTE: The Clamman has a second and equally good location just down the road, on 50 Jagger Lane, also in Southampton, across from Waldbaum's, 283-7705.

✪✪✪✪ **Seafood Shop,** Montauk Hwy., Wainscott, 537-0633. As I like the Clamman, my East Hampton Spy loves the Seafood Shop. She says they are the most reliable fishmarket in the Hamptons—they are very knowledgeable and will have the goods when noone else does!

✪✪✪ **Gosman's Fishmarket,** 484 West Lake Drive, Montauk, 668-2447. Located right next to the award-winning Gosman's Dock Restaurant, this market brings to you the same fresh catch that they serve so well in the restaurant next door. Fresh shark is one of my favorites. Tasty, to be sure, but I'm always glad to be eating the shark instead of the other way around.

✪✪✪ **King Kullen,** Bridgehampton Commons, 537-8103. We mention King Kullen's Bridgehampton Supermarket a number of times in the Guide. Here's another reason: their fish market. Just as with the meat counter, they have a great selection and folks behind the counter who are helpful and know a fin or two about fish.

✪✪✪ **Stuart's Seafood Market, Ltd.,** Amagansett, 267-6700. Heading east on Montauk Highway, just as you near the Mt. Fuji restaurant, you'll see this innocuous little white sign with an arrow pointing down a side street. If you miss the sign, you'll miss one of the best fresh fish markets on the East End.

FLORISTS

The Hamptons are one big garden. From the early crocuses in late February to roses that bloom through October, we are blessed with flowers, flowers everywhere. There are wildflowers to harvest, roadside farm-stands with U-Pick fields, and, of course, whatever you grow at your own place. If you prefer the professional touch, here are the best.

✪✪✪✪ **Yardley Florist,** Hempstead Dr., Sag Harbor, 725-0470. When it came to picking the spot to do our wedding flowers, there were lots of choices. And we talked to several. Yardley got the business because of their great prices, friendly service, and attention to detail. They did a beautiful job!

✪✪✪✪ **Bridgehampton Florist,** Main St., Bridgehampton, 537-7766. Known for the quality of their personal service, imaginative arrangements, and great selection of candles.

✪✪✪ **Artistry in Flowers,** 27 Hampton Rd., Southampton, 283-8200. A very talented staff as well as one of the most complete selections of fresh cut flowers and plants in The Hamptons.

✪✪✪ For something just a little unique and different, try **Topiare Flower Shop** at 51 Jobs Lane in Southampton, 287-3800. Plants and arrangements are the specialties here and they also offer some interesting hand-painted furniture and other gifts.

✪✪ If you'd like something in dried flowers, stop at the **Milk Pail** on Montauk Highway Just north of Water Mill, 537-2565. Amy Halsey specializes in dried flower arrangements with plants she grows and dries herself.

✪✪ **Whitmore's Garden Shop and Nursery,** 1380 Montauk Hwy., Amagansett, 267-3182. In addition to being a wonderful garden shop, Whitmore's is also a full-service floral shop. They can do on-site designing and whip together just what you need for that special occasion.

FRUITS & VEGETABLES

We feature farm stands in our Guide as well as fruit & vegetable markets. What's the difference? It's a difference of walls. A farm stand is open air, a non-permanent, seasonal structure. A fruit and vegetable market has solid walls is meant to be permanent, and is open year-round. Here are THE BEST places to go.

✪✪✪✪ **Schmidt's Produce Co.,** 120 North Sea Rd., Southampton, 283-5777. Schmidt's is the reigning champion of the fruit and vegetable markets out here. Not only do they have the very finest locally grown fruits and vegetables, they import from everywhere; so, in the middle of January you can get vine ripened tomatoes, fresh nectarines, and crisp heads of lettuce. There is a wonderful salad bar, terrific varieties of fresh bread, a deli counter, a well-stocked dairy case, and fresh cut flowers to grace your table. On Fridays and Saturdays, the parking lot is packed. Schmidt's, in total, represents the best in service, quality, and customer care: attributes that I would like to see emulated by all merchants of The Hamptons.

✪✪✪✪ There's another **Schmidt's** in East Hampton, across the street from the Laundry restaurant, on Race Lane, 329-7000. This Schmidt's store has faithfully replicated the quality and service that the Southampton store is known for. Once again, the freshest fruits and vegetables, a full deli counter, a good supply of dairy products, bread, and lots of other goodies. This Schmidt's is run by a nice couple, the Bowden's, who have done a great job with the place.

✪✪✪ But there's more! There's a third **Schmidt's,** this one is owned by another Schmidt, in this case brother Robert. Schmidt's Bridgehampton Country Market, Montauk Hwy., Bridgehampton, across the highway from Bridgehampton Commons and in the spot formerly occupied by the Bridgehampton IGA, 537-1048. Robert has turned the dowdy, old IGA into a replica of the other successful Schmidt-type markets. This store is the biggest of the three. Well worth a visit.

FUEL COMPANIES

✪✪✪✪ **Hardy Fuel Oil, Inc.,** (a division of Southampton Oil, Inc.), 1654 County Road 39, Southampton, 283-9607, fax 283-0286. Oil prices rise and fall, and we all complain when prices go up, of course, but the bottom line is ya gotta have it, so we pay it. But wouldn't it be nice if what we had to pay for was available 24 hours a day, seven days a week from courteous people who care about us? Well, if you get your fuel oil from Hardy Fuel you'll have all that plus budget plans, service contracts and trucks that travel all over the North and South Forks to meet your needs. Best in the Hamptons.

HARDY
Fuel Oil, Inc.
(a division of
Southampton Oil, Inc.)

Serving the North and South Forks

SAME DAY SERVICE
1654 County Road 39, Southampton
283-9607 fax: 283-0286

Other excellent fuel oil companies, by area:

✪✪✪✪ **PETRO** (formerly Southampton Coal, Inc.,) Southampton, 283-0025. Impeccable service and they offer their customers a free, annual, oil burner inspection and a "level pay" plan that allows you to spread your fuel costs over the entire year. That's a nice convenience when you're trying to keep a reasonable monthly budget. PETRO serves the entire East End.

✪✪✪✪ **Pulver Fuel,** Bridgehampton, 537-0930
✪✪✪✪ **Schenck Fuel,** East Hampton, 324-0142

FURNITURE

There are no giant furniture dealers out here—and there probably won't be any time soon; so, don't buy or rent that new home and expect to dash into an IKEA or a Levitz and furnish the whole place in one "swell foop." Won't happen. But there are a number of places out here where you can get most or all of your furnishings. It will pay to shop around, though, and get something here, something there, if you have the patience. And it's also fun! Here are the great places to do just that.

✪✪✪✪ **Hecho a Mano,** 46 Jobs Lane, Southampton, 283-7425. Mea culpa, mea culpa. In last year's "Guide" I incorrectly said they were going out of business. In fact, the business just changed hands. They are very much in business and offering some very fine home furnishings. Mirrors, mirrors everywhere. Plus many specialty items from Mexico and South America. Aluminum and brass serving pieces—great for weddings! Clever "contain me" container for the table that fits standard items like milk cartons and butter rubs. Oh, by the way, it's all hand made—that's what Hecho a Mano means for dummies like me! And check out their website at hechoamano.com.

✪✪✪✪ **Rumrunner,** 14 Main St., East Hampton (324-3444), 22 Main St., Southampton (287-0583). (There is a Montauk store, but it's mostly a curio and knick-knack shop catering to tourists and has no furniture to speak of.) The Southampton store carries a treasure trove of wonderful accessories and some furniture. It's a favorite spot to stop when we're strolling up and down Main Street. The East Hampton store—ah!—here's the really good stuff in furniture. The prices were very reasonable for the high quality of the workmanship.

✪✪✪✪ **Hildreth's,** 51 Main St., Southampton, 283-2300. Commendable for bedroom suites, living room accessories, dining tables and chairs. You can also find it frustratingly hard to locate that odd piece you need to complete a suite here, too. If it's outdoor furniture you want, Hildreth's on Montauk Highway in Bridgehampton is a great choice, too (see "Outdoor Furniture"). Hildreth's also has a furniture clearance center just behind the main store. Check it out—there are some interesting bargains.

✪✪✪ **Fisher's,** Main St., Sag Harbor, 725-0006. Fisher's scours old barns and farmhouses in Europe to find refurbishable treasures, which they will tidy up and gladly sell to you. They have a large selection of other pieces, too, and they'll happily show you all their catalogs.

✪✪✪ **English Country Antiques,** Snake Hollow Rd., Bridgehampton, 537-0606. Yes, they have some pretty good antiques here, but you should stop by and take a look at their new furniture collections, too.

✪✪✪ **Chez Morgan,** Jobs Lane, Southampton, 287-3595. Chez Morgan tries to be both an antique shop and a furniture dealer. They do a pretty good job at both. There are antiques, and some excellent ones, but there are also many reproductions. In this case, that makes for some good furniture selections.

GARAGE SALES

When we have a garage sale, we have a garage sale! Only out here they are called "estate sales." Like most other places, you tend to find them as you're cruising around on Saturday or Sunday mornings. Another good place to look is in *Dan's Papers* and the Southampton and East Hampton "Independent" newspapers (see "Newspapers"). These papers are free and come out every Thursday.

GARBAGE & TRASH
(see also "Dumps & Dumping" and "Rubbish Removal")

We do recycle here on the East End. This can be a royal pain in the fanny sometimes; but, after all the grumbling is done, we are doing our share for the environment and that's a good thing. Southampton, East Hampton, and Sag Harbor have collection centers that accept recyclables, but Southampton has the biggest recycling center (We used to call them "dumps" when I was a kid!). It's located on Major's Path just east of town, off North Sea Road and is open just about every day of the year (except major holidays) from 8:00 AM to 4:00 PM. There is no fee to get rid of your recycled waste, but your non-recycled trash (We used to call that "garbage"!) must be in Town-approved green plastic trash bags. These bags are available at the dumps, darn, I mean "Recycling Centers," and all 7-11s, most pharmacies, and many other retailers around Town. They cost $2 per 30-gallon bag. Recyclables must be separated into the following categories.

cardboard (flattened, please!)
mixed paper (which includes all newspapers, colored papers, magazines, etc.)
glass, plastic, and metal (all in one bin)
hazardous materials which includes paint, paint cans, chemicals,
sprays, etc.

You may, of course, avoid all this fuss by hiring a "local carter." There are several companies (see "Rubbish & Trash removal"). You still have to separate, bundle, wrap, or whatever all your recyclables, and you still have to put up with stinky trashcans. All you do is save the trip to the dump. If you have someone pick up your trash, do not leave your trashcans in an open area at home. We have lots of raccoons, stray cats, and wandering dogs. They will get into your trash. Best to put your trash cans in a bin with a cover or a build a small shed.

GARDEN CENTERS

✪✪✪✪ **Lynch's Garden Center** on North Sea Road in Southampton (283-5515) gets the Gold (again) this year. This operation knows its ilex from its privet hedge. I spend a lot of time in my vegetable garden during the course of the year and I know I can always rely on Lynch's to have what I need: from fertilizer to seedlings. There is also a tremendous selection of bedding plants, both annual and perennial, as well as trees, ornamental shrubs, pots, wild bird accessories, garden tools, hoses, you name it and it's there! You will get your money's worth and you will get quality here. They're great folks and run a great shop.

✪✪✪ **Devonshire,** Main St., Bridgehampton, 537-2661. Not strictly a garden center, but rather one of the finest stores in The Hamptons for gardeners and gardening accessories. You'll go nuts here if you're into plants, planting containers, birdhouses, garden statuary, etc. This store is a real gem and worth a trip to Bridgehampton if you go nowhere else in Bridgehampton!

✪✪✪ **Mecox Gardens,** County Rd. 39A, Southampton, 287-5015. Don't go here for your tomato plants. This is an architectural and interior decorating garden center. "Greeters" welcome you warmly and escort you around the grounds offering helpful and friendly advice. There's a shop with handmade pots from Provence and designer Italian deck chairs. This is one classy garden center. The topiary, walkways, viewing rooms, and planter boxes are filled with exquisite examples of the gardener's art. They also have cut flowers, can make arrangements, will deliver your plants and even help you arrange them on site. Basic soils and garden mixtures are available. Don't plan on leaving here without having spent a few dollars, but you'll love it!

✪✪✪ **Marder's,** Snake Hollow Rd., Bridgehampton, 537-3700. Marder's converted an old barn into a real showcase and they have tons of space—inside and out. Marder's consistently wins many floral, landscaping and decorating prizes. Go here and you'll see why.

✪✪✪ **Whitmore's Garden Shop & Nursery**, Montauk Hwy., Amagansett, 267-3182. A beautiful spot to stop and admire the plants! But I'm sure they'd also be happy if you actually bought something, and you should: from plants to all sorts of flowers, special arrangements to floral gifts. They have an on-site floral designer and delivery service, too.

✪ **Baywoods** on Montauk Highway in Water Mill, 726-5950. Baywoods is one of my favorite places for indoor plants. They also have outdoor plants of all types, but it's the on site expert advice on all kinds of houseplants that makes them stand out, in my mind. They also have a "plant sitting" service for folks who store their most valuable house plants during the winter and they also have particularly expert advice on orchid growing, host orchid shows, etc.

GARDENERS (see "Landscapers")

GARDENS & PRESERVES (see also "Hiking")

Some think the most glorious gardens out here are the ones that are wild and uncultivated: places like the Pine Barrens, or the sedges along the wind swept dunes, or the many fields of wildflowers. Others prefer their gardens cultivated, structured and precise, like the carefully manicured plots along Gin Lane or Georgica Pond. I would argue, wild or tame, the entire East End is a garden. In any case, here are some spots to enjoy our gardens.

✪✪✪✪ **The Madoo Conservancy,** Sagg Main Rd., Sagaponack, 537-8200. Local artist Robert Dash runs this 30-acre preserve with loving care. There are more than 30 mini-gardens here, some of them stocked with very seldom seen plants and flowers. Benches on which to relax, lovely arbors, a great place for a quiet garden stroll. Call ahead for hours.

✪✪✪✪ **LongHouse Reserve & Foundation,** Hands Creek Rd., East Hampton, 329-3568. Sixteen acres of gardens are punctuated with the contemporary sculpture. Landscape feature include a pond, numerous allées and walks, a dune garden, and a one-thousand-foot hemlock hedge that follows boundaries of farm fields that occupied the site until it was abandoned for agricultural use in 19th century. There are collections of bamboo and grasses; an impressive collection of 200 varieties of daffodils with over 1 million blooms; numerous irises, conifers, and broadleaf evergreens. The ground-floor gallery space is reserved for changing exhibits of works by leading craftmakers of today. Sculpture in the Gardens is a growing program at LongHouse. Jack Larsen has assembled a collection of 40 sculptures for the gardens including works of glass by Dale Chihuly, ceramics by Takaezu, and bronzes by Noguchi and Abakanowicz. Works by Ossorio, Claus Bury, Yoko Ono, and Opocensky are also on view, while the recent installation of a Fly's Eye Dome designed by Buckminster Fuller adds an interesting scale and dimension. The large new house was inspired by the 7th century Shinto shrine at Ise, Japan. LongHouse Reserve has been established in 1991 on the property to reflect founder Jack Lenor Larsen's professional interests and his desire to encourage creativity in gardening and in collecting and every day living with art. LongHouse gardens and gallery are open to the public 2–5 p.m. every Wednesday and first and third Saturday (April 29–September 29, 2000). Suggested admission is $10.

✪✪ **Mulford Farmhouse and Gardens,** 10 James Lane, East Hampton, 324-6869 (and only open July & August, 10AM to 5PM). This is mainly a historical tour. There is a living history interpretation in Rachel's Garden, an authentic period garden featuring plants, vegetables, and herbs from the 17th Century—many grown from heirloom seeds.

✪✪ Note: **The Southampton Garden Club** has an annual tour of some of the finest estate gardens in Southampton, usually in June. Call the Southampton Chamber of Commerce details (283-0402).

✪ **Pick-your-own flowers:** there are several roadside stands that grow fields of zinnias, poppies, cornflowers, etc. This can be a lot of fun in July through September. Best places are in Water Mill at Hayground Market and Susie's farm stand, just up the road in Bridgehampton.

✪ **The nature trails at Montauk Point State Park:** Here you'll see the wilder aspect of our East End "gardens." The park and trails are open Memorial Day to Columbus Day, call 668-2544 for more details.

✪ **Second House Museum,** Montauk, 668-5340. In addition to the museum itself, there are rose and herb gardens to enjoy (see also "Museums").

GAS/GASOLINE (see also "Propane")

Gas for the home: The merger of Brooklyn Union Gas and the old LILCO to form the Keyspan Energy Corporation has finally given The Hamptons gas, so to speak. At least it will bring gas to all of the East End. Brooklyn Union has been laying major new lines for several months now. If you're interested in natural gas for your home call "BUG" at 1-800-427-2001. If you're near an existing line, they may be able to run a pipe out to your house. If you and your neighbors want to "get gas," form a "collective" and petition Brooklyn Union to speed up the schedule of getting gas to you. If it's economically feasible, they'll do it.

Gas for your barbecue, pool heater, etc.: This is where you'll use propane gas, so see "Propane."

Gas for your car: Jacking up prices on weekends is a game that many local gas stations love to play with us, especially in summer, and particularly on holiday weekends. And the further out you drive the higher the increase. For example, whatever a station in Southampton is posting per gallon will generally be 20–25% higher than "up-island" (which is outrageous); but, a station in Amagansett, you can bet, will be another 20–25% higher. If you need diesel, you're really in for a shock. Here's how to beat the price gouging.

✪✪✪✪ Fill up or top off up-island. The best places are: The Mobil station off of the Sunrise Highway at Exit 58. Get off and go to the next major stoplight and turn right. The station is on the right. Perhaps the cheapest gas near here for a major brand. Coincidentally, the Exxon station at exit 58 off the LIE also has good prices. So does the Exxon station at Exit 64. After exit 64, you're "in the Hamptons" and Hamptons prices will start to come into play.

✪✪✪ At present, the best gas prices in the Hamptons belong to the several Coastal Stations scattered around. Who is "Coastal?" you say.

Well, they are a major brand knock-off (Mobil). They buy excess production and serve it cheaper because of lower overheads, less advertising, etc. OK, so it's a knock-off. Will it produce just plain "knocks"? No. Not in my experience. Their premium works just as well in my car as any other brand. Here are the Coastal locations:

Rte. 25 in Calverton

626 W. Main, Riverhead

Rte. 39, Southampton

GAY & LESBIAN

We have found the best local resources for information on Gay and Lesbian activities and information to be the following.

EEGO—The East End Gay Organization, Box 708, Bridgehampton, 324-3699. EEGO is certainly an effective political action group for the growing community of East End Gays and Lesbians, but it is also a vital resource for information on events, gay news, and issues that affect the gay community. Membership is strictly confidential, includes a monthly newsletter and invitations to events and fundraisers.

LIGALY—Long Island Gay and Lesbian Youth, contact David Kilmnick, Director, at 665-2300. A social and recreational organization for gay youth.

PFLAG—Parents and Friends of Lesbians and Gays: Contact Arlene, in Riverhead, at 653-9389.

Probably the best known (and "open" about it) restaurant and social club for Gays and Lesbians is the **Swamp Club** on Montauk Highway in Wainscott, 537-3332.

GELATTO (see also "Ice Cream")

✪✪✪✪ **Sant Ambroeus,** Main St., Southampton, 283-1233. I defy you to walk into the gelatto parlor in the front of this fine restaurant and not come out with a big scoop of some exotically crafted frozen treat. This is the way they make it in Italy—and on 18th Avenue in Brooklyn! (only open May to November).

GIFT SHOPS

✪✪✪✪ The gift shop adjacent to the **American Hotel,** Main Street, Sag Harbor, 725-3535. Whoa! Cigars, caviar, smoked salmon, chocolates, world class candies, and fresh-cut long-stemmed roses! This store, part of the award-winning hotel of the same name, has captured the essence of high-class Hamptons gift giving. Folks from the yachts at the pier down the block race up here for the essential tin of caviar to go with the iced vodka. Those of us with "yachts" of a more modest type (can you spell "r-o-w-b-o-a-t"?) can still enjoy the ambience of this great store. All you need is the itch to buy a truly unique something-or-other that will be just right and oh-so-Hamptons.

✪✪✪✪ I know, I know…It's a jewelry store, but **London Jewelers** on Main Street in East Hampton, 329-3939, is much more than a jewelry store. There's a Tiffany's counter with exquisite crystal, pens, and other Fifth Avenue goodies. There's a cigar shop with a walk-in humidor. There are creative and beautiful silk and dried floral arrangements, vases, china and more. It's a very lovely store to stroll—and "troll."

✪✪✪✪ **Lume,** 167 Main St., Amagansett, 267-7551. In the new and popular vernacular, this is a "lifestyle store" which is, I guess, more than a "gift shop"; what the heck…It's a pleasing, eclectic place with many unusual gifts, scented candles, and more. Many of their items are Italian imports. One of our nicest stores.

✪✪✪ **Curly Willow,** 55 Main St., East Hampton, 324-1122. A beautiful little store with a fine selection of gifts and accessories for the home, the garden, and you! I loved the embroidered pillows…especially the one labeled "WWMD." That stands for "What Would Martha Do?"—as in Martha Stewart.

✪✪✪ **Home James,** 55-D Main St., East Hampton, 324-2307. This store is hidden down an alley off Main Street, but it's well worth finding. It's quite small but crammed with interesting little surprises: towels, ornaments, glassware, plates, items in silver, and more. Lots of ideas to fire the imagination and very unique gifts.

✪✪ **Victoria's Mother,** 43 Main St., East Hampton, 324-9507. For something different in gift giving: unique toys, cards, and costume jewelry.

GLASS SERVICE, AUTO

Did an 18-wheeler rolling down the L.I.E. thwack rocks off the windshields of your car? Do you have tiny little spider spreading across your windshield? Insurance policy in hand, drive to this shop.

✪✪✪✪ **Safelite Auto Glass,** #10 Montauk Highway, Bridgehampton, 537-3377, across the highway from the Bridgehampton Commons. Same day, in and out, you've got a new windshield. They handle all the insurance coverage, too. Safelite also has mobile repair service (if your car isn't safe to drive), plus alarms, T-tops, sunroofs, and they're open Saturdays. Great service!

GLASS SERVICE, HOME

✪✪✪✪ **Hampton Glass and Mirror,** 69 Jobs Ln., Southampton, 283-5480. They'll come out and measure, give free estimates, cut to your design specs, and deliver on time for a fair price. Mirrored walls and glass for your table tops plus the usual replacements for busted windows and cracked glass in pictures.

GOLF

We are blessed with some of the country's finest golf courses here in The Hamptons. The problem is that most of them are private clubs. Shinnecock, National, Maidstone, Southampton, Noyac, and the new Atlantic Club are all private. You can probably get on the short list to the Atlantic Club if you have $250,000 to spare for the initial membership fees. Southampton has a long waiting list—and you have to know and be sponsored by a minimum of one Founding Member and probably several other current members. Shinnecock? Forget it...These memberships are so tightly controlled they are passed down from generation to generation. Maidstone? Is your last name Bouvier? Kennedy? Ford? Well, you get the idea.

Now, the good news. There are a number of pretty good public courses that you can play while you're waiting for your check to Atlantic to clear or your 10-year wait to join Southampton to lapse, whichever comes first. In some cases you'll have to fight waiting lists or quirky reservation systems, but you'll get the hang of it after awhile. One of the best resources for golf and some fairly good courses is the Suffolk County Park system. The county operates three golf courses (as well as campgrounds, etc.), the closest and best of which is Indian Island in Riverhead (see below). The secret to getting on these courses and getting reservations is having a "green card." No, you don't have to give up your US citizenship and become a legal alien to play golf here. This Green Key, as the card is officially called, is a membership card for the Suffolk County Department of Parks. It costs $20 and can be obtained by appearing in person at any Park office, golf course, campground, etc., and paying the fee. The catch is that you have to be a resident of Suffolk County—and be able to prove it (usually with a driver's license). If you're a part time resident, become friends with a full time resident and get a Green Key! For more information, call the Suffolk County Parks folks at 244-7275.

✪✪✪✪ **Montauk Downs,** S. Fairview Av., Montauk, 668-5000. Located in Montauk Downs State Park, this course is consistently in the "Top 100" of the best American public courses—sometimes it creeps into the "Top 25." It is a lovely course, offering some very nice views. It is a links course, 18 holes, par 72, and about 6,700 yards. The course has been around a long time but was redesigned in 1968 by Robert Trent Jones. There is a phone reservations system. It used to be that you either had to get in line at 3 AM (or at least send an unlucky surrogate) or simply show up and wait 5 to 6 hours in order to play. It's better than that now with the new phone system, but it's still a challenge to get on during the summer months. Best times to play are March, April, October, and November. The green fees are also quite reasonable, and that attracts a lot of players. Year round, daily, dawn to dusk.

✪✪✪✪ **Long Island National,** 1793 Northville Turnpike, Riverhead, 727-4653. Yes, it's Riverhead, not the Hamptons, but, hey, if you wanna play golf and you can't get onto Maidsonte or Shinnecock, you can't be too choosy. Besides, this is a brand new course and it's located just a few minutes from the Hamptons. Par 71, 6,800 yards and designed by Robert Trent Jones, Jr. It will challenge you! Lots of rolling hills, 55 bunkers, 3 large lakes, and tons of tall grass. Bring extra balls...Open 7 days. $90 weekdays, $100 Friday through Sunday, but the fees are all inclusive; that is, green fees, cart and driving range for the day.

✪✪✪ **Calverton Golf Links,** Edwards Ave., Calverton, 369-5200—just north of exit 71 off the L.I.E. This is a 9-hole course that opened in 1996. If you want to get in a few quick holes, or tune up your game before playing somewhere else, this is an OK place to go. The greens and fairways are in very good shape, and there is an excellent driving range (upper and lower decks). Calverton also has a good miniature golf course, a clubhouse, and a snack bar, pro shop and golf instructors. It's not crowded! Hurry! Year round, open daily, 7AM to dark, about $25 for 18 holes (going around twice). Flash!: Calverton is expanding to 18 holes! Construction on a new "back nine" has begun. They expect to open holes as they are completed, with the entire 18 holes being ready by Fall, '00.

✪✪ **Indian Island,** Riverhead, 727-7776. As mentioned above, this is one of the Suffolk County courses. It's a pretty fair course: long, challenging in parts, and scenic with a couple of very pretty holes along Peconic Bay. If there is any drawback, it is that it is pretty well used and can get "beat up" from time to time. It is 18 holes, about 7,000 yards, and can take walkers or carts. Use the Green Key system to get a reservation up to seven days in advance. The club has a nice pro shop, instructors, a good coffee shop and bar. Course is open year round, weather permitting, 7AM to 6PM.

✪✪ There's a little nine-hole course in Bridgehampton called **Poxabogue,** right on Montauk Highway, 537-0025. It's open all year and will not be a challenge for serious golfers. For someone who shoots under 100 consistently, this will seem more like a "pitch and putt" course. But you know what? You can drop by here and play just about any time with no waiting. There's also a great driving range and a very respectable café. The course did some major renovation last year and improved the driving range, too.

✪ **Rocky Hill Golf and Country Club,** Clancy Road, Manorville (near exit 70 off the LIE), 878-2250. A pretty good course, open May through October, and has a pro shop and driving range, 18-hole, par 71.

✪ Also near the LIE and just west of Manorville is **Pine Hills,** 162 Wading River Road (exit 69), 878-4343. 18-hole, par 73 with driving range. Course open April through October. BUT! Pine Hills is trying to go "private" as we go to press. Call to be sure you can still get on…

Oh, how about miniature golf?

✪✪✪✪ **Lynch's Links** in Southampton, on David White's Path, just off County Rd. 39, behind the Suffolk Lighting Center. A wonderful little spot to just relax and have some fun. Not your typical, "junky," "touristy," miniature golf spot either. This one was designed with class. About $6.50 per adult. Call 283-0049 for details.

GROCERIES/GROCERY STORES
(see also "Supermarkets")

What's a "grocery store" versus a "supermarket"? Well, as you might deduce, "super" translates to "big" and "grocery" means "neighborhood," "local," smaller and "friendly." We have lots of good grocery stores out here. Let me give you some of the best in your local communities.

Bridgehampton

✪✪✪ **Schmidt's Bridgehampton Country Market,** Montauk Hwy, Bridgehampton (537-1048), across the highway from Bridgehampton Commons and in the spot formerly occupied by the Bridgehampton IGA. A first-class country market and grocery store. Check it out!

Sagaponack

✪✪✪✪ **Sagg Main Store,** 542 Sagg Main Road, 537-6036 (it's attached to the Post Office!). Fresh bagels, all sorts of condiments, salads, meats, cheeses and grocery items. Reminds me of an old-fashioned country store.

Sag Harbor

✪✪✪✪ **Schiavoni's Market,** Main St., 725-0366. Schiavoni's is an IGA, but not like most IGA's you may have been to. They've completed a rather radical modernization program. They certainly have all the conventional groceries you may want, but they also have a complete meat department, deli, and bakery. There's also a rather nice selection of gourmet foods, health foods, and organic products. All this in a "country" setting, right on an old-fashioned, picturesque main street.

✪✪✪✪ **Cromer's,** Country Market, 3500 Noyac Rd., 725-9004. This is where I got the prize-winning 70-pound pig I barbecued. Man, was it terrific! And I love this store! It's cramped and crowded, wacky and wonderful. They have a very complete line of groceries and a great deli section. Homemade pies, cold beer, soda, party platters, home delivery and they're open 365 days a year!

Southampton

I'd recommend taking the short trip to our award-winning King Kullen Supermarket in Bridgehampton (see "Supermarkets").

HAIRDRESSERS (see "Beauty")

HARDWARE STORES

✪✪✪✪ Can't beat **Herrick's** at 41 Main Street in Southampton (283-0026). It's small for a major hardware store (although it is an Ace affiliate) but what it lacks in size it more than makes up for in terms of how well they've stocked the limited space. And the expertise of all, and I mean all, of their very friendly and helpful staff continuously amazes me. I've even walked in with challenges just to see if they're on their toes: "Spindle gouges"…(Answer) "Next aisle, lower right" "OK, fluted parting tools"…(Answer) "right or left handed?" Well, you get the idea. They've been around forever and the store is just a wonderful place to spend an idyllic hour—if you're into hardware stores, like I am. It never fails...I go in looking for something particular. I end up wandering around and suddenly remember that I need this or that and I come out with twelve items instead of the two I went in to get. No matter. It's fun. And don't forget to get your fresh roasted peanuts, here, too.

✪✪✪✪ **Water Mill True Value Hardware,** Montauk Hwy., Water Mill, 726-4493 and **Emporium True Value Hardware,** Main Street, Sag Harbor (725-0103). Both stores are owned by the same folks. If they don't have it, they will get it. If they can't get it, they'll tell you where you can get it. I've been dealing with the Water Mill store for years and they really are quite helpful. Large selections, many "weekend specials."

✪✪ **Riverhead Building Supply,** Southampton, near the LIRR Station (283-2000). Riverhead Building Supply has several stores on the East End and the Southampton store is the newest, having taken over from the old Southampton Lumber Company. They've done a nice job and their folks are friendly and helpful. This store has more of a "wood & lumber" feel to it than Herrick's, which is natural, I guess, since it is so much bigger, has a warehouse, storage yard, cutting services, etc. It's where I go when I want personal help with large wood orders, pipe, paint, or such projects.

HEALTH CLUBS

The health-club craze is all over the East End, big time. There are a number of really good choices for your workouts. All these clubs cater to fulltime residents as well as part-timers and offer membership programs that meet the needs of each. An annual exercise membership at all clubs is running about the same this year: around $425. You can, of course, buy seasonal memberships and, in some cases, even join for just the day.

✪✪✪✪ **East Hampton Gym,** 2 Fithian Lane, East Hampton, 324-4499. This facility is smaller than some of your other choices, but the equipment is first-rate and the place is squeaky clean. It's right behind the Windmill Deli and across the street from London Jewelers.

✪✪✪✪ **Omnihealth & Racquet Club,** County Road 39A (Montauk Highway), Southampton (283-4770). Extensive weight and workout facilities, indoor pool and Jacuzzi, racquetball court, day care and baby-sitting, plus a full schedule of exercise and aerobics classes. Good but sometimes limited parking.

✪✪✪✪ **World Gym,** 250 West Montauk Hwy., in the King Kullen Shopping Center, Hampton Bays, 723-3174. Brand new and first rate. Tons of equipment, lots of classes and instructors, and (hooray!) plenty of easy parking.

✪ **The American Fitness Factories:** 15 Hill St., Southampton, 283-0707 and Bay St., Sag Harbor, 725-0707 (next to the Bay Street Theatre). The Factories are great for weights, aerobic exercise, conditioning, and checking out the opposite sex in workout gear.

HEALTH STORES / HOLISTIC HEALTH PRODUCTS

Hey, a few lungfuls of clean, country air and a walk on the beach ought to do wonders for you, but if you need more, here are the best places in The Hamptons for your health and beauty needs.

✪✪✪✪ **Second Nature Markets:** one in Southampton at 29 Main St., 283-8117 and one at 41 Newtown Ln., East Hampton, 324-5257. The best selection in The Hamptons for health foods. They also stock a full range of vitamins, including Solgar, and an excellent selection of face and body products, including Kiehl's.

HEATING CONTRACTORS AND SERVICE

There are a fair number of heating contractors and service companies out here. Sadly, there are a few rip-off artists. Here are some good folks you can rely on when the heat is on; or, more likely, off.

✪✪✪✪ **Hardy Plumbing & Heating,** 1654 County Rd. 39-A, Southampton, 283-9333; 486 Montauk Highway, East Hampton, 329-1333; and 27 No. Ferry Rd, Shelter Island, 749-9333. Hardy guarantees same day service and has the personnel and locations to do it. They do boilers, water heaters, radiant heaters, coils, etc., etc. They are our company and we have only had the best in service and support.

✪✪✪ **Matz,** 219 W. Montauk Highway, Hampton Bays (but serving all the East End). Sales: 728-0661. Service: 728-0055. They can be there 24 hours a day, seven days a week and offer service agreements and service all brands of heating devices.

✪✪ **North Sea Plumbing & Heating,** 524 County Rd. 39A, Southampton, 283-3876. Also have 24-hour service and offer free estimates. Their specialty is in water and steam installations.

HIKING

There are a number of excellent choices for hikers here on the East End.

First, the terrain is, for the most part, blessedly flat. Second, there is a move afoot (pun intended), now being assisted by the National Park Service, to complete the long overdue Paumanok Trail. Maybe this year. Once completed, you'll be able to hike almost 100 miles from Rocky Point to Montauk. Forty miles of the trail is available now via the Long Island Pine Barrens Trail that starts in Rocky Point.

Here's where to get lots of information on East End hiking.

Long Island Greenbelt Trail Conference, a nonprofit group that you can call for the latest information on hiking trails as well as scheduled nature walks: 360-0753.

East Hampton Trails Preservation Society, 324-1127. They organize over 100 free guided hikes each year from Sag Harbor to Montauk. You can also write the Society for info. at PO Box 2344, Amagansett, 11930.

The South Fork–Shelter Island chapter of the **Nature Conservancy,** 329-7689. They sponsor walking tours through many East End parks and preserves. Special hikes for children, too!

The South Fork Natural History Society, PO Box Nature, Amagansett, 11930, prints a regular newsletter with information on the Long Pond Greenbelt.

Here are, in my opinion, the best hikes:

✪✪✪✪ For the best hiking trail around these parts, get thee to the **Mashomack Preserve on Shelter Island** (see "Ferries"). The Nature Conservancy runs the Preserve and provides trails ranging from short loop walks in the woods to five and ten mile treks. You'll see lots of typical East End flora and fauna along the self-guided trails. Maps with the means to identify what you're walking by or through are provided. The Preserve is free, but donations are appreciated—and well deserved. For hours and information, call the Nature Conservancy at 329-7689.

✪✪✪✪ **Long Pond Greenbelt,** starting in Sag Harbor and stretching 6.2 miles to the Atlantic. This hike has been described as "otherworldly." Hikers go from one lovely pond to another along trails that were cut for supply wagons during the Colonial Era. Clear water, painted turtles sunning themselves, ospreys wheeling above you, cool breezes fanning your face. You'll see life as it was like before the $1,000 cocktail party.

✪✪✪✪ Go to the beach! We have some of the world's finest beaches here on the East End. You can walk, literally, for miles in either direction. Here are two walks that are grand:

(1) Go to **Flying Point Beach** (see "Beaches") and park the car. As you face the surf, turn right. About two miles down the beach, after passing some of the grandest ocean front homes in the East, you'll come to the Southampton Beach Club. Get off the beach there and head up South Main Street (Agawam Lake will be on your left). Half a mile later you'll be in Southampton Village. Have lunch. Turn around and walk back.

(2) Drive to **Montauk** (take Old Montauk Highway to make it a little more scenic). Park downtown anywhere that's legal. I suggest a right on Essex Street to Surfside Place. Get on the beach. As you face the surf, turn left. You can walk, literally, for about five miles on the beach: all the way to the Montauk Lighthouse if you like.

✪✪✪✪ **The Walking Dunes,** Montauk: go out Montauk Highway to Montauk and just before Cyril's take Napeague Harbor Road to your left. Cross the railroad tracks and go about a mile to the sign that says "Walking Dunes Trail." Stop and park. You're on the edge of Napeague Harbor. You can walk the trail all the way out to Goff Point and back (about 2.5 miles). Spectacular scenery, and, would you believe?—cranberry bogs!

✪✪✪ **Grace Estate,** Northwest Harbor, East Hampton (call East Hampton Trails Preservation Society, 324-1127). These 516 acres of public parks have some 20 miles of hiking trails. The estate used to belong to the W.R. Grace of the legendary company of the same name. Red maples and oak abound along with deer, fox, and song-birds of all types. This area also used to be East Hampton's main port in Revolutionary War days, but all of that construction has long since been re-claimed by Nature.

✪✪✪ Speaking of Montauk...Here's a hike for those who wear tennis shoes, don't like sand in their shoes, and want to avoid all dirt and bushes. It's a hike for non-hikers. Go to **Montauk Point State Park.** Park in the paid lot ($4). Visit the Lighthouse (originally commissioned by George Washington!) and the museum. The trek up and down the hill to the lighthouse and the lighthouse steps themselves will get your heart pumping. If that's not enough walking for your day, take a spin around the lighthouse road and parking lot. It's a level, gentle loop walk of about a half mile.

✪✪ **Northwest Path,** East Hampton, starting at Rte. 114 and Edwards Hole Rd. No parking lot, but you can park on Edwards Hole Rd. This 7-mile trail is marked and blazed. You can get a map at the East Hampton Town Clerk's Office, 324-4143. The trail winds through hickory forest and blueberry bushes, pitch pine, and mountain laurel. At the end of the trail you'll be at a wetlands, where you can spot migrating waterfowl in Spring and Fall. There is an abundance of native bird life, white-tailed deer, and red-tailed hawks here, too.

✪✪ **Red Creek Park,** Rte. 24, Old Riverhead Rd., Hampton Bays, 283-6000 ex. 233 (Town Parks Dept.). This is a 5-mile loop trail, where you can see birds and deer; and, in October, migrating Monarch butterflies. It's mostly mixed woods with maple, pitch pine, oak, tupelo, and wild sedges. Maps are available at the park entrance.

HISTORICAL SITES

My friend Nelson DeMille, the best selling author, has chided me rightfully about the dearth of information in my Guide concerning the wealth of history that we have here on the East End. Both Nelson and I are historians by education and training, and, Nelson, you're right, I need to pay more attention to this area. My only excuse for this lack of concern is that, like most everyone else out here, we've been too busy basing our concerns on the present. Living life in the fast lane, lavishly spending our money on homes and possessions, has allowed many of us to conveniently forget a great deal of our heritage. Mea culpa. Now, donning my historically accurate "hair shirt" let me tell you where you can find some great history.

✪✪✪✪ **The Montauk Lighthouse,** Montauk State Park. Basically, get on Montauk Highway and head east until you run out of road. The lighthouse was actually commissioned by George Washington during his first term as President. It was completed in 1797 and still serves today (although the light itself is now automated). The museum on the lighthouse grounds, though small, is filled with the history of Montauk Point, tales of tragic shipwrecks, stories of the hardy men who manned the light, and so forth. The lighthouse is well worth a trip—and you can pack a picnic lunch. New to the park is the Lost at Sea Memorial. It's inside the park grounds and is a memorial to all those lost at sea. It's quite sobering. There is a nice park with picnic tables and barbecue pits just across the street (Parking $4). Open year round, but only on weekends during the winter, 668-2544.

✪✪✪✪ **Mulford Farm,** East Hampton, run by the East Hampton Historical Society, 324-1850. Who needs Colonial Williamsburg! We have our own mini-version right here in East Hampton. This circa-1680's home, abode for more than ten generations of Mulford's, is filled with period furniture. It stands next to an 18th century barn tended to by costumed folks doing Colonial era chores. No Brooklyn accents either! Nearby, and also run by the society, is the Georgian-style old Clinton Academy. This was the very first secondary school in New York State to admit female students. Today, the school is closed, but the building now houses a major collection of historical documents and decorative arts. Great place for a rainy day excursion.

✪✪✪ **Water Mill Museum,** Old Mill Rd., Water Mill, 726-4625. Open from May through September, this mill dates from 1644—and it's still grinding grains today (for exhibition only, of course)! It's a seldom seen slice of colonial life that dates to the earliest settlers of New York. The museum is informative, entertaining, and has periodic art, photo, and handmade quilt shows.

✪✪✪ **East Hampton Town Marine Museum,** Bluff Rd., Amagansett, 267-6544. Highlights the history of the fishing and whaling industry on the East End with particular emphasis on the lives and struggles of the "Bonnackers." These early residents of the Acabonac Creek area of East Hampton (thus, "Bonnackers") were the area's first full-time fishermen. There are still a few families who proudly keep the tradition alive. They have been wresting a living from the sea for 350 years. Some literally lived in shacks on the beach. Their saga is commemorated here.

✪✪ **The Halsey House,** S. Main St., Southampton, 283-3527. See what a typical home from the 1640s looked like. This is the oldest existing homestead in New York State. And this was, for its time, a rather luxurious house. Most summer renters would be glad to have this much space.

✪✪ **Southampton Historical Museum,** 17 Meeting House Ln., Southampton, 283-2494. Located just behind Main Street, across the street from the 1st Presbyterian Church parking lot. This museum does a pretty fair job of representing several aspects of 17th and 18th century life here in The Hamptons. If you happen to catch the annual craft fair (usually in August) you'll get an extra bonus.

✪✪ **Home Sweet Home Museum,** Main St., East Hampton, 324-0713. See two real windmills up close on this historic property. Don't expect Don Quixote to come whizzing by, though.

✪✪ **The Shinnecock Nation** maintains a Cultural Center and museum on the reservation grounds in Southampton. Call 287-4923. And don't miss the annual Pow-Wow held every Labor Day Weekend! Indian crafts, native celebrations, dances, story telling, and exhibits.

HORSEBACK RIDING

Eastern Long Island is one of a dwindling number of places in the East where you can find extensive riding trails and enjoy the rare treat of riding on the beach. Pull on your boots and get to.

✪✪✪✪ **Deep Hollow Ranch,** Rte. 27, just past the town of Montauk, 668-2744. Deep Hollow holds the unique distinction of being the oldest cattle ranch in the US. Really. No kidding. They offer beach and trail rides covering thousands of acres, beginner to advanced. They also have pony rides for the children, a petting farm, wagon rides, and Texas style family barbecues. They also welcome weddings, corporate parties, and other special occasions.

✪✪✪ Also in Montauk are the lovely and well-outfitted **Rita's Stables,** on West Lake Drive, 668-5453. Rita's also has a petting farm, pony rides for the kids, and carriage rides for the whole family! I also hear that Rita's doing "Prairie B-B-Q's" this year, too. That could be interesting.

✪✪ Sears Bellows County Park (see "Parks"), in Hampton Bays, also has a riding stable, 723-3554.

✪✪ Want your little ones to learn to ride? Kids 4 and up can learn to ride at the Red Pony Camp at Rosewood farms in Southampton. Dial 329-TROT.

HOSPITALS

Southampton Hospital, Meeting House Ln., Southampton, main phone number 726-8200. This is the only hospital on the South Fork, it is the biggest single structure on the East End, and it is the Hamptons' largest employer (at the moment). But, oh boy, what else to say? Well, it is true that it's been a difficult couple of years for this hospital. Just two years ago the hospital was seemingly the picture of health: happy patients (if being in the hospital can be a happy experience), busy doctors and nurses, robust finances, gala benefit parties each summer, and local social climbers scrambling for seats on the Hospital Board. Unfortunately, behind that rosy cheeked glow, a cancer was eating away at the hospital's vital innards. The true nature of the disease? Fiscal mismanagement. Or more properly put, fiscal stupidity. The Board rubber-stamped everything the hospital's then popular director, himself a doctor, proposed. The auditors, somehow, signed off on the hospital's financials without ever asking any probing questions. Then—Bang!—the bottom fell out. Suddenly, somehow, the hospital went from being, supposedly, "in the black" to being millions and millions in debt. How? Why? The former director was not, thank goodness, putting unearned money in his own pocket. He was just covering up what he didn't know and understand: how to properly manage the books. Eventually, it'll catch up with you and it did with him. He's gone now, has been replaced by professional management, and the Board has been recon-stituted (i.e., told to ask the &^%$#@ questions!).

Unfortunately, when something that seems as good as this goes bad, it really goes bad. The financial irregularities—overnight—spawned horror stories about the hospital's staff and its practices, too. I was standing in a popular shop on Jobs Lane not long ago perusing the goods when I over-heard a conversation between three gentlemen concerning the hospital. One man was swearing that one of his good friends told him about another friend, twice removed, who went in to Southampton for gall bladder surgery and came out with a large pair of forceps sewn into his abdomen. True or false…I don't know, but it didn't hit the local papers, I can tell you. And, these days, if true, a story like that would be Page One around here.

HOTELS & MOTELS (see "Accommodations")

HOT TUBS (see "Spas")

HOUSEKEEPERS

✪✪✪✪ We finally found a housekeeping service that's better than their promotional materials. **Carol D. Mason,** of Hampton Bays, 728-5236. They are thorough and, equally important, dependable. Carol will come out and estimate the service for free. She also tries very hard to assign regular staff to your home instead of using a "revolving door" approach. That way the cleaners don't have to be told every time how you like things done.

HOUSE NUMBERS

It used to be (until 1995) that you did not have to post your house number on your property. That has changed. The small, graceful house signs with cutesy names must now have the number of the house posted, too. Some of my favorites: Done Rovin', Azure Rest, Hardscrabble House, The Bonus, Tooth Acres (a local dentist), etc.

HOUSE RENTALS (see "Rentals—Houses")

HOUSES, UNSAFE & UNSANITARY

Hard to imagine that you'd ever run across a situation where you'd be stuck with an unsafe or unsanitary home or rental; or, an unsafe or unsanitary neighbor, but it has happened. If you find yourself in this situation call the Suffolk County Division of Health, Environmental Protection Office at 852-2069 during the day or 853-5555 for evening or weekend emergencies. This office is responsible for "surveillance and regulation of food establishments, housing and general sanitation, as well as radiation control." (I hope that means "radon" and not "plutonium!")

HOUSEWARES

In this category we're going to refer you to some places where you can stock up on those "things" you absolutely can't live without. Goodies that will complement your "Hamptons Lifestyle."

✪✪✪✪✪ **Hildreth's Department Store,** 51 Main St., Southampton, 283-2300. See a complete description of Hildreth's under "Department Stores"; but, you cannot beat Hildreth's for the most complete and wonderful selection of housewares.

✪✪✪✪ **Pier 1,** 54 Montauk Hwy., Water Mill, 726-2032. Pier 1 has come a long way in the past couple of years toward providing a first-class selection of really nice items for the home. I think their selections at this store are better now than they have ever been. You really should give them a try.

✪✪✪ **Zona,** 2 Newtown Lane, East Hampton, 324-4100, fax 324-4102. Zona is classified as a "lifestyle store." I guess that means they have things to complement your lifestyle. All I know is that you come home with an armful of cool stuff if you shop at Zona.

HUNTING

There are lots of places out here where you can still hunt. Actually, you can hunt anywhere that's not posted and is more than 500 yards from any occupied building. More and more postings are going up, though, and there are certainly more and more structures. There's also a lot of debate going on about hunting out here, as you might well expect. Animal activists oppose it on all grounds. Many homeowners oppose it for safety reasons. The deer are certainly not in favor of it, but as yet they have been unsuccessful in organizing a union.... Hunters do have accidents, unfortunately, but there has been only one documented fatality from hunting on Long Island, ever. Conversely, five people have been killed in just the last three years in traffic accidents involving deer and cars. You make the call.

Perhaps the best deer-hunting areas are on Shelter Island and in North Haven, where, in season, deer are taken regularly. The deer season starts

November 1st and runs for about three months. Only bow hunting is permitted in November and December. In January, there's a special three-week firearms season, but only shotguns and muzzle loading rifles are permitted. No high-powered rifles, M-16's, Thompson submachine guns, Uzi's, etc.

Hunters can also go after Canadian geese, duck, pheasant, and grouse from November 20th to January 20th. Again, by shotgun only; or, if you're really a Robin Hood, the bow's OK, too. Whatever type of hunting you do, be sure to get a permit from the local wildlife officials. Permits are required!

There is also one good hunting preserve, **Spring Farm,** which is on Clay Pits Road in Sag Harbor, 725-0038. In season (best to call and ask) you can trek out with several dozen of your closest buddies and blast away at pheasant, quail, duck, and whatever else the farm has raised in its large bird enclosures. The birds are all released on a specified signal, and the hunters are all arranged in carefully situated enclosures that the birds must fly by or over. It's not quite like shooting "ducks in a barrel," so to speak, but I imagine these birds must feel somewhat like Custer at the Last Stand. Their only consolation is that if they successfully fly through this gauntlet they are then free. I'm told, though, (and how dumb is this?!) that most of the birds that make it to freedom actually wander back to the enclosures! Most of them were born and raised there and they know the pens as a reliable source of food.

HURRICANE INFORMATION

We have been very fortunate the past few years. The last really bad "blow" to come through The Hamptons was Hurricane Bob in 1991. We had a couple of scares last year but got lucky again. But make no mistake: we have hurricanes and they can be bad, bad, bad. And the time to prepare for one is NOT when you see the CNN radar image of the storm barreling down on Long Island.

We are now such an "Information Society" that it would be hard to imagine not knowing days in advance that a hurricane is pointed in our direction. Peak season is August through November. This is such an important issue that we are going to take the time and space to reiterate the New York State issued information contained in the Citizen's Guide for Preparedness on hurricanes. There is some really good advice in here—some of it you probably never would have thought about, so PLEASE read this section at least once.

Important Phone Numbers:
Local Emergency Management: 852-4900
Red Cross: 924-6700

Before the hurricane season:

- develop a family plan for survival
- plan what you will do with your pet
- inventory your personal property (instant photos are a good way)
- have materials handy to protect your doors and windows (pre-fitted plywood sheets are the best, but masking or duct tape are good, too)
- trim tree branches and move any yard debris that could blow around
- check the roof for leaks, tears, missing shingles, etc.
- make sure you have at least one good-sized fire extinguisher
- identify a friend or family member that you will keep informed of your whereabouts, safety, etc. Make sure they aren't in the hurricane area!
- put together a family survival kit. Here are the basics.
  portable radio with extra (fresh) batteries
  flashlights with extra (fresh) batteries
  first Aid kit
  portable ice chest
  canned and non-perishable food for a week
  emergency cooking supplies/utensils
  drinking water storage containers
  several gallons of emergency drinking water (plastic jugs are OK)
  emergency repair supplies
  extra medicines and sanitary supplies (diapers??)
  extra eyeglasses
  phone directory for those you need to reach

When a hurricane threatens:

- monitor local radio and CNN or weather channel
- re-check all your emergency supplies (you should think of being self-sufficient for two weeks!)
- fill your car's fuel tank and check the water, oil & battery
- secure the windows with plywood or tape to prevent flying glass
- locate the cutoff switches for electricity, water, gas. Secure any propane tanks
- secure all essential records and documents in a safe place
- if you don't have a car, arrange to go with someone to a shelter
- be prepared to evacuate as soon as notice is given!

During a hurricane watch or warning:

- closely monitor the radio, CNN, or the weather channel

- secure any and all outside objects, furniture, etc.
- don't drain the pool but add extra chlorine to reduce contamination
- turn off electrical connections to the pool
- remove pool pump, if possible, or at least cover it with plastic
- turn all refrigerators and freezers to the coldest possible settings
- lower any outside antennas, masts, flagpoles, etc.
- use the phone only when necessary
- DIAL 9-1-1 ONLY FOR EMERGENCIES!!
- fill the bathtub (for when the water goes off)
- set aside 1 gallon of water per person per day for drinking
- if you evacuate anywhere, call your contact person!

During the hurricane:

- monitor the radio but listen to only official broadcasts
- stay indoors but retreat to the most protected area of the house, away from doors and windows
- if the eye of the hurricane passes over, don't be fooled! Don't think the storm has passed! The winds will return with equal ferocity from the opposite direction! Stay indoors until the entire storm has passed!
- turn off the internal electricity and gas
- stay indoors until the "all clear" is issued by proper authority

Evacuation:

If proper authority deems that evacuation is necessary:
- be prepared to leave early
- select and confirm your destination before leaving
- take detailed maps of your destination
- monitor the local media
- fill your car's tank FIRST
- check all the car's fluid levels
- check the spare tire
- take adequate food and water with you
- bring sufficient cash

After the storm:

- pay attention to the local authorities
- stay away from the disaster areas—don't "sight see"
- If you must drive, use extra caution; for example, treat a broken stop light as if you were at a four-way stop

- advise interested parties that you are safe
- use caution when using food from appliances that have been off during the storm
- avoid all downed power lines! Assume they are "hot"!
- check all your connections before turning on water, power, etc.
- do not use any water until the authorities have indicated it is safe

In summary, just like good scouts, "be prepared"!

ICE CREAM

Isn't this a delightful topic (except maybe in January)! Here are the best places.

✪✪✪✪ **Snowflake Ice Cream Bar & Grill,** 277 Pantigo Road, 329-7867. Old fashioned, real ice cream that slops over the side of the cone. The scoops are big! Plus, you get a picnic table to sit at where you can try and keep up with the melt as it dribbles down the side of the cone—and your chin. The only way to eat ice cream.

✪✪✪ **Fletcher's,** 590 County Road 39-A, Southampton, 283-4141, near the Southampton Golf Club. Lots of homemade ice cream, both traditional and soft types. Very unique cones to cram the sweet stuff into as well as bowls made out of sugar-cones. And check out their newest feature: ice cream made from different herbal teas! No sugar, no lactose, and delicious! Fletcher's has also thoughtfully provided a small but cozy seating area indoors.

✪✪ Of course we have a **Ben & Jerry's**! It's on Flamingo Rd. in Montauk, 668-9425, and they dispense all the best that Ben &

Jerry can dream up. (My favorite is Cherry Garcia: (1) because of the clever name honoring someone who's gone long before his time and (2) the flavor!)

✪✪ **Sip 'N Soda,** 40 Hampton Rd., Southampton, 283-9752. Yes! We have a real soda fountain with all the 50's funk you could want. In addition to great ice cream, you can get egg creams and lime rickeys and vanilla cokes and....

Best ready-made ice cream in the Hamptons:

✪✪✪✪ The absolute BEST ice cream I have ever had out of a carton, no joke, is the wonderfully smooth and creamy concoctions that come from **Essay Ice Cream** under the Cream of the Hamptons brand. Pick up some today and you'll see what I mean! Yum!

INNS (see "Accommodations")

INSECTS

There are only three insects you really need to worry about out here. Two are mostly nuisances, the other is a potentially serious little bugger. The nuisance pests are the mosquito and the fruit fly. Both are around in droves from June through the first cool days of Fall. They are most prevalent during the sometimes hot and sticky days of August.

You can minimize mosquitoes by making sure there's no standing water on your property. Mosquitoes lay eggs and breed in stagnant pools of rainwater or ponds where there is little flushing action. Get rid of the puddles and turn over the buckets you left out in the rain. Pools, by the way, won't attract mosquitoes. Too many chemicals and too much motion. Most pools are constantly being stirred up thanks to swimmers, pool pumps, and so forth. Bug zappers—those stupid, noisy, purple, light things don't work against mosquitoes. In fact, some people think they actually attract mosquitoes. The best protection is slopping on some Avon Skin-So-Soft or dousing yourself with Off anti-

mosquito spray. If the air is still (the constant breezes out here tend to foil mosquitoes) citronella torches or citronella candles are effective. If you get bit (and you will, no matter what you do) rub a little white wine vinegar on the bite. You may smell like a salad for a while but it'll relieve the itch, and the slight acidity of the
vinegar is also a mild antiseptic.

Fruit flies! Ugh! They're everywhere, but, thankfully, they're harmless. At least they don't bite. They'll go after any fruit (and, don't forget, tomatoes are fruit and fruit flies love tomatoes!) you leave uncovered. Same goes for soft drinks left untended and—do these little buggers have taste or what?—your glass of wine. I've sat on the deck with a delightful glass of Chardonnay, gotten up to take a quick you-know-what and come back to see a tiny, dead fruit fly, little legs up in the air, floating around in my glass. It's not that they drink that much, what really galls me are the broad smiles on their little dead faces as they float around in what, to them, must be the equivalent of an entire swimming pool full of alcohol. Some way to go, I guess. In any case, minimize the fruit flies by putting your fruit and any-thing sweet and sticky in the fridge or a properly closed container. And don't sip your wine slowly. Chug it.

The much more serious insect problem has to do with the deer tick. (OK, OK...It was pointed out to me that the deer tick is really an arachnid—i.e., a spider—not a true insect, but who the heck knows that? I mean, I didn't and obviously you didn't since you're reading about them under "Insects," so we'll leave it here, in this section. The information herein is no less impor-tant! These nasty little bastards are small, hard to spot, and prevalent. Why are they so bad? Most of them carry Lyme Disease (see also "Lyme Disease"). Lyme Disease is nothing to fool around with. Though seldom fatal, it is very debilitating and it can take a long time to overcome. Sometimes it takes months or even years just to detect and diagnose. If you keep the grass short and don't put up with a lot of weeds on your property, you will mini-mize your exposure to the deer tick. The deer tick likes thick grasses, woods, high hedges, etc. And if those cute little deer we have out here wander onto your property, feed them at your risk. These pests aren't called "deer" ticks for nothin'. Also, be wary of your own pets. If you allow them to wander off in the brush, deer ticks will find them like iron filings to a magnet. Check your pets very carefully every day. If you see what you think might be a tick burrowed deep within the fur of dear old Rover or Miss Kitty, don't fool around. Get the pet to a vet—and don't try to remove the tick yourself!

If you want to wander around in the woods or stroll the fields, take some preventive measures. As stupid as it looks, tuck your trousers or slacks into the tops of your socks. Wear some anti-insect goo. And when you return, carefully undress and examine any areas you think have been exposed to the woods.

One almost sure sign that this dreaded tick has bitten you is a small red bite that has another red ring around the bite area. If you see this type of bite it doesn't always mean you will develop Lyme disease (not all ticks are infected) but it is nothing to fool around with. Get thee to a doctor immediately—one who is experienced with treating Lyme disease.

Most local doctors' offices, as well as the Southampton Hospital, have brochures on Lyme disease, what to do, how to handle it, and so forth.

INSURANCE (General)

For you renters, for heaven's sake, cover your butts with a renter's policy—one that includes accidental damage and personal liability. All it takes is one crazy friend slipping on your pool deck to ruin your summer—and a friendship. If you're going to invest several thousands of dollars in a rental or a "share," what's a few more dollars to protect yourself? Call your regular insurance agent and get a rider or floater for the summer.

For you permanent residents, in addition to your standard or required homeowners coverage, you might give some serious consideration to hurricane coverage and flood insurance. If you are fortunate enough to live along or near the water, be sure you know where the water table under your property is and how far your house is above it. Your home may not get blown away in a hurricane, but the waters do rise out here after big storms. Many a homeowner has awoken the day after a bad storm to find the nice, dry cellar looking more like an indoor pool. Hurricane and flood insurance are expensive, but read your current policy carefully: rising ocean waters that create that unwanted pool in the basement are considered "flood waters" and you might want to be sure you're covered.

INSURANCE AGENTS (Auto and General)

If you're not careful, and don't shop for rates, you can get stung out here. Here are some folks you can rely on for service and decent rates.

✪✪✪✪ **GEICO,** local number 1-800-841-7475 (and they do have a local office on Long Island). After many, many years with one auto insurance carrier I decided to test my loyalty and actually shop around for some rates. Much to my shock and surprise, I found my loyalty was not being rewarded. GEICO offered me a much better rate, by about 15% less. I switched! Then, last winter, I had a slippery confrontation with some bushes by the side of the road. GEICO was Johnny-on-the-spot with a rental car, adjuster, and a repair check.

✪✪✪✪ **Lighthouse Insurance,** 1730 North Highway, County Rd. 39A, Southampton, 283-7000. Heard some good reports about these folks. Mostly auto insurance.

✪✪✪✪ **Allstate,** Michael R. Haines, 3420 Montauk Highway, Wainscott/Sagaponack, 537-3540. More good reports. A full service agent, all lines.

By the way, have you tried the Internet? Have you tried Select-Quote? I know, neither resource is a Hamptons resource, but, hey, we're here to help each other out, right? Again, throwing tradition to the winds, I surfed the 'net and also called Select-Quote. Got a great term life policy for a great rate.

INTERIOR DECORATORS

With all the new homes and seemingly abundant resources to spend on them, we have a flourishing interior decorating business in The Hamptons. Our local decorators see many homes out here, understand the lighting, weather, what holds up, what doesn't, etc. You ought to try my favorite.

✪✪✪✪ How can you beat **Hildreth's,** Main Street, Southampton, 283-2300? The best department store in the Hamptons has everything you'll need to decorate every room in the house. Great prices, great people and they deliver, too.

✪✪✪✪ **Windows & Walls,** 375 North Hwy, Southampton, 287-1515 (also see their listing under "Window Treatments"). The husband and wife team of Paul and Linda have done many beautiful fabric walls in bedrooms and dens plus window treatments, wallpaper for bathrooms, etc., all over the East End. Their service is excellent and their prices are fair. If something isn't right they'll work at it until it is. That's good service in an environment where all too often the merchant is only interested in getting in, getting out, and keeping your money…

INVESTMENTS & INVESTMENT SPECIALISTS
(see "Stockbrokers")

j

JEWELRY & JEWELERS

✪✪✪✪ **Hollis Reh & Shariff Estate Jewelers,** 2 Jobs Lane, Southampton, 283-6653: Hollis Reh and Sal Shariff (husband and wife) have actually been very much a part of the local merchant scene for many years, opening their first store in 1986. They now have a wonderful shop on Jobs Lane. My goodness! What an exquisite store! They specialize in Art Deco and 1940's jewelry and other objets d'art. They have an on-site master jeweler and they do repairs, too. Gorgeous antique diamond bracelets and necklaces. I found exactly two items I could afford on the limit of my credit card; but, what the heck, it's fun to look. Wait until you see the white and yellow diamond necklace that can be converted into two bracelets. Only $125,000!

✪✪✪✪ **Corwin's Jewelers,** 61 Main St., Southampton, 283-1980. Talk about a family business! Corwin's was established 121 years ago and it's still in the family, now run by Timothy Corwin. When Myra and I went looking for that special ring that she'll—I hope—wear forever, we thought about going "up island" or perhaps to the diamond district in Manhattan. Better prices, we thought. But, there we were, strolling Main Street one beautiful day last Fall, and we poked our noses into Corwin's, just to take a look. Lo and behold, we found the perfect combination of diamonds and bands right there in Corwin's. And we were able to strike the right price! Tony, Alexis, and Tim were very, very helpful—and patient, too. If they don't have something in stock they'll do their best to find it. Tim does expert repairs on site and you should also look at their very fine collection of estate jewelry, pearls, and other fine jewelry.

✪✪✪✪ **Jobs Lane Jewelers,** 50 Hampton Rd., Southampton, 283-2841. No, despite their name, they are not on Jobs Lane, though they used to be. They have had a couple of moves over the past few years, but now they are happily ensconced in a renovated Colonial on Windmill Lane, across form the Fire Department. Beautiful location! I've always gotten excellent jewelry service here (cleaning, tightening, restringing pearls, etc.), and I feel like I am being treated well by people who want my business. Prices are fair, they have an excellent selection of gold, diamonds, and watches, and they do appraisals. And—are you ready for this?—this is where I got my ear pierced last year. Yes, even at my age.

✪✪✪✪ **London Jewelers,** 2 Main St., East Hampton, 329-3939. Fifth Avenue has come to The Hamptons. But this is not just a jewelry store: it's a showcase for Rolex, Tiffany, fine porcelain, handcrafted furniture, and much more. They even have a walk-in humidor and selection of great cigars. These folks also believe in service, attention to detail, and making the customer feel special. We like that!

✪✪✪ **Second Chance Antiques,** 45 Main St., Southampton, 283-2988. This is a first-rate second-hand store. Lots of antiques, furniture, linens, and so forth. They obtain a lot of their merchandise from estates and estate sales. Out here, that could mean a great find. It's worth your time to check it out. Myra now has an antique, hand-carved, 100-year-old cameo with 18-K gold backing that I got here. A real bargain!

THE  PROMISE

SINCE 1879

JEWELERS
OF SOUTHAMPTON

WE PROMISE YOU QUALITY

Quality you can count on—well-designed, well-made jewelry
for you and everyone in your family.

WE PROMISE YOU VALUE

Value you can trust. Prices that make sense, sale prices that are true.

WE PROMISE YOU SERVICE

Service that's prompt, service that's friendly,
service that's courteous and respectful.

IT'S ALL PART OF OUR TRADITION

A tradition that began in 1879...
and carried on each day now for five generations.

American Gem Society

61 Main Street, Southampton, NY   283-1980

KAYAKING (see "Canoeing")

KENNELS (see "Pet Boarding")

KIDS! KIDS! KIDS!

"What do we do with the Kids!!!" Do you cringe when you hear the dreaded, "Mom, Dad! We're B-O-R-E-D!!!" Herewith are some of the best ideas for the young ones who, after all, can only take so much beach time.

Art Related Activities

Call the Art Barge in Amagansett, 267-3172 (See also "Art," above). There are lots of topnotch classes here for kids interested in collage, painting, drawing, and sculpture. Separate workshops for ages 5–8 and 9–12, then special young adults' classes for 13–16 year olds.

Birthday Parties (spectacular ones!)

East Hampton Historical Society, 101 Main St., East Hampton, 324-6850. Want to throw a special birthday party? Call these folks: cavort in a haystack and play 18th Century children's birthday party games. They also have clowns, balloon sculpture, face painting, puppets, magic tricks, live animals, costumed characters and more! Oh, and the kids might even learn something. Wouldn't that be a nice bonus!

Day Camps

Pathfinder Country Day Camp, Second House Rd., Montauk: 668-2080
Southampton College, 5–12 years, usually June through August:
287-8316

Fun Stuff

The East End Children's Museum: this is a "hands-on" museum devoted to kids having fun and interacting with all kinds of East End related "stuff." Drag the kids in and they won't want to come out! The museum has been moving from place to place (Shelter Island, The Parrish Art Museum) and is looking for a permanent home. Call 726-6501 to see where they will be this year.

Hiking

The South Fork-Shelter Island chapter of the Nature Conservancy, 329-7689. They sponsor walking tours through many East End parks and preserves. Special hikes for children!

Horseback Riding

The little ones (ages 4 and up) can learn to ride at **Red Pony Camp** at Rosewood Farms in Southampton. Dial 329-TROT. The other kids (and the kid in you) should check out our listings under "Horseback Riding." Get on a trail or a hayride and have some old-fashioned fun!

Piano Festival

For your budding Van Cliburn, there's **Pianofest.** This is a very serious piano camp for very serious piano students. Classes will be held in East Hampton and at Southampton College. Usually June through mid-August. For information, call 283-2044.

Sports Camps:

Lacrosse Day Camp, ages 7–13, Southampton, 653-5658
Basketball Camp for Girls: 736-7523
Soccer Camps, Girls and Boys: 283-2909
Gymnastics (sleepover and day camps): 666-6999
Volleyball Camp, ages 10–18, boys & girls, 723-9910
Tennis: Future Kids, Green Hollow Tennis Camp, East Hampton, ages 5–16, beginners to advanced, call for information and a brochure at 324-0297.

Whales and Seals

Look under our "Ten Most Fun Things to Do in the Hamptons" category for information on whale and seal watching. Depending on the time of year, you can do one or the other, mostly in Montauk.

Youth Centers

East Hampton Youth Center, East Hampton, 324-8704. The Center offers tutoring (during the school year) by licensed teachers, has a drop-in lounge, youth employment services, drama workshops, karate, and Saturday night programs.

KITCHENWARE

With all the cooking and entertaining being done out here, it's good to know where you can find quality cooking utensils and housewares. Here are the best.

✪✪✪✪ **Williams-Sonoma,** Bridgehampton Commons, Bridgehampton, 537-3040. I LOVE this store, which says a lot since I HATE to shop. But I do love to cook, and this is a store for serious cooks. This would be one of my personal "Top Three," best-of-the-best stores in The Hamptons. The quality of the merchandise is just five-star. The selection of gadgets and cookware could keep me occupied for hours.

✪✪✪✪ **Bar-Boy,** 218 W. Montauk Hwy., Hampton Bays, 728-7100. Another place I love. Man, can you get lost in gadget heaven here! I mean, there's everything for the kitchen and the bar somewhere in these aisles!

✪✪✪ **Fishs Eddy,** 50 Jobs Lane, Southampton, 287-2993. This is more of a chinaware shop, but I'm putting it under kitchenware, too, because it's a fun place to find odd plates, glasses, and so forth for the kitchen.

✪✪✪ **Sylvester & Co.,** Main St., Sag Harbor, 725-5012. "A Contemporary General Store." Another place I like a lot. Fresh coffee beans, specialty food items and numerous gadgets and knick-knacks for the kitchen. Nice selection of candles, linens, and napkins, too.

✪✪✪ **Lechter's,** Bridgehampton Commons, 537-2196. If I can't find it at Williams-Sonoma, or need some little doo-dad at a cheaper price, I'll walk across the parking lot to Lechter's. They've got every kitchen gadget imaginable.

LANDSCAPERS

Sometimes it seems like every other truck on the highway, between March and October, is a landscaper's truck. There are lots of 'em out here. All you need is a pickup, a rake, and a power mower and you're in business. There are many good ones but be careful: there are some who are more interested in the "green" in your pocket that the green in your lawn. Here's someone we know is great.

✪✪✪✪ **John Leuthardt,** PO Box 104, East Moriches, 878-1387. He does impeccable work. His crews mow the lawn without having to be called. The grass gets fertilized, the weeds get pulled, the trees get trimmed, and in the winter your driveway is plowed just about as soon as it stops snowing. John is also great for getting new plants, fixing things, hauling firewood, and just about anything else you need. In short, your lawn will look as good as the fairways at Shinnecock, and you'll never have to worry about anything relative to yard work except the stuff you want to do yourself. What more could you ask for?

LAUNDRIES/LAUNDROMATS

Herewith we provide relief from stacks of wet beach towels and damp bathing suits. This is also a list of places where you can get your regular laundry done, for that matter, if your landlord was too cheap to put in a washer and dryer.

Amagansett
Amagansett Laundromat, Montauk Highway, 267-7725
Hampton Bays,
Tony's Tubs, 218 W. Montauk Hwy., 728-1046
Montauk
Montauk Laundromat, 45 S. Elmwood, 668-4349

Sag Harbor

Sag Harbor Launderette, 20 Main St., 725-5830

Southampton

Tuckahoe Launderette, 376 North Hwy., 283-0153

LAWYERS & LEGAL HELP

There are a lot of lawyers out here, as you might expect, since there are a lot of lawyers everywhere! Now, now, no lawyer jokes. Well, maybe just one: "Did you know that attorney egos are in direct proportion to the size of their yellow page ads?" 'Court jesting' aside, here are a few lawyers we can recommend to you; we give you the best by area of expertise.

Accidents & Personal Injury:

✪✪✪✪ Barry H. Feldman, 27 Bowden Sq., Southampton, 287-8700.

Bankruptcy:

✪✪✪✪ Bennett & Read, 212 Windmill Ln., Southampton, 283-9696.

Criminal Law:

✪✪✪✪ Barry H. Feldman, 27 Bowden Sq., Southampton, 287-8700.

Divorce:

✪✪✪✪ Richard S. Fernan, 592 Hampton Rd., Southampton, 283-3510.

Professional Corporations:

✪✪✪✪ William H. Duggan, Jr., 40-A Newtown Ln., East Hampton, 324-0512.

Real Estate:

✪✪✪✪ Marty Gilmartin, 200 North Sea Rd., Southampton, 283-1800.
Marty I can vouch for personally. He's thorough and he's the best!

✪✪✪✪ William H. Duggan, Jr., 40-A Newtown Ln., East Hampton, 324-0512.

✪✪✪✪ Nancy Tainiter, Southampton, 283-7804

Traffic, DUI, etc.:

✪✪✪✪ Richard S. Fernan, 592 Hampton Rd., Southampton, 283-3510.

Wills and Estate Planning:

✪✪✪✪ Marty Gilmartin, 200 North Sea Rd., Southampton, 283-1800.

✪✪✪✪ Mary Jane Asato, 83 Jobs Lane, Southampton, 283-0046.

Zoning:

✪✪✪✪ Gilbert Flanagan, 83 Jobs Lane, Southampton, 283-0046.

✪✪✪✪ Marty Gilmartin, 200 North Sea Rd., Southampton, 283-1800.

LEATHER & LEATHER GOODS

✪✪✪✪ **The Coach Factory Stores**: 69 Main St., East Hampton, 329-1777, Main St. in Amagansett, 267-3340 and now in the Tanger Mall, 369-4670: Coach is one of the defining stores of The Hamptons. Coach cannot be beat for the quality of their leather offerings in belts, handbags, portfolios, briefcases, gloves, and so forth. East Hampton and Amagansett offer many "seconds" at greatly reduced prices. These are otherwise beautiful leather pieces with some sort of small defect or another. I can never tell, though, as hard as I've tried.

LIBRARIES

The two main libraries in our part of the East End are: the **Rogers Memorial Library,** 9 Jobs Lane, Southampton, 283-0774; and, **The John Jermain Memorial Library,** Main St., Sag Harbor, 725-0049.

The venerable old Rogers is open Monday through Thursday from 10 AM to 9 PM, Fri. and Sat. from 10 AM to 5 PM and on Sundays, May to October, from 1 PM to 5 PM. The building is old and the collections are bursting at the seams because of lack of space, but you'll find a very up-to-date library with video, CD's, books on tape, online databases and, yes, books! The Rogers is going to get out of its current space and move to larger quarters a few blocks away on Windmill Lane. Expect an opening late in 2000 or maybe early 2001.

The Jermain is smaller but serviceable and is open Mon. to Sat. from 10 AM to 5 PM and Thurs. evenings to 9 PM.

LICENSES

Motor Vehicles:

It's time to get your driver's license renewed. Ugh! What a chore. Now imagine being able to walk in, walk up to the counter, fill out the forms, get your picture taken, pay the fee and be out of there in under 30 minutes?! Impossible? No! It happens every day at the DMV office in Riverhead, 200 Rte. 58. Even the people running this DMV office are nice. Maybe it's because they don't have to work at any of the other DMV offices! You can take care of license plates and other standard DMV matters here, too.

Marriage:

The urge has struck you! You're actually going to do it! Well, out here, it's not Vegas. There isn't a single spot you can run away to, find a Justice of the Peace, and simply tie the knot. You're going to have to apply for a license, wait a few hours, cool off, make sure it's the right thing to do, and then plunge in. Marriage licenses are available from the Town Halls in East Hampton (324-4142) and Southampton (283-6000). Basically, you'll (both) need to appear at the Clerk's office, have picture ID (driver's license is OK) copies of your divorce papers if you've been married before, and $25. There's a 24-hour waiting period before the license becomes valid (don't know if that's a wise "cooling off" period or the time needed to process the paper!). The license is good for 60 days from issuance just in case you want to take even more time to think about it. Hours are from 8:30 AM to 4 PM.

LIGHTS/LIGHTING/FIXTURES

✪✪✪✪ There's a really great lighting fixtures store in Southampton at 455 County Road 39A: **Suffolk Lighting,** 283-4800. Huge selection of chandeliers, lamps, bulbs, you-name-it. You should definitely go the one or two times a year they have their biggest sales (early spring, late fall) and absolutely go when they have their tent sale (mid-summer).

✪✪✪✪ For lighting supplies, **REVCO** can't be beat. This is REVCO Electrical Supply, not Revco Pharmacy. There are two stores, one on County Road 39-A in Southampton, 283-3600 and on Gingerbread Lane in East Hampton, 329-4600. It's primarily a builder's resource, but they've got the bulbs, fixtures, and electrical supplies you're going to need!

LIMOS

The yellow page listings for limos in this part of the world are almost as garish as the listings for lawyers! What does that tell you? In any case, like the attorneys, there are some good ones.

✪✪✪✪ **Hampton Jitney Limousine Service,** Southampton, 287-4000. These are the same folks who bring you our "Gold" bus service to Manhattan. Their limo service is equally good. They serve the city and all major airports. Daily and hourly rates, and corporate accounts are welcome.

✪✪✪✪ **Southampton Limousine Service,** Southampton, 287-0001. Ask for Mollie. Another great limo company with service to all the airports, the City, parties, 24-hours a day, you name it. They also have corporate accounts. I have hired Mollie and her drivers for years now and have found them to be reliable, on-time, and capable.

✪✪✪✪ **Town Car Express,** 33 Flying Point Rd., Southampton, 287-5568: Todd keeps his cars clean, shiny, and ready to ride. Give him a call! They'll take you wherever you want to go in the Hamptons—in style and comfort.

LIQUOR (see also "Wine Shops")

All the liquor stores I've been to also carry wines, and vice versa, but some stores are better at one or the other. Here are my selections for the best liquor stores and I encourage you to also see our selections under "Wine Shops." Not surprisingly, some of them are the same as you'll see here.

✪✪✪✪ Well, there just is not a better place out here than **Herbert & Rist,** 63 Jobs Ln., Southampton, 283-2030. Their folks are helpful, friendly, courteous, and very, very knowledgeable about their wares. Their selection is terrific and the prices and selections here are as good as anywhere. Herbert & Rist will deliver on larger orders and offer case discounts on wine—even on mixed cases. They have specials often, and when they do, they can't be beat.

✪✪✪ **Southampton Wines & Liquors,** in the Water Mill Shoppes, Montauk Hwy., Water Mill, 283-6315. The nice lady who owns this store used to be in the mini-mall next to Carvel Ice Cream on the corner of Hampton Road and Montauk Highway. She moved to this new site when the Water Mill Shoppes first opened. It's a much larger store and one you should visit.

✪✪✪ **Amagansett Wines & Spirits,** Main Street, Amagansett, 267-3939. Known primarily for their wines, they also have a very good selection of liquors. Good prices, too, especially when they are having one of their frequent sales.

LOCKSMITHS

Some of the most dreaded words you can hear are: "Honey, do you have the keys?!" In case neither of you can come up with them, call one of these folks.

✪✪✪✪ **Champion Locksmiths,** 293 Montauk Highway, Southampton, 287-0500. They "virtually guarantee" 15 minute service on all emergency calls, 24-hours a day, 7 days a week. Well, they're quick. They do homes, cars, boats, and safes.

✪✪✪ **East End Locksmiths,** 59 Maple St., Southampton, 283-0763.

✪✪ **John's Locksmith,** Sag Harbor, 725-4738

LUMBER

Unless you're a contractor or building your own home, lumber prices are not going to be competitive compared to some of the "super depot" stores up-island; but, you have to weigh convenience against driving time, gas, etc. I come down in favor of buying my lumber here unless it's just a super-large quantity for a big project (paneling your den or sheet-rocking your basement fall into this category). Here's where to go.

✪✪✪✪ **Riverhead Building Supply:** in Southampton, 40 Powell Ave. (near the LIRR Station), 283-2000. In East Hampton, 21 Railroad Ave., 324-0300. In Hampton Bays, 165 W. Montauk Hwy., 728-0307.

✪✪✪✪ **Water Mill Lumber:** in Water Mill, Montauk Highway, just before Scuttle Hole Road, 726-4493. They also have an outlet in Montauk, also on Montauk Highway, 668-6800.

LYME DISEASE (see also "Insects")

(see also "Insects") Lyme disease is a problem that has begun to plague our little slice of paradise. This awful and sometimes (though rarely) fatal disease is carried by the tiny, insignificant, common deer tick (which is actually a spider). And they are everywhere—especially in wooded areas and areas with lots of grass and shrubs. How can you tell a deer tick from a regular tick? You can't usually, unless, you're an entomologist or afflicted with deer tick paranoia. Best to treat any tick bite seriously; or, better yet, exercise caution by minimizing exposure to these mean little buggers. Wear protective clothing while walking in the woods or tall-grass areas. This means, unfortunately, wearing long pants tucked into the tops of your socks, long sleeved shirts, etc. It also helps to rub on some commercial insect repellent. I know that you want to look like you just posed for a Calvin Klein ad when you're ditzing around out here, but, believe me, Calvin wouldn't mind. He lives here, too. And if you want a good lesson for why you should not go naked in the woods trying to look like a model, talk with Christie Brinkley. She got Lyme disease in her (former) backyard in Amagansett (she's OK, though).

Golfers need to be especially conscious of the potential for Lyme disease. The little ticks absolutely love running around on the links as much as you do. Most of our course superintendents have picked up on ways to minimize the ticks, but it wouldn't hurt for you to "drive defensively." Again, use a commercial insect spray, especially from the knees down. Shorts are great in good golf weather, but long pants are better. After your round, do a tick check. Susceptible areas are behind the knees, under the collar of your oh-so-chic Polo golf shirt, the beltline, scalp, groin, and those sweaty armpits.

OK, so you're not a golfer. Doesn't matter. After your idyllic walk in the woods, take off all your clothes and do a self-exam, like above. If you suspect you have been bitten by a deer tick—or, worse, find one of the little bloodsuckers buried in your calf—don't mess around. Get a pair of tweezers and nab that little SOB as close to its head and as close to your skin as you can. Yank it out. Apply some antiseptic to the site. If you get the tick within 24 hours of attachment, you are much less likely to be infected. If you're still concerned, go immediately to a doctor who knows something about Lyme disease (you can call Southampton Hospital for a referral). An almost 100% sure indicator of a Lyme bite is a small red mark surrounded by another red circular ring. Not all deer ticks carry Lyme disease, but are you willing to take the risk? Ain't worth it...Go to the doc.

Symptoms of Lyme disease (which can sometimes take a long time to develop) include fatigue, listlessness, lack of energy, headaches, dizziness, fevers, and a general overall sense that you feel like crap. Sometimes you don't get all the symptoms. It's a bitch of a disease. If you don't get it diagnosed and treated in a timely fashion you may be stuck with it—including many blood transfusions or worse—for months or years. Untreated, Lyme disease can lead to chronic arthritis and heart and nervous system abnormalities.

Most local doctors' offices carry pamphlets on Lyme disease, as does Southampton Hospital. They're free, of course, and it's a good idea to have one in your kitchen junk drawer with all the takeout menus. A new SmithKline-Beecham vaccine has been recommended for approval for Lyme disease. It's called Lymerix and is available now for those of us between the ages of 15 and 70. Three inoculations over a 12-month period are required and the vaccine has been shown to reduce immunity in 8 out of 10 people. See your doc for details!

MAGAZINES

For the best selection go to.

✪✪✪✪ **Book Hampton,** all three locations, in East Hampton, Southampton and soon to be in Sag Harbor. 93 Main St. in Southampton (283-0270) and 20 Main St. in East Hampton (324-4939).

✪✪✪ Get your magazines with your groceries, or just come by for newspapers and magazines at **King Kullen** in the Bridgehampton Commons, 537-8103. Be sure to wear your sunglasses and a knit cap if you're picking up the latest *Enquirer.*

MAID SERVICES (see "Housekeepers")

MALLS

Shopping malls are inconsistent with the image of "The Hamptons," or so it would seem; but, you know what? We have a couple of malls that are pretty good!

✪✪✪✪ **The Tanger Outlet Mall,** 369-2732, Riverhead, 1770 W. Main. OK. OK...Riverhead is not The Hamptons, but once you've been to the Tanger Mall, you'll stop quibbling. Conveniently located just off of Exit 72 on the L.I.E. (next-to-last exit), it's a place to stop on the way out or on the way back. This is one of the largest malls in America, by the way. A real fix for "mall-a-holics." Our favorite Tanger stores are:
The GAP, Nike, Mikasa, Levi's, Greg Norman, L'Eggs/Hanes, Brooks Brothers, Off 5th (Saks outlet), J. Crew, Donna Karan, Old Navy, Bass Shoes, Tommy Hilfiger, Lenox, J. Peterman, the Cosmetics Company Store, Camp Coleman, the French Connection, Lindt Chocolates, and Skechers (shoes). But there are many more. There

are food courts and ATMs, too. You can spend the whole day there kissing your entire paycheck goodbye.

✪✪✪ **Bridgehampton Commons,** Montauk Highway, Bridgehampton, information at 537-2174. This is not, strictly speaking, a mall but more of a traditional shopping center. Nonetheless, it's got some great stores. You'll find a King Kullen supermarket that is trying to be everything from a grocery to a dry cleaners (and succeeding pretty well at it). There's also a new K-Mart, GAP, GNC Nutrition, Radio Shack, and, my two personal favorites, a Williams-Sonoma outlet store and Razzano's Italian deli and restaurant.

MANICURISTS (see "Beauty")

MANHOLE COVERS

If you have a problem with a manhole cover, try to read the inscription on it...if it's right side up, that is. The name of the "owner" is stamped on the cover. If it's not right side up, don't try and turn it over. You'll get a hernia. If you can read the name, call the owner. Most likely it will be Suffolk County Water (324-0959). If you can't read the name, think for a second, remember where you are, and call that town's public works department.

MAPS

You'll notice that we elected not to include any maps in the "Guide" (but we do try to give general directions to most of the places we feature). I HATE folding those damn map pages back into books like this! And they never fold back properly, plus they tear easily. Thankfully there are some really good maps of The Hamptons. I'd recommend the Streetwise Maps—available in Southampton and East Hampton versions. They are "plasticized" so they won't tear, and—bless them!—they fold up automatically! Available in many retail shops, 7-11's, etc., but if you can't find them, call Streetwise in Amagansett at 267-8617.

MARRIAGE LICENSES (see "Licenses")

MASSAGES

Ooh, what we do to ourselves with stress. Get the kinks out with some expert massage therapy! There are lots of people out here providing massages. In some cases, you go to their place of business. In other cases, they will come to you. Whom to trust? First, anyone providing massage therapy (with very few exceptions) MUST be licensed and registered with the State of New York. If you have any questions, call the State Education Department, Division of Professional Licensing Services, 800-342-3729. Four years ago a local "massage parlor" was apparently rubbing more than just lower backs...They got busted. Many citizens cheered...some cried.

In any case, here are the best (and totally honorable) folks on the East End for that oh-so-needed massage.

✪✪✪✪✪ **Naturopathica,** Red Horse Plaza, 74 Montauk Hwy., East Hampton, 329-2525: Massage therapy? How about Swedish, Deep Tissue, Aromatherapy, Trager, Myofacial Release, and Four-Handed massages? Even massages for pregnant women. We've tried a couple of these wonderful massages and they are the best! And they also have spa treatments (see "Spas").

✪✪✪✪✪ **Ron Esposito, LMT,** (that's "Licensed Massage Therapist," if you didn't guess!), 287-3362: Ron has been practicing his art for 20 years, the last 12 here in the Hamptons. He's really good... talented with an innate quality of touch. Ron knows his anatomy; or more importantly, yours! Ron will do Swedish massage, deep tissue, and Myofacial technique, too. If you want the best, call Ron. By appointment only, either at his Southampton office location or your residence. Ron will also make trips to the City in the off-season from September to May.

✪✪✪✪ **Massage In The Hamptons,** Kevin Reynolds, licensed massage therapist, (LMT), 324-2201. Kevin does Swedish, deep-tissue and shiatsu. He also works with pregnant women, infants, and those of you who have medical and sports related massage requirements. Kevin lives in East Hampton during the summer and St. John, in the Virgin Islands, during the winter. This guy must be good!

✪✪✪ **Gurney's Inn,** Old Montauk Highway, Montauk, Health Spa number, 668-2509. Massages delivered the old fashioned way: lying on a hard table, in semidarkness, naked as a jay bird except for your towel, and some hard-knuckled pro wrestling the kinks out of your tired ol' body. Men's and women's massage facilities, spas, pools, sauna and, of course, the ocean to jump into after your massage. Ahhhh….

✪✪✪ **Michael Mezzatesta,** LMT, 145 W. Montauk Hwy., Hampton Bays, 723-2540 and Southampton, 283-3780. Michael does sports, European, and medical massage therapy and will also do house calls.

MATERNAL & CHILD CARE

No political statements here…just a little advice on where to go to get information, depending on your needs.

Birthright: free pregnancy tests, confidential counseling, referrals for reduced cost medical care, baby & maternity clothes: nonprofit, staffed by trained volunteers, 929-3447.

Lamaze: prepared childbirth, education, counseling, partnering, "learning to share in the childbirth experience," 360-6667

Parents Anonymous: support group for parents under stress. Day and evening groups. Some child care available, 265-3311

Planned Parenthood: birth control and comprehensive gynecological care for women of all ages. Special services for teens. Pregnancy testing and counseling. Fees on a sliding scale, 267-6818.

MEATS (see also "Poultry")

Looking for something that's "a cut above"? Something for that special dinner or barbecue? Try one of these.

✪✪✪✪ **Cromer's,** Country Market, 3500 Noyac Rd., 725-9004. This is one fine meat market. The butchers here know what they're doing and they have the best cuts of just about everything. You can order ahead, too, especially for the holidays.

✪✪✪✪ **Dreesen's Excelsior Market,** 33 Newtown Ln., East Hampton, 324-0465. Prime meats are a specialty—and they deliver! Consistently one of the finest shops in The Hamptons.

✪✪✪✪ **King Kullen,** Bridgehampton Commons, 537-8103. The meat department here may be in a big super market but the service feels like a real neighborhood meat market.

✪✪✪ **Catena's,** 143 Main St., Southampton, 283-3456. Wonderful roasts, prime cuts of meat, and you can order ahead. (Psst! A secret! It's Catena's Porterhouse that gets marinated and served on Friday nights at Fellingham's.)

MEN'S CLOTHING (see also "Malls")

If you're used to buying your "threads" at Burberry's or Brooks Brothers, well, that's hard to beat. But there are some good shops out here and you just might be surprised to find that the prices in these stores are no worse than in The City and in some cases better.

✪✪✪✪ **Saks Men's Store,** Main St., Southampton, 283-3500: What used to be a very small department of the main store was relocated to a much larger store down the block on Main Street. There's an excellent collection of men's furnishings here. The selection tends to the casual, in keeping with the informal and somewhat "country" nature of The Hamptons. We like this store a bunch.

✪✪✪✪ **Latham House,** 117 Main St., Sag Harbor, 725-1973. You walk in here to a working fireplace and shopping warmth to match it. This is what I would call "distinguished weekend country clothes." Think: sport coats, slacks, turtlenecks, and pipe smokers. Beautiful suede jackets, too, along with flannel shirts and corduroy slacks.

✪✪✪✪ **Blanc Bleu,** Main St., East Hampton, 329-2552. This is a fabulous store. Its entire line of men's and women's clothing is, just as the store's name suggests, mostly white or blue. Wonderful, French-style sportswear: classical, updated, and nautical. There's definitely a "sailor's touch" and a whiff of salt air and seaspray in this shop. The chain originated in Paris and has several stores there, plus shops in Cannes, Nice, St. Tropez and other spots. There are (as yet) only two stores in the US: this one, in East Hampton, and one on Rodeo Drive in Beverly Hills. Does that give you a clue as to what we have here?

✪✪✪✪ **Titano,** 22 Nugent St., Southampton, 287-4123, on-line at www.titanoonline.com and www.bestselections.com: Oooh, I like this store! Men's and women's shirts, hand stitched from pure

Egyptian cotton—French cuffs, too! They also have silk ties, great knit sweaters and an exclusive collection of coordinated women's knits, skirts and pants. All of their goods are imported from Italy. Not inexpensive, but you deserve it!

✪✪✪✪ **Polo Country Store,** 33 Main St., East Hampton, 324-1222. All of the great "Ralph" stuff in a country atmosphere. This is a very classy store.

✪✪✪✪ **Eddie Bauer,** Bridgehampton Commons, Bridgehampton, 537-0299. Wonderful for sweaters, outerwear, and casual clothes for both country and city.

✪✪✪✪ **The Gap,** also at Bridgehampton Commons, 537-2762. Would we be complete without a Gap?

✪✪✪ **Banana Republic** has two stores in The Hamptons. One in East Hampton and one in the Bridgehampton Commons in Bridgehampton, 537-5534. Only the Bridgehampton store has the great men's casual clothes for your Hamptons seasonal lifestyle. The East Hampton store is just for women's clothes.

MENTAL HEALTH (see also "Physicians")

Being out here, in The Hamptons, is supposed to be "mental health" enough, right? Well, sometimes you need a little more help. Here's some advice and a few places to call.

AMI of eastern Long Island: East Hampton—support for the families of the mentally ill. No fees—324-2046

Catholic Charities: Bridgehampton—Licensed outpatient mental care workers, alcohol problems, fees based on a sliding scale, generally 9 AM to 5 PM, except Monday 9–9, 537-1159

Family Counseling Service: Westhampton Beach—nonprofit, nonsectarian. Individual, family and group counseling. Substance abuse, prevention and treatment; life transition; bereavement; domestic violence and child abuse. Sliding scale fees—288-1954

Jewish Community Services: Center Moriches—outpatient services to Suffolk residents; individual, marital, family and group counseling; psychological testing; psychiatric placements; family life institutes. Staffed by psychiatrists, psychologists, and certified social workers—874-2700.

Kings Park Psychiatric Center—Support, direction and referrals for any kind of psychiatric emergency, 24 hours a day, seven days a week, emergency hotline, 544-2222

Recovery, Inc.: Southampton—self-help aftercare program for people with emotional problems—no fees 264-0589

RESPONSE: Hotline—24 hours, 7 days, a crisis intervention service that operates solely by phone. Offers immediate accessibility to trained volunteers. Not-for-profit and strictly confidential—751-7500

Suffolk County Dept. of Health, Division of Community Mental Health Services—Hauppauge—"services are available to any person residing in Suffolk County and include psychosocial evaluation, psychological evaluation, diagnosis and treatment, individual and group psychotherapy, chemotherapy, family therapy and consultation services." Application can be made by phone; referrals may be made, 853-3114.

MONEY ORDERS

Best (and least expensive) place to get money orders is at any of the Post Offices (see "Post Offices").

MORTGAGES

Usually, the best place to go for a mortgage is where you have the rest of your banking relationships, especially if you have a personal banker. It's much easier to negotiate rates, points, etc. with someone you know— someone who knows your net worth. It's also important to know, in case you didn't, that assumption of mortgages is not allowed in New York State. So, it doesn't matter, and has no value to the re-sale of a property, that someone still has a 6%, 30-year loan, with 10 years remaining. Bummer. But it keeps the mortgage companies and real estate attorneys happy. Oh, here's another tip for you, in case you hadn't heard it, for retiring that 30-year mortgage: Make 13 mortgage payments a year if you can afford it. Apply the 13th payment "to principal." At today's rates, making 13 payments a year will reduce your 30-year mortgage to roughly 15 years. Do the math. Believe me, it works. If you'd like a couple of ideas on people to talk to that know the local market here they are.

✪✪✪✪ **First Network Mortgage,** 71 Hill St., Southampton, 287-6000:
See my friend Cal Lutz. First Network has a sterling reputation locally and they deal with dozens of banks all over the area to find

you the best deals.

✪✪✪✪ **Manhattan Mortgage Company,** 670 Montauk Hwy., Water Mill, 726-7700 (just behind the Water Mill Post Office).

✪✪✪✪ **Park Avenue Mortgage Group,** 2415 Montauk Hwy., Bridgehampton, 537-9055.

✪✪✪✪ **IPI,** 2487 Main St., Bridgehampton, 537-9500.

Notice I didn't mention any of our local banks? Well, that's because they operate like, well, banks, when it comes to mortgages. We have found better deals with the local mortgage brokers, like the folks listed above. If you have a good relationship with your banker, you should definitely get him or her to quote a loan, though.

MOSQUITOES (see comments under "Insects")

MOTOR VEHICLES

The DMV (affectionately known elsewhere as the "Dreaded, Motionless Venue") has a branch in Riverhead (200 Rte. 58). Here, you can actually see a state worker smile and get something accomplished within the car's current registration period. It's one of the best kept secrets of The Hamptons that you can get or renew your driver's license in your own lifetime here as well as get plates for your car before antique plates are required (see also "Licenses"). General information (this number is hopelessly helpless, but it's not the Riverhead office, so don't get the wrong impression. I think it's staffed by the same guys that the State has making the license plates), 800-342-5368. Don't bother calling, just go. There are no long lines like at other DMV offices. Best way to get there is to go to Riverhead, go all the way east down Main Street to the end. You'll come to Route 58. The DMV is to your left, but you can't turn left just there. You'll have to go right then do a quick U-turn at the next intersection.

MOVIE THEATERS (see "Theaters")

Here's a convenient listing of all the local movie theaters, so you'll have their numbers handy. For more detailed information on these theaters, including which ones we think are the best, go to the "Theaters" section of the Guide, below.

Amagansett: None
Bridgehampton: None
East Hampton: United Artists, Main St.: 324-0448
Montauk: Montauk Movie, 3 Edgemere: 668-2393
Hampton Bays: United Artists, 119 W. Montauk Hwy.: 728-8676
Sag Harbor: Sag Harbor Cinema, Main St.: 725-0010
Southampton: United Artists, Hill St.: 287-2774
Westhampton Breach: Loews, Brook Rd.: 288-2600

MOVING COMPANIES

✪✪✪✪ **Mark Press Moving & Storage, Inc.,** Southampton, 283-2110.
Very personal service, extra-careful handling of your household
goods, and courteous workers highlight the service provided by
Mark Press and his staff. And they've been doing it since 1950!
Mark shows up in person at most of the moves to ensure a smooth
operation. Mark has moved a number of the "rich and famous," but
he doesn't charge extra. Storage facilities, too (see "Self Storage").

✪✪✪ **Despatch,** 554 Hill St., Southampton, 283-3000 and
Bridgehampton, at 537-4500. Despatch comes highly recommended by some folks we know that have used their services.

MUSEUMS (see also "Art Museums" and "History")

These museums are well worth your time.

✪✪✪✪ **Montauk Point Lighthouse Museum,** Montauk, 668-2544. The
Lighthouse and its park have already been mentioned elsewhere in
this Guide (see "History" and "Hiking"). This note is for the lighthouse museum itself. It's located in the actual lighthouse and provides a concise, fascinating history of what lighthouse life was like
from 1797 (when this lighthouse was actually built) to today (the
lighthouse still works, though it's on an automatic beacon). It's well
worth the excursion to Montauk. Just get in your car and drive as
far east as you can. I love the local Montauk bumper stickers:
"Montauk: The End" and "Montauk: The Last Resort." That about
sums it up!

✪✪✪ **Sag Harbor Whaling and Historical Museum,** Main St., Sag
Harbor, 725-0770. The name is about as big as the museum itself,

but it's a cute spot. Gives you a pretty good idea of what it was like to have a "bone in your teeth," walk "the widow's walk," and otherwise find out what life was like in a roaring whaling town of a hundred and fifty years ago. Sag Harbor? Roaring? Well, maybe not like New Bedford, but close!

✪✪✪ **Amagansett Historical Society,** Montauk Highway and Windmill Lane, Amagansett, 267-3020. Open summers only, Thursday through Sunday, 9 AM to 1 PM. The 1725 Miss Amelia Cottage Museum has changing exhibits on what life in Amagansett was like from Colonial times to the early 20th Century. The cottage is furnished with locally made furniture and early clocks. On the same site is the Roy K. Lester Carriage Museum with 28 fascinating horse-drawn vehicles. There is a small fee.

✪✪✪ **East Hampton Historical Society,** across from Village Green, East Hampton, 324-6850. Start at Mulford House at 10 James Lane. This is a four-acre, 17th Century farm with an 18th Century English style barn. Nearby is Clinton Academy, the state's first chartered academy (circa 1784), where you can see displays of decorative arts. Town House, next to the Academy, is a one-room 18th Century schoolhouse. Another part of the Society's exhibits is the Town Marine Museum on Bluff Rd. in Amagansett. Lastly, there is the Boat Shop, 42 Gann Ln., East Hampton, offering classes in wooden boat building. Tours are available for all exhibits. Small fee.

✪✪ **Second House,** Third House, and Pharaoh Indian Museum, Montauk. Second House is located on Montauk Highway and was, literally, the second house built in Montauk—about 1746. (The First House, by the way, was destroyed many years ago). It's open May to September, Thursday through Tuesday, 668-5340. The house was used primarily by early cattle herders. Bet you didn't know that Montauk was the site of the first cattle ranch in America and where the term "cowboy" was coined! Take that, Texas! Second House is next to Fort Pond. Five rooms have been decorated by *Victoria* magazine and there are herb and rose gardens to poke around in.

Any guesses on what **Third House** might be? You're right! This home was built in 1747 and was also used by "them herders." Third House, in Theodore Roosevelt Park (ex–Montauk County Park), 852-7878, was rebuilt in the 1800s, however, and was even used as a restaurant in the 1950s. Another claim to its fame is that this house was used by Teddy Roosevelt. He used to hunt out here, trained his Rough Riders here, and used this spot as a recuperative area after his adventures in Cuba, post–Spanish-American War. There's a turn-of-the-century Montauk diorama and some neat period photos.

The **Pharaoh Indian Museum** is right behind Third House in Roosevelt Park, 852-7878, and houses prehistoric Indian artifacts recovered from a dig started in the Park over 10 years ago.

Visit all three sites as an afternoon package!

MUSIC—CONCERTS & FESTIVALS

A ton of talented musicians live and/or frolic out here. But it's only recently (like in the past couple of years) that they seem to have gotten off their collective beach chairs to make any great music for the rest of us! Happily, that trend is now building. I have pretty eclectic tastes in music. When I sit down to write this Guide (mostly between 4:30 and 7:00 AM any given morning) I like to put on a classical CD. The garden party brings out the MTV Dance Mix CD's along with Celine, Sir Elton, and Tina. More mellow dinner parties are apt to have a mix of Enya, Bryan Ferry, and Winton Marsalis. The Hamptons music scene is very eclectic, too. It makes it fun. Here are some good bets.

✪✪✪✪ **Bridgehampton Chamber Music Festival,** 537-6368: This festival started some 15 years ago with a paltry budget, four musicians, and a few devoted attendees. Today, it's got a $300,000 plus budget, 25 musicians, and a legion of fans. Most concerts are held in the 440-seat Bridgehampton Presbyterian Church on Main Street. Last year's programs heralded Bach and Mozart but there were many other wonderful offerings from composers as diverse as Gershwin, Debussy, Vivier, and Astor Piazzolla. Since the concerts are not held in "great halls," the feeling is one of intimacy with the audience, the way chamber music is supposed to be. The Festival usually begins mid-August.

✪✪✪ At the end of summer Long Island University's Southampton Campus puts on an outdoor concert "under the stars." There have been some memorable evenings: Tina Turner, Tony Bennett, Jimmy Buffet, twice, Rod Stewart (and, man, can Rod rock a crowd!). The concerts are on the lawn, so bring a blanket and beach chairs, unless, that is, you buy the $200 tickets which allow you to sit up front and have access to the VIP tent. Me, I prefer sitting in the back and letting the music roll over me. So, who's on tap for this summer? Don't know yet. The gig is usually announced late Spring (after we go to press). Call Southampton College, 283-4000, and ask for concert info after May 1st.

✪✪✪ **The Perlman Training Program** (formerly the Hamptons Summer Music Festival), East Hampton. Yes t*hat* Perlman, as in Itzhak Perlman. The program is a training camp for gifted precollege musicians hand-picked by Mr. Perlman and his wife Toby (how great could that be for a young musician, to be "hand-picked" by Itzhak Perlman!). Usually in late August. The students, directed by Mr. Perlman, present several concerts. Call the East Hampton Chamber for details, 324-0362.

✪✪ **Pianofest in the Hamptons,** presented by Southampton College, usually in mid-August. The Pianofest is a series of master classes for about 30 gifted students from around the world, who range in age from 16 to 27. The students give public concerts, so call the College for details (283-4000).

MUSICIANS

If you want a truly talented group of musicians that will "make" your party or private affair call the following.

✪✪✪✪ **Grindle Entertainment,** 287-5190. Troy Grindle is in charge and he's done everything from weddings on the beach at dawn, attired in black tie, to finding bagpipers. Classical, jazz, rock, the piano, harps, they can do it all. Book early.

MUSIC—LIVE

✪✪✪✪ **The Stephen Talkhouse** on Main Street in Amagansett, 267-3117. Music breaks out here most any night, and you never know what's going to happen. Local artists honing their acts for the "big time" can be found here along with local musicians who don't give a damn about the "big time." Phil Ochs will drop by or maybe Jimmy Buffett or even Billy Joel. You just never know. Anyway, it's fun, eclectic, and very up beat. Call ahead to see who's on the playbill.

✪✪✪✪ **Belle's Café,** Westhampton Beach, at Gabreski Field, 288-3927. Every Thursday, year round, there's a free Blues jam. There's live Jazz on Friday and Saturday, too.

✪✪✪ **The Wild Rose Café,** Sag Harbor-Bridgehampton Turnpike, Bridgehampton, 537-5050. A mix of live music, sometimes DJ's (call ahead to find out which), all situated in a laid-back and mellow little club. This is where a lot of the locals go on Saturday nights.

Note: almost all the nightclubs we have in the Guide (see "Clubs") have live music or DJ's every weekend, in season.

MUSIC—STORES

✪✪✪✪ **Coconuts,** Bridgehampton Commons, Bridgehampton, 537-7555. Myra knows more about pop music and artists than anyone, I swear! (She's also a fabulous flute player, but I'm not supposed to let you know that!) Anyway, this is her favorite spot for CD's and tapes. Biggest, best, and most current selection in the Hamptons.

✪✪✪✪ For something very different, try **Ned Parkhouse,** Main St., Sag Harbor, 725-4074. This store has collector's CD's and tapes includ-

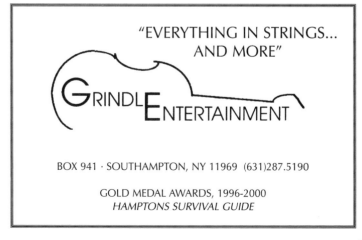

ing the best classical music, boxed sets of Judy Garland collections, Sinatra, and much more.

✪✪✪ **Long Island Sound** has two locations: 34 Main St. in East Hampton, 324-2660 and 76 Jobs Lane in Southampton, 283-6683. Excellent selection and they handle most popular concert tickets.

✪✪✪ **Sam Goody,** 14 Main St., Southampton, 287-7119. This is the biggest spot out here for CD's, tapes, and so forth (does anyone buy "records" anymore, I wonder? Can you even get them, except at garage sales?). The selection is quite large and they have all the latest tunes.

NAILS (see "Beauty")

NEWSPAPERS (and local magazines)

"Where can I pick up *The Times*?" The answer is just about everywhere, but not from the newspaper vending machine you may be used to. There are very few of those tacky boxes out here...violates certain esthetic ordinances, don't you know. Just about all the delis have the most popular papers, as do the bagel shops and all the 7-11's.

The Local Press:

✪✪✪✪ *The New York Times.* Of course they are not a "local" paper but *The Times* is just the best paper in the World. I am also adding them to our list of winners because they have significantly upgraded their coverage of Long Island with a very fine Long Island section, published each Saturday. The Long Island section does a good job of listing many of the local events. *The Times* also highlights, in typical NYT style, many of our local restaurants, wineries, and so forth.

I also want to commend the Long Island staff writers who are now turning out real news that affects the East End. You can get home service everywhere here, and alter it to your lifestyle: 7 days, weekends only, seasonal, etc., Call 1-800-631-2500.

✪✪✪ East Hampton has the *Star* which is quite credible about publishing the news of their part of the East End (East Hampton, Springs, Amagansett, etc.). *The Star* also supports local school sports teams and has a very fine arts section promoting local artists, writers, and so forth.

✪✪✪ In Southampton and East Hampton, **The Independent(s).** *The Independent* is a sort of alternative newspaper. Like *Dan's*, it's published weekly and it's distributed free of charge; but, unlike *Dan's*, *The Independent* is trying to be a real newspaper. I don't know the owners and editors, but it seems to me that they have a healthy sense of moral outrage and community mindedness that will only add to the local newspaper scene. They are worth picking up and stuffing in the grocery bag.

✪✪ **The Southampton Press:** It's not a bad paper, really, and does a faithful job of reporting the "real" local news (as opposed to *Dan's* social news). They even get down to the high school softball scores. It's exactly the kind of paper you'd want in your hometown for one-dollar, please, published every Thursday.

✪✪ The best known of the local is **Dan's Papers.** Published just about every Thursday, year round, and free. It is a source for local goings on, gossip, and Dan's never-ending editorial diatribe. There is a "Dan," as in Dan Rattiner, who has been faithfully publishing his paper for 39 years. Dan is a constant presence in the Hamptons, lending his local fame to all sorts of causes and parties. *Dan's* is mostly advertising. And in an ironic sort of way, the advertising in *Dan's* is the news. By watching who is placing ads and how big the ads are, you'll be able to keep track of which establishments are coming or going, the new places on the scene, and so on. Maybe Dan should change the name to *Dan's* Ads. Nobody would mind. We'd still pick up the paper anyway…Force of habit.

The Local Magazines:

✪✪✪✪ *Hamptons After Dark,* the brainchild of my friend Rob Dec, 287-9212. *After Dark* is really well done and the advertisers should thank Rob for putting a quality product in front of us. *After Dark* is a simple but comprehensive listing of clubs, restaurants and "after dark" places to socialize. Rob publishes twice a year, a premier issue for "the season" and a smaller version for the holidays. Rob doesn't compete with us (thank goodness!) because he doesn't provide reviews or opinions. *After Dark* is just a good reference that you should have in your kitchen drawer (next to your copy of the "Guide" of course!).

✪✪✪✪ **The Hamptons Catalog,** 725-2351. is an excellent shoppers guide to some of the finest stores in the Hamptons. Distributed free throughout the Hamptons, it's an effective vehicle for many of our local advertisers to get their products in front of you, and it's an excellent way for you to shop some of the Hamptons finest merchants before you ever get in your car!

✪✪ The two best known local magazines, both of which are "give-aways," are Randy Schindler's **Hamptons** magazine and Joe DeChristofaro's newer **Hamptons Country** magazine. And we have a real war going on out here between the two of them. They are both, on the surface at least, slick and sassy paeans to the lifestyles of the rich and famous. Scantily clad (and, at least to me, seemingly seriously undernourished) young ladies grace most of the covers of both magazines. While these two mags furiously go at it, from April through October, we are treated to scads of colorful pages featuring photos from the best parties along with lots of social gossip. There's always a running "soap opera" in *Hamptons.* Last year had the saga of "A" who was married to "B" but "B" was cheating on "A" with "C." I mean, this "breathless drama" was full of sex, drugs, and rock-and-roll! From week to week we were supposed to try and figure out who "A-B-and-C" were and really care, deep down, about pathetic and shallow fools. Man, what drivel.

Randy Schindler has been publishing *Hamptons* for many years. *Country* is newer and backed by the company that publishes the very credible *Cigar Aficionado.*

There are no serious attempts at journalism here, but, that's OK. That's the way these magazines have been designed. If you want to be connected to what's happening on the oh-so-social Hamptons Summer scene, that's what these publications are all about. I have to say, though, and I could be wrong, I don't think that's what The Hamptons are about—at least not anymore. Oh, of course, there are still fabulous summer parties and lots of money—new and old—being tossed around out here, but we've really matured beyond a lot of that. There are more families and young couples who want to plant roots here now than there are "wannabes" looking for the all the hot parties. Oh, well, I digress.

NIGHTCLUBS (see "Clubs")

NOTARIES

You forgot to get that blasted power of attorney notarized before you came out...Where do you go? (Note: charge is usually $2 per signature.)

Bridgehampton
Ocean Copies, Snake Hollow Road, 537-1220, just at the east end of the Bridgehampton Commons shopping area near Dapper Dog.

Sag Harbor
George Heine Realty, 3495 Noyack Rd., 725-9001.

Southampton
Chase Bank, Main St., Southampton, 935-9935.
Southampton Stationary, 18 Hampton Rd., 283-1964.

O

ON-LINE SERVICES

What a revolution the Internet has brought to our society! Where will it end? What will life be like five years from now? What was it like five years ago before we all started using the Internet so extensively? Can you remember? Anyway, should you want to "get wired" out here there are national as well as local service providers to help you. Phone lines are handled by Bell Atlantic (890-6611 for home service, 890-1598 or 1-800-722-2300 for business service). Some phone lines operate only to a maximum of 28-K, sometimes you'll connect at even less depending on local phone line load, so your new 58-K or 124-K modem may be useless unless you get a high-speed line. If you need or simply want a high-speed phone line you could call Bell Atlantic for ISDN (1-800-GET-ISDN). You can get T-1 lines, but that's probably overkill (and very expensive) unless you're setting up an ISP (Internet Service Provider) business in your basement. Another alternative is "DSL" or direct subscriber line. It's fast and reliable. Call Peconic On-line for DSL (see below). Still another alternative to getting to the Internet now exists via cable. Cablevision, the only cable provider for the East End, now offers Internet access at high speed with no waiting or "busy" signals. It's also a little on the expensive side. Call Cablevision at 727-6300 in Riverhead or 267-9600 in Amagansett.

For local service I highly recommend the following:

✪✪✪✪ **Peconic Online,** (www.peconiconline.com) 287-4004. The best of our local on-line service providers. Peconic's rates are $19.95 per month or $17.95 per month if paid one year in advance. Either way, it's unlimited monthly usage. They offer dialup access to accommodate any modem, DSL ($49/month) and they're good at website design, too! They also offer a free trial of their service.

✪✪✪ **Hamptons Online,** Southampton, 287-6630. "hamptons.com" offers subscribers total access to the Internet, and many if not most of the services of the better known providers for an unlimited usage fee of $18 per month. The home page offers a raft of neat stuff on The Hamptons and the owner has started a "surf shop" at his location for novices to learn to surf (the Internet, of course)!

OPTICIANS/OPTOMETRISTS

Optician…Optometrist…I can never keep straight who does what. Look, if you need an eye exam, eye care, glasses, or contact lenses, this is the best I know.

✪✪✪✪ **the Drs. T.J. Calabrese** (yes, that's plural—there's a father and son team, both are "T.J. Calabrese") with offices in Southampton at 414 County Rd. 39A (across from the Omni), 283-6226 and in Amagansett, 145 Main St., 329-3838. Both "T.J.s" handle emergency cases, do routine exams, take care of glasses and repairs, and fit you for contacts. Good prices, and they accept a number of eye care plans.

OUTDOOR CLOTHING

✪✪✪ **Outdoors of Amagansett** (formerly La Carruba's), 171 Main St., Amagansett, 267-3620. This is one of the finest little stores in The Hamptons, and they've been around a long time. Outdoors offers a superb collection of clothing and accessories for playing around in the Great Outdoors. It's solid "Down east" stuff. Just the kind of gear you need to go with the new Lincoln Navigator or Mercedes SUV!

OUTDOOR FURNITURE

Patio tables and chairs, pool lounges, hammocks…all de rigeur if you're spending any time in The Hamptons. Buy it here. You won't find a better selection and you'll certainly get much more personal service than going to one of the stores up island that just wants to get your credit card in hand.

✪✪✪✪ **Hildreth's** operates two locations where you can shop for top of the line outdoor furniture. First, they have an outdoor furniture department in their main store on Main St. in Southampton (283-2300). They also have a specialty store just for house and garden products. It's on Montauk Highway in Bridgehampton, across the road from the Bridgehampton Commons, 537-1616.

✪✪✪✪ **Thayer's,** Main St., Bridgehampton, 537-0077. I don't know why it took us so long to discover this store, but we didn't really wander in until last Fall. It's great! Especially their wonderful selection of wooden outdoor furniture. They also have hammocks, umbrellas, wicker, BBQ grills, and accessories. I noticed, too, that they carry or can get a number of replacement items: stuff like extra pillows, cushions, new rope hammocks, etc.

✪✪ **Treasure Island,** Wainscott Village Center, Montauk Highway., 537-0073. Treasure Island's store in Wainscott is quite large and they have practically everything for the deck, backyard, grilling, etc. This is all they do (except Christmas decorations in the winter). The selection is excellent, and if they don't have something in stock in Wainscott, they can get it from one of their other stores.

OUTDOOR TOYS

✪✪✪✪ **Recreational Concepts,** call 726-2020. Here's where to go for all your swing sets, slides, basketball hoops, trampolines, pool toys, outdoor game tables, and more!

PAINT (Where can I buy it?!)

✪✪✪✪ **Janovic,** 352 Montauk Hwy., Wainscott, 537-9700: Those of you who live in The City know about the Janovic Stores. They are the best for paint and paint supplies. Happily, they've opened up a store out here and it's a great one. They carry several brands of first-rate paints including Pratt & Lambert, Martha Stewart, and Calvin Klein. And when it comes to supplies to use with that wonderful paint, they have it all.

✪✪✪ I would also recommend the paint department at **Water Mill True Value,** Montauk Hwy., Water Mill, 726-4493. They know what they're doing, have an excellent selection and knowledgeable people to mix and match your paints.

PAINTERS/PAINTING

There are lots of painters out here…some of them good, some of them pitiable dribblers. Just about anyone can buy a beat-up old station wagon, an extension ladder, some buckets and brushes and call himself or herself a "painter." Here is a category where you definitely should get a referral from someone who's had a happy experience.

Something else to be aware of: mildew and power washing. Even the best paint will eventually mildew out here, given the atmospheric conditions. Many people unnecessarily restain or re-paint as soon as mildew shows up. Some people also contract power washers (at exorbitant rates) to come in and water-blast the stuff off the house. May not be necessary. The first time extensive mildew shows up, get yourself a 5-gallon sprayer. Fill it with a mix of one part plain, cheap bleach and four parts water. Spray the mildewed areas, wait a few minutes, and then wash it off (gently) with a garden hose. The mildew will be gone, and you'll probably not have to re-paint for at least another year. If you do hire someone to do the power washing, make sure they do your decks and deck furniture, too! As a rule of thumb, you shouldn't have to do this but every other year and you should pay about $350 for a 3,000 square foot house.

Now, the good news: we've found a couple of great painters to recommend to you.

✪✪✪✪ **Peter's Home Service,** Peter Girardi, Southampton, 283-4667. A truly fine paint job is 90% preparation and 10% paint. Careful preparation of all the surfaces, which a lot of painters don't bother to do very well, is what Peter does well. Man, the sanding and patching and taping these guys do would drive me nuts!

✪✪✪✪ **Gaeton Berube,** 399-2274. Gaeton is primarily known for his superb remodeling work, but he also does both interior and exterior painting.

PARKING LOTS

No...We're not referring to the L.I.E. at 5 PM on Friday night. We're talking about where you can park your car to do a little shopping, dining, etc.

Amagansett is generally not too crowded except in Summer, of course. Best place to park is in the large (free) lot just behind the Coach Leather Outlet store at the east edge of Town.

Bridgehampton is very problematic for parking on busy weekends and in Summer. Main Street has lots of spaces, but they're often full. I don't like having to jump in and out of the car while traffic is whizzing by anyway; so, try this: just as you come into Bridgehampton (from the west) turn left at the flashing light by the Candy Kitchen. There are some good parking spots down this road. You could also park at the Bridgehampton Commons lot and walk—great exercise! It's about a mile up and back.

East Hampton has provided a fairly large lot just behind their main shopping area, next to the Waldbaum's and directly behind Main Street. Time there is limited, and they will ticket! If you're a little more ambitious and like to walk, drive the half-mile to the train station. You can park near the station all day, walk to town, get your exercise, and walk back. If you're not so ambitious, park near the railroad station anyway at the Lumber Lane Parking Lot (watch for the signs). The Village of East Hampton runs a free shuttle bus to Main Street all summer long!

Hampton Bays can sometimes be a bottleneck at busy times, and there's very limited parking along the main street. Try the lot in front of the new UA Cinema or the large lot behind the 7-11.

Montauk generally has few parking problems. There are lots of spaces down the side streets off of Montauk Highway. If you go down to Montauk Dock and visit the shops, beach, piers, and restaurants, there's plenty of space in the large municipal lot across the street from Gosman's Dock.

Sag Harbor: there is pretty good parking along Main Street, but the spaces don't "turn" very quickly in season. And when they do, it's a "demo derby" of impatient motorists trying to zip into the empty spots. Be careful! There's a large lot behind Main Street along the bay. There's also a Municipal lot at the North end of Main Street behind the Suffolk County Bank Building. Just a note: the Sag Harbor Traffic cops are especially diligent in ticketing for overtime.

Southampton: Parking is very scarce. One of the best spots central to Main Street is just behind Main Street; in particular, just behind Hildreth's and Herrick's. You can park in some spots all day—24 hours, in fact. A few spots are limited to 2 hours, so check the signs. There's also a smaller, no-limit lot just behind the Chamber of Commerce building and another even smaller lot behind Chase Bank. If you want to cheat a little, you can park at the IGA lot on the corner of Hampton and North Sea Roads (across from Saks), but try and limit your time there, because it really is for the shoppers in that lot. Likewise, you can use the Waldbaum's lot a block to the north. There's also a nice, less well-known lot behind the Southampton Cinema. It's only a short walk to Jobs Lane. You can also park in the Presbyterian Church parking lot at the end of Main Street, behind the church—any day but Sunday, that is. If you're parked there on Sunday, you had better be in a pew!

Water Mill has parking space behind the Post Office as well as in the new Water Mill Shoppes complex—just turn left at the new (and only!) traffic light in town.

Westhampton Beach has lots of parking on Main Street and in extra lots at both ends of town.

General note on parking: Southampton and East Hampton have very efficient traffic control officers with long, chalk-tipped wands. They stroll up and down the streets marking your tires. If you're more than the allotted time—bingo!—you've got a ticket. Same thing for the parking meters. It seems as soon as they click over to "violation" there's a meter maid/guy standing there, ticket book open, grinning.

PARKS

We have lots of parks, some of which are truly great parks, where the beauty of the East End has been captured. Here are the best bets.

✪✪✪✪ **Hither Hills** gets a Gold for sheer beauty, open space, beaches, camping, tent sites, showers, a general store, picnic facilities, athletic fields, playing fields, and fishing. Hither Hills is a State Park and is easily reached by driving down Old Montauk Highway in Montauk. Call 668-2461 for information. The park has 1,755 glorious acres, all situated on one of the finest white sand beaches you'll ever see. If the temperature were 80 degrees year round, this beach would belong in the Caribbean. Take a picnic; better yet, pack a Sunday Brunch (hide the champagne, though, no alcohol officially allowed). Walk the sands...You'll feel great.

✪✪✪ **Montauk Point State Park** is just breathtaking. On a clear day you can see forever, as the song goes. And it's awesome to stand on the Point itself and stare off into the Atlantic. But there are 724 other acres to wander, a food stand, good parking ($4 a day), fishing, hiking, and picnicking. Then, of course, there's the Montauk Lighthouse and Museum. Call 668-3781 for information.

✪✪✪ Here's a hidden gem: **Cedar Point County Park.** Its 608 acres are located down a long and winding road in East Hampton. Call 852-7620 for information. There are great nature walks, secluded walks along the water, trailer and tent camping, picnic tables (with grills—a rarity!), fishing, rowboats for hire, horseback trails (bring your own horse!), in-season duck hunting, facilities for the handicapped, and a bike hostel area. Bring the Sunday paper and a flask of hot coffee from the Golden Pear in East Hampton.

✪✪ There's a little park tucked away at the end of Jobs Lane in Southampton called **Agawam Park** that you'll like, especially if you have kids. To call it a "park" on the scale of the others we have mentioned above is too generous. It's really just a great big lawn sandwiched between private mansions and Agawam Lake. The toddlers can run their little legs off (thereby granting you a peaceful afternoon nap) or swing the swings, shoot the slides, and all that fun stuff you'd like to do yourself if no one was looking and you could still fit in the swing seat. Feed the ducks! The Village has a few concerts there in the summer, too, and you shouldn't miss the Christmas Tree lighting ceremony in early December (call the Southampton Chamber, 283-0402, for date)—it's a real slice of small town life.

✪ **Sears Bellows County Park** gets a nod, too, for 693 well appointed acres where you can also horseback ride. Sears Bellows is in Hampton Bays, just off the connector road to Riverhead, exit 65 (east) from Rte. 27. Park information is at 852-8290 and the stable's number is 723-3554. It's also right near "The Big Duck" which is somewhat of a County legend.

✪ We have mentioned **Montauk Downs State Park** in relation to its incredibly lovely public golf course (see "Golf"), but we should not pass without a mention of its other acreage. You can wander, play tennis, or enjoy the large pool. Call 668-5000 for information.

✪ One place that always gets passed by, except for those that like their parks unspoiled and wild as a badger, is **Shinnecock County Park** in Southampton. The east park is strictly outer beach camping and there are no "facilities"—just the sound of the surf and the gentle winds. The west park (the two parks are separate) is strictly for surfing and surfcasting. It is an unprotected recreation area, which means "wild and woolly." No facilities here, either. Call 854-4949 for information on either or both parks.

PARTY HELP

Would you like to actually enjoy the party you've worked so hard on instead of running around cleaning up spills, refilling party platters, and washing the dishes?

✪✪✪✪ **"Just Us" Party Service**. Ask for Moira. 724-9553. Moira and her helpers are spectacular. They show up, take over, keep the food served, clean up as they go, and make it possible for you to have fun at your own events!

PARTY SUPPLIES/PARTY RENTALS

This is a busy topic—especially in the summer months, as you might imagine. A word of advice: if you are planning a large party, wedding, etc., you should get signed up several months in advance.

✪✪✪✪ **Water Mill Party Rentals,** Willow Rd., just off Montauk Highway, Water Mill, 726-6664. They seem to have just about everything you'll need. Tents, dance floors, tables & chairs, linens, china, silverware, glassware, chaffers, grills, and so forth. They are on time—both setting up and taking down—and their equipment is in good shape (not always the case with some of the party rental services). They also have full time party consultants on site. Call Kathy or Rose. They're great to work with.

✪✪✪ **Bar-Boy,** 218 W. Montauk Hwy., Hampton Bays, 728-7100. Everything you could possibly need for the pool party, beach party, yard party, or whatever. Glassware, paper products, and all your bar supplies. Great spot for those indispensable plastic champagne glasses that you can actually take in the spa and not worry about broken glass under your toes.

✪✪✪ **Long Island Party Rentals,** 670 Montauk Hwy., Water Mill Square, Water Mill, 239-0707.

PARTY SUPPLIES/TENTS

Most large outdoor parties in the Hamptons are held under a tent. Why? Well, the weather can be pretty capricious, for one thing. For another, tents are romantic! For your party tent call the best.

✪✪✪✪ **P. J. McBride,** 694-1939: They rent all over the Hamptons, from the tiny tent for twelve to the giant extravaganza tents that could easily hold the entire circus!

PASSPORTS

You can get passports done out here, but only in Southampton. Go to the Post Office, 39 Nugent St., just off Main Street, 283-0268. Passports are only done between 10 AM and 1 PM Monday through Friday and 8:30 AM to 11:30 AM on Saturday. You'll need:

1. Certified copy of your birth certificate with the raised seal.

2. Driver's license, or naturalization papers, or expired passport, whichever is appropriate.

3. Two non-glossy passport photos, 2" x 2," head and shoulder shots, black and white or color.

4. Money. If you're over 18 years of age, it's $65 for a new passport and $55 for a renewal. If you're under 18 the fee is $40. Checks are OK or a money order or good old cash, too.

PEST CONTROL

Pest control out here usually involves not letting the doofus on the bar stool next to you buy you a drink.

In the more traditional forms of pest control we usually think of ticks (see "Insects"), termites, fleas, silverfish, mice, rats, and roaches (Gasp! rats and roaches?! In The Hamptons?!). Ticks and mice are the biggest pest control concerns and the most prevalent pests. Other than that, remember: this is "the country." The bugs and field mice were here long before people were and they aren't leaving anytime soon. Having to put up with a few spiders and mosquitoes, raccoons and crickets is a normal part of life out here. If you see more than a few pests (and if you see a lot of feral cats —see "Cats"), or if you see sawdust appearing in odd places and suspect termites, you might want to call a professional pest control company. The secrets to controlling pests are: (1) run a "tight ship"—clean up after yourselves promptly and frequently. Don't let the party leavings linger about too long and don't leave your trashcans uncovered. (2) If you have a problem, you can't just treat it once. You'll probably have to undergo a series of treatments every few weeks or monthly until the problem is eradicated. Here are the best folks to consider.

✪✪✪✪ **Nardy Pest Control**—726-4777 in Water Mill and 324-7474 in East Hampton. The family has been serving the East End for 40 years, they know their "pests," and give prompt, reliable, service for a fair price.

✪✪✪ **South Fork Pest Control,** 723-3427—Licensed and insured, they offer free estimates and serve all The Hamptons.

✪✪ **Wild Life Consultants,** 726-9309. Use these folks for humane removal of bigger pests like feral cats, raccoons, squirrels, bats, moles, etc.

P.S. I've been here almost ten years now and I have yet to see a single rat or roach. I know they're here, but I haven't seen them.

PET BOARDING

Not too many choices here, and, be warned, there aren't too many homeowners who want to rent to pet owners. Be sure to consult with your rental agent for the very few listings where pets are welcome. Fido may have to stay in The City...the best we've heard of.

✪✪✪✪ **Dr. John Turetsky,** DVM, 3 Good Friend Dr., East Hampton, 329-6235.

You might also try:
Sag Harbor: **Northwest Kennels,** 725-1090
Wainscott: **South Fork Animal Hospital,** 537-0035.

PET GROOMING

Alas, we have no pets, so we have no first-hand experience in these pet categories, but we have friends who do. Here's what they tell me about the best in this category.

✪✪✪✪ **The Classy Canine,** 478 North Hwy., County Rd. 39, Southampton, 283-1306.

✪✪✪✪ **Dapper Dog,** Bridgehampton, 537-3355
✪✪✪✪ **Paws & Claws,** 17 Newtown Mews, Southampton, 324-8995

PET SITTING

Rather not confine Snookums to the kennel?

✪✪✪✪ **Erica's Eclectic Enterprises,** 34 Center Ave., Southampton, 283-2475. They'll "puppysit" for you!…or "kittysit," too (don't try to say that five times fast!).

PET STORES

We hear that the best places to get pet supplies and stock up on doggie treats are the following:

✪✪✪✪ **Pet Hampton,** on Montauk Highway in Wainscott, 537-7387. They seem to have it all, not only the supplies, but the pets, too, including tropical fish, small mammals, exotic birds, and even reptiles.

✪✪✪ **One Stop Pet Shop** has three handy locations and discount pet food and supplies. The locations are:
Amagansett, 136 Main St., 267-7535
Southampton, 20 Hampton Rd., 287-6001
Westhampton Beach, 29 Old Riverhead Rd., 288-6765

PHARMACIES

Chains are merging and independents are being bought out by the big chains. It seems the time of the small, independent pharmacist may be coming to an end. One of the oldest and best pharmacies in Southampton, Cancellieri's, was bought by CVS three years back. Rite Aid took over one of the old supermarkets in town and turned it into a pharmacy super store. It's rumored that Genovese is trying to open next to Pier 1 on Montauk Highway in Water Mill. Whew! Keeping up with these guys is getting to be like taking castor oil! Anyway, if you need a "good dose," here's where to go.

✪✪✪✪ If you want the personal touch from a family that has been operating a local pharmacy in Southampton since 1874, go to **Corwith's,** 56 Hampton Rd., Southampton, 283-0001 (must have gotten the first phone in the 283- exchange, too!). Corwith's accepts most insurance plans, has a fairly broad selection of all the major brands of over-the-counter remedies; but, unlike any other place I've seen out here, they also have a subspecialty in homeopathic remedies.

✪✪✪✪ Also in Southampton, you can go to **South Thrifty Drugs,** 54 Jagger Lane, 283-1506 (across from Waldbaum's). They are proud of their "personal touches," including free health care screenings, senior and group discounts, savings on generic drugs, and even special pre-schooler discounts. They accept most insurance plans.

✪✪✪ **Rite-Aid,** Hampton Rd and Windmill Lane, Southampton, 283-2604 and in the Bridgehampton Commons next to K-Mart, 537-2890. If you favor the large, super store pharmacy, this is where to go. Selection is excellent and the prices are chain store prices, with many specials every week. Full service pharmacy (both locations) accepting just about all insurance plans.

✪✪✪ Another good choice in the large-store category is the new **CVS** store in East Hampton, 38 Pantigo Road, 324-8587. Their shelves are stocked with everything from magazines to lipstick, and they also have a full-service pharmacy.

✪✪✪ **White's,** on the Plaza, Montauk, 668-2994: This is a complete department store as well as a drug store, with full service pharmacy. As you wait for your Viagra, you can check out the inflatable beach toys, T-shirts, and magazines.

Now, since getting your prescriptions filled is important, we are going to list some other pharmacies in locations convenient to you. We have NOT personally visited or patronized these stores, therefore, they are not rated. They are listed as a convenience to you, but if you do use them, please tell us about your experiences and how you would rate them.

East Hampton:
Park Place Chemists, 58 Park Pl., 324-6600
White's, 81 Main, 324-0082
Hampton Bays:
Bangston Pharmacy, 15 W. Montauk Hwy., 728-1331
Center Island Pharmacies, 254 W. Montauk Hwy., 728-3300

Genovese, 190 W. Montauk Hwy., 728-2566

Liggett, 39 W. Montauk Hwy., 728-4030

Sag Harbor:

Sag Harbor Pharmacy, Main St., 725-0074

Shelter Island:

Shelter Island Heights Pharmacy, Grand Ave., 749-0445

Westhampton Beach:

Barth's Drug Store, 58 Sunset Ave., 288-4345

Speed's, 72 Main, 288-1880

PHOTOGRAPHERS

We've seen some truly beautiful work from some of our local photographers, but we had to make a very important decision last year on our wedding pictures. After talking to a lot of folks, and investigating a lot of photographers, we decided on one fabulous photographer.

✪✪✪✪ **Deborah Kalas,** 22 Indian Hill Rd., East Hampton, 324-1862. Debbie is just the best! Patient, reliable, and professional. You should see the extraordinary pictures she took of our wedding. It was a chilly November afternoon at the Ram's Head Inn, but the sun set almost on cue, right behind us, and Myra was just stunning. Debbie even managed to make me look good!

PHOTO FINISHING

You can get fairly inexpensive and reasonably fast photo finishing at several of the large chain stores like: Rite-Aid in Southampton, CVS in East Hampton, or King Kullen in Bridgehampton, and any of these stores will do a fine job. None of them have "1-Hour" service, however, if you're in that much of a hurry.

If you'd like a little more personal touch, most with one-hour or rapid service, here are three places we think are very good.

✪✪✪✪ **Reed's Photoshop,** 54 Newtown Ln., East Hampton, 324-1067. Drop off your film, go strolling in East Hampton for an hour and come back and pick up your prints!

✪✪✪ **Hampton Photo Arts,** Bridgehampton Commons, Bridgehampton, across from King Kullen, 537-7373 (and they also do framing, offer art supplies and sell cameras and film).

✪✪✪ **Chelsea Crossing,** West Water St., Sag Harbor, 725-5802. As with Reed's, you can drop off your film, go shopping or have lunch in Sag Harbor, come back an hour later and look at your prints.

✪✪ **Hampton Bays One Hour Photo,** 266 W. Montauk Hwy., Hampton Bays, in the King Kullen Plaza, 723-0242. Lots of services and open seven days!

PHYSICAL THERAPY

Your best resource for physical therapists is absolutely your physician; but, we have checked with some doctors we know, and some folks who have had need of a therapist and here's who they recommend as being among the best.

✪✪✪✪ **Bernard A. Finnerty,** MA, PT, OCS, Hampton Bays, Hampton Atrium Condominium across from the Sterns Department Store, 728-6377. Bernie and his staff of four (count 'em, four!) licensed and Board Certified therapists are unique. First, they believe that physical therapy is "hands on." Therapy should be a one-on-one experience, not something dependent on a few quick twists from the therapist followed by endless hours on machines. You'll like them…they have aqua therapy, arthritis treatments, help for back pain and sports injuries, too. All therapists are licensed and bonded and they accept most insurance.

PHYSICIANS & SURGEONS

As the quality of life here on the East End draws us, so it draws a goodly number of excellent doctors. Where we know of good docs we have used or had friends use, we are listing them in the appropriate specialty below. These are all "Gold" level winners. (Somehow, the thought of recommending less than a Gold level Doctor didn't appeal to me.)

✪✪✪✪ If you want a great resource for additional reliable referrals, call the Southampton Hospital Physician Referral Service at 726-8282. This service has access to more than 120 physicians, dentists, and allied health professionals representing over 30 different specialties. And you know what? Call them now—when you don't need a doctor. Ask for a referral before you frantically need one!

✪✪✪✪ A place where you can walk into anytime without an appointment! Wainscott Walk-In Medical Care, Montauk Hwy., Wainscott, 537-1892. Physicals, stitches, all sorts of injuries, Lyme Disease, shots, EKG's, etc.

✪✪✪✪ The Gold Level "Docs" we would recommend to you, by specialty.

Allergy/Immunology:
Dr. Russell Cancellieri, Southampton, 283-3300
Cardiology:
Dr. Alan DeCarlo, Southampton, 283-8888
Family Practice:
Dr. Merritt White, 537-3765
Gastroenterology:
Dr. Charles Casale, Southampton, 287-7100 and
Hampton Bays at 723-2905
Dr. Rodney Ryan, Southampton, 283-7090
General Practice:
Dr. Blake Kerr, Wainscott, 537-1892
Dr. Merritt White, Bridgehampton, 537-3765
Gynecology:
Dr. William Shuell, Southampton, 287-5500
Internist:
Dr. Richard Panebianco, 283-2100
Obstetrics & Gynecology:
Hamptons OB/GYN, 283-0918
Osteopathy:
Dr. Merritt White, 537-3765

Pediatrics:
Dr. Gail Schonfeld, East Hampton, 324-8030 (as well as the entire staff of East End Pediatrics, all at the same number).

Plastic Surgery:
Dr. John Anton, Southampton, 283-9100

Psychiatry:
Dr. Robert Hauben, 283-9191

Surgeons:
(General) Dr. Medhat Allam, 287-6202
Dr. Anthony Petrillo, 283-2100*
Dr. Arne Skilbred, 283-0535 or 723-0223
(Vascular) Dr. Leslaw Gredysa, Southampton, 287-1433

   *Dr. Petrillo also runs the Breast Center at Southampton Hospital, a special place where the goal is to prevent breast surgery as much as possible. The Breast Center sees referrals and conducts mammograms and needle biopsies, the results of which are immediately available. Dr. Petrillo has opened another new clinic, a Wound Clinic (also at Southampton Hospital), that will be of great comfort to folks afflicted with open wounds, especially the diabetic type.

PIANO (Tuning)

If you've invested in one of these "ebony monsters," you need to remember that we live by the ocean: salt air is going to do bad things to your piano (like rust the strings!) unless you take extra precautions. Keep it tuned, and I'd also suggest installing a relatively inexpensive piano dehumidifier.

✪✪✪✪ **The Piano Barn,** ask for Mike: 726-4640.

PICTURE FRAMING

✪✪✪✪ **Harrison & Harrison,** Main Street, Bridgehampton, 537-7474. Mr. Harrison is truly an artist in the framing business. And I typically spend far more on the framing, believe it or not, than I do on my posters and paintings! Why? Because I'm cheap? No…I just can't quite afford that first Picasso yet. But when I can, I'm taking it here. Victor has over 40 years in the business. By the way, if you're looking for Hamptons Classics posters, he's got them all (18 years worth!), and he's the official framer for the Classic.

PIZZA

Boy, this can create a lot of friendly argument: "Who's got the best pizza???" Well, I have a personal favorite, and I do think it's the best pizza in all The Hamptons.

✪✪✪✪✪ **La Parmigiana,** Southampton, 283-8030. Home made dough and sauce, fresh toppings, cooked to your specifications, always, always wonderful. No delivery service, but part of the fun is going to pick it up. There is no better pizza out here.

Now, I realize zipping to Southampton for pizza isn't going to be easy for all of you reading this "Guide," so here are some other great pizza places by location.

Bridgehampton:
✪✪✪✪ Our second favorite pizza pie in The Hamptons is **World Pie,** 537-7999.

East Hampton:
✪✪✪✪ Sam's on Newtown Lane, 324-5900.

Montauk:
✪✪✪✪ Poppy's Pizzeria, 668-1144

Sag Harbor:
✪✪✪✪ Espresso, 184 Division St., 725-4433.

Wainscott:
✪✪✪✪ La Capannina, Montauk Hwy., 537-2626

Westhampton Beach:
✪✪✪✪ Baby Moon, Montauk Hwy., 288-6350

PLUMBERS

✪✪✪✪ **Hardy Plumbing & Heating,** 283-9333. Hardy goes from Southampton to Montauk with its 20 (+) fully stocked trucks and capable plumbers. They can almost always get to you the same day you call and will try very hard to get there immediately if you have an emergency. I have found their people to be knowledgeable and courteous.

✪✪✪ **North Sea Plumbing & Heating,** 283-3876. North Sea specializes in 24-hour a day emergency service. They also have an extensive parts shop for do-it-yourself-ers as well as a fixture showroom.

✪✪ **G.F. Schiavoni,** Sag Harbor, 725-0466. They've been serving The Hamptons for over 50 years. They do residential and commercial work and the all-important "back-flow testing." If you don't know what that is, see "Backflow Testing." It's a must for homeowners.

POISON/POISONING

The emergency number for all manners of poisons or suspected poisoning is 542-2323.

POISON IVY/OAK/SUMAC

You can call the poison number listed above (542-2323), especially if some-one has ingested any of these nasty flora. Generally, none of these are a big problem out here. Poison ivy is the most prolific, and poison ivy can twine and creep. Those beautiful red and gold leaves that look so pretty in the Fall, the ones climbing that tree trunk, could be poison ivy. And they still have oil in them. Pick them and you'll be itching! The best cure is still good old calamine lotion. If more than just small case, go to a dermatologist.

POLICE

The police situation gets a little confusing in Southampton, where you have Town Police and Village Police and the Sheriff. All three are separate police forces. You kind of have to know where you are when you call, but if you get the wrong one, don't worry, they won't hang up on you. They'll get you to the right department. The Village Police patrol and cover the Village of Southampton. The Town Police actually cover the outlying areas including Town property, Water Mill, Bridgehampton, Wainscott, and Sagaponack. The Sheriff covers the whole of Suffolk County, of course, but rarely gets involved in local police business unless asked. There are separate police forces for Sag Harbor, Shelter Island, and East Hampton.

You can always call 9-1-1 for any Police emergency, but for non-emergencies, here are the local numbers.

Amagansett, 324-0024 (East Hampton Town Police)
Bridgehampton, 728-5000 (Southampton Town Police)
East HamptonTown, 324-0024
East Hampton Village, 324-0077
Hampton Bays, 728-5000 (Southampton Town Police)
Montauk, 324-0024 (East Hampton Town Police
Sagaponack, 728-5000 (Southampton Town Police)
Sag Harbor, 725-0058
Shelter Island, 749-0600
Southampton Town, 728-5000 (Southampton Town Police)
Southampton Village, 283-0056
Springs, 324-0024 (East Hampton Town Police)
Wainscott, 728-5000 (Southampton Town Police)
Water Mill, 728-5000 (Southampton Town Police)
Westhampton Beach, 288-3444

POOLS—CONSTRUCTION

Boy, this is a tough one. Seen from the air, The Hamptons looks like a sea of green that's suddenly gotten a bad case of aqua colored polka dots. And since there are so many pools, there is a gaggle of pool companies. Some of them are quite good—many others are just plain rip-offs. And pools ain't cheap. There are two basic types of in-ground pools out here (We're not even going to discuss above ground pools. Putting in an above ground pool out here would cause your entire neighborhood to collectively faint). There are pools with vinyl liners and pools constructed of concrete, or, more accurately, "gunite." Vinyl pools are about 50% less expensive to construct than gunite pools, and some say they are easier to maintain and clean. It's basically a huge plastic baggie sunk into the ground. Gunite is more expensive, but it's a lot longer lasting than vinyl. I also happen to think it's more attractive and classier looking, but, hey, that's just me. Permanent pools come in all sizes, of course, but the fairly standard so-called "Olympic size" pool is about a $30,000 job, minimally. If you start adding rocks and fountains, well, the cost will accelerate from there. Some advice based on hard-won experience: a pool heater (propane) is definitely worth the expense. You'll get much more use out of your pool during the crucial summer months. DO NOT, however, run the thing all the time. You'll go through $3,000 (+) worth of propane in a summer if you do. Best thing to do is keep the heater on a clock or timer so that it minimally heats the pool when you're not around (to 75 degrees, say) and then cranks it up a little on the weekends. How about a solar cover? Costs run $1,500 (+) depending on the cover. It's a good idea, I think, but get a cover with an electric or hand cranked reel. Oh, in case you didn't know, when you have a pool out here it MUST be surrounded, in some fashion, by fencing at least four feet high. This is a local law for the protection of children, who might wander into your yard and fall into your pool. You can surround the entire yard with fencing (see "Fencing" for allowable types, etc.) or just surround the pool itself. It's up to you, but the pool must be entirely closed off. Gates to the pool are, of course, allowed. Some people go the extra mile and install the so-called "hard covers" or childproof covers over their pools. These are generally electrically operated and retract on command. They can double as solar covers, too. That's a lot of expense to go through, since it will not relieve you of the obligation to build a pool fence anyway. And if you're worried more about your kids falling in the pool by accident, as opposed to the neighbor's kids, why even have a pool if you haven't taught your kids to swim? If you're going to have a pool, there's no excuse for not teaching your kids to swim. They even teach teeny babies to swim these days for heaven's sake! In any case, when you're ready to build the pool here are the best companies to work with.

✪✪✪✪ **J. Tortorella Swimming Pools, Inc.,** 1764 North Highway, Southampton, 283-7373. Tortorella is known for their unique designs and the quality of their work. Whether its a regular ol' gunite rectangular job or a free-form design with cascading waterfalls and little brooks trickling over rocks, these are the folks to talk to. They have designed and built many of the more "famous" pools in The Hamptons.

✪✪✪ **Pools by Jack Anthony,** 1724 North Highway (showroom), Southampton, 283-8101 and 324-2066 in East Hampton, another company with a very fine reputation. They can do gunite or vinyl, steel or concrete walls, and also offer a full line of heaters, covers, supplies, etc.

POOLS—SERVICE

It's best to get a referral from someone who's happy with his or her pool service. It's also a good sign if the referred company services more than one pool on your street. The service tends to be more reliable and cost efficient if a pool company can service a number of pools in an area. You want a company that understands the word "clean." If their idea of a "sparkling pool" is where you can see through the thin green film on the top of the water, bail out.

✪✪✪✪ **Recreational Concepts,** Montauk Highway and Scuttle Hole Rd., Water Mill, 726-2020. Hank Katz, the owner, has always been responsive to his customers. The service people are competent and on time. They do the little extra things like fix the straps on the solar cover, store pool pumps for the winter, find covers for pool heaters, etc. I also think Hank's prices are very fair for service, openings, closings, acid washes, and so forth. These guys are the best.

POST OFFICES

The phone numbers and zip codes for all the post office locations in the Hamptons are as follows:

Phone	Zip Code
Amagansett: 267-3344	11930
Bridgehampton: 537-1090	11932
East Hampton: 324-0790	11937
Hampton Bays: 728-0371	11946
Montauk: 668-2218	11954
Sagaponack: 537-1140	11962
Sag Harbor: 725-0108	11963
Shelter Island: 749-0250	11964
Shelter Is. Heights: 749-1115	11965
Southampton: 283-0268	11968 & 11969
Wainscott: 537-3636	11975
Water Mill: 726-4811	11976
Westhampton: 288-2828	11977
Westhampton Beach: 288-1238	11978

Some post offices are better than others. I do a lot of direct mail during the course of any given year and there are weeks when I think I'm servicing the Post Office's debt. In any case, I end up dealing, in some way or another, with most of the Post Offices out here. It absolutely boggles my mind some of the laziness that does occur with some PO's out here. Two PO's that shall remain nameless (but I'd love to name them!) are particularly offensive. I did one particular mailing for a client not long ago wherein there were two addressees where we had street addresses, but the mail merge program did not pick up the PO Boxes for these two businesses for whatever reason. One business was literally right next door to this particular post office on one side and the other business was two doors down on the other side. The piece of mail to the business "right next door" was returned marked "Insufficient address—no PO Box." The piece of mail to the business two doors away was returned "Addressee Unknown." Now, you tell me: how does this happen?! Was there someone brand new to the Post Office sorting the mail that day? Are you kidding? The people who work in this particular post office have more seniority in Federal Service than Strom Thurmond! It was just plain laziness!!!

Anyway, enough of that. There are some really good post offices to balance out the ones that should be hosed out and re-staffed. And they are:

✪✪✪✪ **The Shelter Island Post Office,** 749-0250, right across from Town Hall. If you're a resident of the Island, your PO Box is free, now finally here's a deal from the "Feds!" Mary is there most days and ever helpful. I get too much mail, but she never yells at me. She just sets it aside and when I come by I don't even have to ask. She just smiles and hands it over. Now I realize it's a stretch to go to Shelter Island to get or post your mail, but if you do, it's always pleasant and never, never crowded.

✪✪✪✪ **The Water Mill Post Office,** Montauk Highway, Water Mill, across the street from the old Mill itself. You get real help with a smile at this branch office and extra measures of service every time. It's a great group.

POTHOLES

Minor crater suddenly appears in your street? Busted curb (usually the result of a bad winter and lots of snow plowing)? Anything else that relates to the repair of the road surfaces in your neighborhood? Call your local Highway Department.

East Hampton Highway Department: 324-0925.
Southampton Town or Village: 728-3600.

POULTRY

✪✪✪✪ **North Sea Farms,** Noyac Rd., Southampton, 283-0735. The absolute best place to get your fresh turkey, chicken, and, yes, pheasant, goose, and other exotic birds. Did you know this is Kathleen's dad? Yes, the Kathleen as in the Bakery.

PREGNANCY

Here we're talking about help with a pregnancy that's already underway. There's a real dearth of OB/GYNs on the East End. There is, however, one very good resource in Southampton, and that's Hamptons Gynecology & Obstetrics, 283-6088, 595 Hampton Road. They are staffed by several MDs as well as Physician Assistants. (Also check out their website at www.hamptonsobgyn.com.) Another good resource for help and information is: Birthright of Peconic in Southampton at 287-6456 or in Hampton Bays at 728-8900. Birthright provides free pregnancy testing and confidential counseling. They are non-profit, non-sectarian, and staffed by trained volunteers. They can also provide baby layettes, maternity clothes, and reduced fee medical referrals. The Southampton group also operates a Thrift Store at 17 Flying Point Rd.

PRINTERS & PRINTING

Want that printing job done right—the first time? Then you should talk with these folks. Pine Barrens can do all your work, but they specialize in the "big" jobs. Printhampton can take care of your normal, everyday needs, like small runs, stationery, and stuff like that.

✪✪✪✪ **North Fork Press**, 132 Front St., Greenport, 477-1250. I don't think there's much Rita and her fine crew can't do—and they do it in a timely fashion for an excellent price. Creative, too! Most times I don't know what I really want, but by the time Rita's done with it she makes me look like a genius!

✪✪✪✪ **Pine Barrens Printing**, 351-1 Riverhead Rd., Westhampton Beach, 288-5200, fax 288-1036 and email at pinebarrens@peconic.net. Mike Lennon and his crew can do it all, from design and layout to printing the final product. They've done some of the nicest work I've seen, and many local companies with large printing needs count on Pine Barrens.

✪✪✪✪ **Printhampton,** 42 Hampton Rd., Southampton, 283-9572. They can print typical small to medium sized jobs, do typesetting and graphic design. Good folks for stationery, the flyer for school, business cards and the like.

PRODUCE (see "Farm Stands" and "Fruits and Vegetables")

PROPANE

✪✪✪✪ **Pulver Gas,** Main St., Bridgehampton, 537-0930. A good company for service and they also have a nice selection of gas grills and maybe more important for grilling fanatics (like me!)—spare grill parts!

✪✪ Need a quick fill-up for your grill's propane tank? Best place to get that done in a jiffy is the **Mobil** station on Montauk Highway Just north of Water Mill and before the Water Mill True Value Hardware Store.

QUIET

Open your window…Isn't it wonderful out here?

QUILTS

This art, a staple of Colonial America, has been much neglected in recent years. Some of the finest examples of the current state-of-the-art can be found at:

✪✪✪✪ **Water Mill Museum,** Old Mill Rd., Water Mill, 726-4625. There are examples of the quilting art on display and the ladies of the museum make a beautiful quilt annually to be raffled off for the benefit of the Museum. Seasonal. Call for hours.

RABIES

New York had a single, fatal case of rabies four years ago (from a bat bite!) and that was after many years of zero deaths from rabies. It is, as I am sure you know, a horrible disease. If not treated promptly, it is 100% fatal. Rabies, in humans, is caused by animal bites from animals infected with the virus. What is your chance of getting rabies out here on the East End? About as likely as hearing Howard Stern do one single show without a four-letter word. But there's always a chance, slim though it may be. The most likely culprits to transmit rabies to humans are infected dogs and raccoons but also cats, rats, and bats (oh, my!). The wisest thing to do is to treat any animal bite as a potential case of rabies—get to the hospital immediately. Are you willing to take a chance? Not me. Now the good news: we haven't seen or heard of any rabid animals out here in many a moon.

RADIO STATIONS

The East End is one saturated radio dial! There's lots of competition, both local and national, as well as some Connecticut "interlopers" who are pitching their powerful signals across the sound. (Well, actually, some of our stations are pitching our sounds back to Connecticut, too, so I guess that's only fair!) Here are our favorite stations and some people who are definitely "doing it right."

✪✪✪✪ **WBEA** (104.7 FM) and **WEHM** (96.7 FM), Hamptons Radio Corporation, 267-7800. My good friend Suzanne took me to task after last year's "Guide" came out. She wanted to know why the heck these two great stations were not in the "Guide." Well, uh, I really didn't have a good answer, so we're correcting that oversight here and now! And these are two excellent stations. Around here 104.7 is known as "Beach Radio." The Hot Adult-Contemporary format is, indeed, the perfect companion for the beach—or while you're zipping around town with the top down. You'll hear

"Hamptons Hot" music here: Jewel, Sugar Ray, Matchbox 20, Alanis Morissette, Sheryl Crow, Madonna et al. Beach Radio's sister station, 96.7, is Progressive Adult Rock: cool, laid back, very sophisticated—the best of the 70s rock with a blues influence and a 90s–00s "current" twist. This is "Hamptons Cool" with Van Morrison, Bruce Springsteen, Bonnie Raitt, Tom Petty, Neil Young, Bob Dylan, Joni Mitchell, Sarah McLachlan, and more! This is live radio, designed for the Hamptons. All features and news stories focus on the Hamptons. I encourage you to pre-set these stations on your radio dial (why do we still say "dial?") and enjoy.

✪✪✪✪ **WBSQ,** 102.5 FM and **WBAZ,** 101.7 FM. Two more sister stations both owned by MAK Communications and a very fine gentleman by the name of Mal Kahn. "Q-Bright," 102.5 FM in Bridgehampton is 80s & 90s Radio. The format is really very pleasant. It's contemporary but not overpowering. The current principal on-air personality, Ed Wright, is excellent. He brings a local touch to the hosting of his morning show that complements the top-rated CNN news broadcasts and the other programs that round out the day. You'll get Mariah Carey, Jewel, Alanis Morrisette, David Bowie, and most of the "Top 10" Rock, Pop, and Contemporary artists. Casey Kasem's "Top 20" show can also be found here every Saturday morning. Both WBSQ and WBAZ carry Joe Cioffi's weather forecasts (frequently) and two very helpful features: "Health Talk" and "You and Your Money." WBAZ, 101.7 FM is in Southold. Known as "The Lite on the Bays," BAZ provides a slightly lighter mix of contemporary music than BSQ. BAZ has excellent programming, talented announcers, and numerous local news broadcasts supplemented by CNN News. Ted Schreiber is the principal anchor here (mornings, 5–10) and Ted simulcasts the local news on both BAZ and BSQ. I also like George Morton, who does some news and local commentary, and I like Dave Malow, who does some fill-in work and has a great Sunday morning "Pops" show. If you're here during January, you should tune in on Saturday mornings to BAZ's "Bargains by the Bays." It's a live, on-air auction of some really valuable goods and services from local merchants. You can snap up some real bargains! BAZ also has Martha Stewart every day with those oh-so-correct "good things" and Dave Koz on Jazz, Sundays 10 to noon.

✪✪✪✪ **WLNG,** 92.1 FM, Sag Harbor. You thought live radio was dead? Not at LNG! This is 24-hour live radio, my friends. And has been for 36 years! If you want true East End flavor all year round, this is the place on the dial to find it. WLNG plays a very eclectic mix of music, mostly the rock-'n-roll classics of the 50's. This is the East End's original, pioneering station. On-air (and well known locally) personalities Paul Sydney, Rusty Potz, and Gary Sapian keep rockin' with a blend that pleases. This is where to find coverage of local stories, local sports, and local news. And whenever any kind of weather threatens, these folks will be talking about it—and talking you through it! And have you seen LNG's new mobile studio? This brightly colored mega-bus cruises the Hamptons in search of the best remote broadcasts and the most candid interviews. LNG—check it out, it's a "hoot."

✪✪✪ **WSHU** 103.3 FM, Public Radio broadcasting from the south shore of Connecticut but easily picked up here because of a remote re-broadcast transmitter in Noyac. Classical all day. And just about your only choice for classical out here. "Sunday Morning Baroque" is a great program as is "Sunday Matinee" with David Bouchet. But my favorite program on 103.3, by far, is the Sunday evening program "Echoes," wonderful new-age music hosted by John DiLoberto. Starts about 6 PM. In the early morning each day you'll get PBS's "Early Edition" news broadcasts and each afternoon you'll hear the excellent news program "All Things Considered."

✪✪ **WLIU** 88.3 FM, **WLIU,** which is broadcast from the grounds of our own Long Island University campus in Southampton. If you like jazz this is where you need to be!

RAILROADS

We only have one out here "The L-I-R-R"; The Long Island Railroad: Local info: 231-5477. From Manhattan: 718-217-5477. I've been pretty hard on the LIRR over the past five years, but I'm pleased to report that things are much better this year—finally! During the last year the LIRR purchased 134 new coaches and 23 new dual-mode engines and have now put most of this new equipment in service on the Hamptons and Greenport lines. They have also been upgrading the station platforms to accommodate the new cars. The new equipment is both diesel and electric, which means they can operate on both types of tracks. That means, in turn, that the new trains will be able to go all the way from the East End directly into Penn Station without making that annoying change of trains at Jamaica Station (from Jamaica into Penn Station the rail lines are electric only). That hasn't occurred yet, but it should soon.

Now, the next step is to work on the schedules. God Bless you if you have to commute to the City from The Hamptons on the LIRR! If you want to commute to The City and get there by "normal working hours," you have to leave Southampton at 6:15 in the morning. That is currently the one and only express train to Penn Station for East End commuters. The rest of the schedule makes a bazillion stops between here and The City. But it gets worse. If you can't leave Penn Station by 4:15 PM—the last eastbound express—you probably can't get back home before 9:30. What kind of service is that for the local commuter? What company is going to allow you to get to the office at 10:00 AM and leave at 3:30 PM to catch the last express? It's nuts.

The round trip peak fare is about $20.00 from Southampton. If you come out on Friday nights, call ahead and reserve the Parlor Car. For an extra $16.00 you still get a seat in a "private" car. There's cocktail and snack service in the Parlor Cars (cocktails and snacks extra, of course).

RAINY DAYS

What could you do on a rainy day around here? Well, fortunately we don't have too many rainy days in Summer, but if you do get stuck with a rainy day in Summer (or anytime for that matter) here are my favorite rainy day activities in The Hamptons.

✪✪✪✪ Catch a good movie at the East Hampton Cinema preceded or followed by lunch at Rowdy Hall, topped off by a visit to London Jewelers to ogle the expensive trinkets (leave the Platinum card at home today!). Then stop next door at Book Hampton to pick up a good book to read while it rains! All of these spots are on the same block, so you won't get too wet!

✪✪✪✪ Grab lunch at the Driver's Seat or Le Chef at Jobs Lane in Southampton then run up the block to the Parrish Art Museum to check out the latest exhibit. After that, run back down the Lane to the Southampton Cinema for the latest show. (Get a cigar at Doug & Besim's on Jobs Lane and pick up a bottle of champagne at Herbert & Rist for later.)

HAMPTONS HOT

Jewel
Sugar Ray
Matchbox 20
Alanis Morissette
Sheryl Crow
Madonna
Goo-Goo Dolls
Melissa Etheridge
Third Eye Blind

HAMPTONS COOL

96.7
WEHM
Hamptons Radio

Van Morrison
Bruce Springsteen
Bonnie Raitt
Tom Petty
Neil Young
Bob Dylan
Dave Matthews
Joni Mitchell
Sarah McLachlan

The "Hamptons"

Loves

* *Ted Schreiber*
* *Ed Wright*
* *Great Car Tunes*
* *Latest Weather*
* *CNN Biz Minute*
* *Casey Kasem*
* *CNN Sports*

WBS Q 102.5 FM
Today's Hits... Yesterday's Favorites

WBAZ 101.7 FM
Z-Lite On The Bays

✪✪✪✪ What's the very best thing you can do on a rainy day, especially if you have kids? Pick up lunch at one of our recommended delis, pick up a board game (not an electronic game!) at one of our favorite toy stores, and pick up a good book you can read to your kids at one of the BookHampton stores. Go home, spread a picnic on the living room floor, read your kids a story, then everyone plays a board game for hours.

✪✪✪ Stop for lunch at Gosman's in Montauk then spend some time strolling around the shops at Gosman's Dock. (Bring an umbrella—the shops are not connected.) After that, drive up the road to Montauk Point and take in the Museum and lighthouse.

✪✪✪ See what's going on at the Art Barge in Amagansett. Maybe you can drop by for an impromptu class in sculpting or watercolors or whatever happens to be going on that day.

REAL ESTATE (Agents and Brokers)

A good real estate firm is important, but a really good real estate professional is critical. Find the right person first—the firm will follow. How do you find the right person? The very best way I know is talk to a couple of your friends or trusted business associates who've purchased real estate out here. The best agents and brokers rise to the top in this fashion. Next best resource is right in your hands! These folks have been thoroughly checked out and have kept rising to the top of the list again and again.

✪✪✪✪ **Melanie Ross, Cook Pony Farm Real Estate,** East Hampton, 324-9600: Cook Pony Farm also has offices in Amagansett (267-7700), Bridgehampton (537-7773), Sag Harbor (725-5252), Southampton (283-9600) and Westhampton Beach (288-6900). Melanie is the President of Cook Pony Farm and she's quite a story: she started out (how many years ago, Melanie?) as a secretary, answering phones. Now she runs the whole show! I am very impressed with the quality of their offerings, the knowledge of her associates, and the service they provide. You can call any office, or Melanie, and she'll refer you to one of her best.

✪✪✪✪ **Margot R. Horn of We Lead the Hunt, Ltd.,** Southampton, 283-8020, fax 283-8048. Margot is a delightful lady with 28 years of

real estate experience and a solid-gold reputation for honesty and hard work. She knows the local real estate scene inside and out and has dealt with some of the most exclusive properties in The Hamptons. Even more, she knows how to structure a deal and get it done.

✪✪✪✪ **Pat Petrillo of Sotheby's,** 50 Nugent St., Southampton (283-0600). Now I know you think that Sotheby's is only going to handle the 50-room ocean front mansion. They certainly can, but many people don't realize that they do a very good job in the $400,000 to $1 million range, too. Pat Petrillo is a friend of ours and we know how hard she works and how dedicated she is to her clients.

✪✪✪ **Punch up Hamptons Real Estate Online,** www.hreo.com. (Also at 288-8833, fax 288-3194). This website is a compendium of all the best properties available in The Hamptons! Shop for a house without leaving your desk! Once you find one or a bunch of places you want to see, call up the broker listed or (better yet) call one of our award winning real estate people above!

RECYCLING (See "Garbage & Trash")

RENTALS: HOUSES

Finding the summer rental is only half the fun. If you're going to be renting a home out here for the season or any part of the year, there are three, and only three, ways to do it.

First and best way: rent from someone you know. Knowing someone willing to rent a home to you is going to save you money (agent's fees) and you're going to know what you're getting before you get there. If you want to keep this owner as a friend, though, you're going to have to be a good renter.

Two: most people who rent for the season do rent through a broker. There is a fee in the rental cost, paid by the owner, but who do you think really pays it? You do, of course. Just like buying a house, getting a good broker is the key to having a pleasant rental experience. Many brokers do both sales and rentals but there are some that specialize in rentals. Herewith for your edification are those that we think can be most helpful to you in a summer rental.

✪✪✪✪ **Margot Horn, We Lead the Hunt,** Southampton, 283-8020
✪✪✪✪ **Melanie Ross, Cook Pony Farm,** 324-9600
✪✪✪ **Main Street Properties,** East Hampton, 324-1800

Three: if you want a short-term rental, one or two weeks, you really should call:

✪✪✪✪ **Accommodations Plus,** 324-1858, fax 329-0762, website: www.hamptonsvacations.com. Accommodations Plus has eight 3 and 4 bedroom homes available for short-term rental. All the homes are in East Hampton. They are turnkey rentals: they have everything you'll need. Three of the homes have pools. All utilities are included and they can arrange beach passes, make dinner reservations, and book golf or tennis times. The words "complete" and "immaculate" keep popping up when we have asked about the services of Accommodations Plus. And the Kaufmanns, who own the company, are really nice folks. Call them. The properties go for $3000 to $4500 per week.

RENTALS: PARTY (see "Party Rentals," above)

RENTALS: TOOLS & STUFF

Two good resources here:

✪✪✪✪ **One Source Tool Supply,** 823 North Hwy., Southampton, 283-8700
✪✪✪✪ **Village Hardware of East Hampton,** 32 Newtown Lane, 324-2456

RENTER'S PROBLEMS

If you're an owner and are experiencing problems with a renter, and the problem is a matter of public safety or an emergency call the Sheriff's Department and ask for help from a patrol officer (852-2205).

If your problem is of a "nuisance" nature (too many people sharing, renters refusing to honor a commitment in the lease, etc.), it is best to call an attorney (see "Lawyers").

If you're a renter and you're having problems with your landlord and it's a matter of safety (dangerous electrical wiring, etc.) or of an emergency nature (no water, for example), call the Suffolk County Health Department, 852-2069.

RESTAURANTS

We're going to tell you where to go to eat great food and be treated well. It's just that simple. We have many, many fine restaurants out here. At last count, there were over 325 eating establishments associated with The Hamptons. Plus, my informal poll indicates that ten to fifteen percent of all these restaurants are turning over all the time. We have a dozen or so new openings every year, a dozen or so closings, and a few places changing names or ownership. If you wanted to search for the best of this bunch you'd spend a fortune in the process and probably go home looking like the Goodyear blimp. We're here to help you out.

We will give you what we think are the "Best of the Best." The research we conduct is based on first-hand experience. Each restaurant we review is done clandestinely. After we leave, we immediately fill out a scoring sheet that awards points for each of fourteen categories. Possible points range from 1 (really "low") to 10 ("extraordinary"). You must score a minimum of 75 to get an Honorable Mention, 80 to obtain a Bronze Award, 85 to earn a Silver Award, 90 to win a Gold, and a Platinum Award winner must score at least 95 out of a possible 100. Platinum awards are reserved for the absolute best restaurants in The Hamptons.

The winners are listed alphabetically by town or village, and then by level of award. We also indicate if they are "plain" or "fancy," the type of cuisine, something about the restaurant, when during the year they are open (if not all year), basic hours of operation. Credit cards accepted by each winner are listed along with the reservation policy (if there is one).

Fine Dining Awards (listed as "Fine Dining"): These are the restaurants where one goes to impress, or be impressed, and where you should expect to spend serious money on fine food and drink. There isn't any restaurant in The Hamptons that I know of that requires a coat and tie, but there are places that will turn you away if your attire is too informal. These Fine Dining establishments are "informal" but I wouldn't wear jeans or shorts to any of these spots.

Family/Fun/Casual Dining Awards (listed as "Casual"): These are the restaurants where you go to have fun, have a quick meal, or to engage in really informal dining. These are the places where you can wear jeans or shorts. Most of them are also great places for the entire family.

A Special Note on Reservations:

The Hamptons Restaurant Reservations Nightmare (in season) has gotten even worse: some of the more popular places have simply thrown up their hands and are no longer taking reservations at all!! If you want a table on Friday or Saturday, you can: (1) show up at 5 PM and get seated fairly quickly (2) wait for one to two hours if you show up at 7:30 PM, or (3) eat at midnight. The best way around this is to find the one or two places you really love, spend serious money on food and drink, take the receipt to the maitre d', show it to him or her and say "I would like a table here next Saturday night at eight." Chances are, you'll get a table when you show up. (Oh, don't forget to wink and slip the maitre d' a $20.) By the way, this is not cheating, in my view. I think restauranteurs are entitled to treat their best and most regular customers with a certain level of preference. No matter what your profession, don't you treat your customers the same way?

For those places still taking reservations, you know, of course, that the most popular restaurants will be packed all the time in season. It has not been uncommon for me to hear a host or hostess ask in what week or month you want to reserve, not just what day and time. If you get a reservation, please keep it or cancel it in a timely fashion—not an hour before you are supposed to be there. If we all do this, the restaurant craziness we have seen out here of late may abate. For example, I know people who make several reservations at different restaurants then go to the one they feel like going to that night and never cancel the other reservations. Some restaurants are asking for a credit card deposit in order to guarantee you keep your reservation or cancel it in a timely manner. If you don't, they keep a fee! This whole situation is nuts and it's gotten out of hand, although I can certainly see both sides of the issue. So, patrons! Do your part! Pick where you want to go, keep the date or cancel well in advance (at least 48 hours would be nice!).

Here we go! The best restaurants in The Hamptons for 2000! Enjoy!

Wow, has there been change this year! First of all, the top of our list, the very best of the very best, has flip-flopped around a bunch. One of the most hopeful new stars in the Hamptons restaurant firmament didn't even make it through its first season (Maya's). And, with the rising popularity of the North Fork as a destination for wandering Hamptonites, we've added a few North Fork spots to our list. I've also decided to do something a little different with this section this year. It's just plain hard—darn near impossible, in fact— to pick the very best, Numero Uno, top banana restaurant in the Hamptons. It used to be easier but now there are so many wonderful eateries that I feel I'd be doing you a disservice by picking just one very best place. So, this year, for the first time, we're going to pick the very best restaurant in each major area of the Hamptons. This will be fun! The very best restaurants will receive our Top Award: the "Platinum."

A Platinum winner is, de facto, the very best restaurant in that town or village and one of the top ten restaurants in the Hamptons for this edition of the Guide.

And now, our Award Winners, by Location.

Amagansett

✪✪✪✪ **Pacific East** (Seafood) ("Fine Dining"), 415 Main Street, 267-7770. This very modern and beautiful spot has firmly planted itself among our favorites. As its name might suggest to you, the restaurant looks and feels like Marina Del Rey or Laguna Beach. It's open, airy, and has a very friendly bar (and bar scene!). The dishes are reminiscent of a menu that you might find in a trendy beach spot on the Left Coast…er…West Coast. There are some wonderful shrimp, fresh local seafood, excellent side dishes, and great desserts. I wonder…if these folks opened a place in San Diego, say, would they call it "Atlantic West"? [Seasonal, April–Oct., 7 days, AMEX, V, MC, Reservations recommended]

✪✪✪ **Mt. Fuji**—(Japanese) ("Casual") there are two of them: this original spot on Montauk Highway in Amagansett, 267-7600 and 1678 North Highway in Southampton, 287-1700 (on your way into town). Myra and I are connoisseurs of sushi and sashimi and we rate Mt. Fuji right up there with the best. Service is excellent, too. You can dine at regular tables, tatami tables, or at the sushi bar. Be sure you have clean socks if you want to sit Japanese style. [Year round, 7-days, AMEX, MC, V, Reservations suggested]

Bridgehampton

✪✪✪✪✪ **Henry's** (Bistro Style) ("Fine Dining"), 2495 Montauk Highway, next to the Monument at the end of Main Street, 537-5665. Clearly one of the Top Ten. The atmosphere is seductive, the bar and dining room are well laid out and spacious, and the ambiance is top notch. Noel Love, who runs this wonderful place, is gracious and accommodating. Now, read this and see if you don't hear your stomach start rumbling: "Loup de Mer," grilled

whole wolf fish, flown in from France; braised brisket of beef (but nothin' like Grandma's pot roast—this is ten times better!); monkfish stew with cockles and root vegetables in a saffron broth; and, for carnivores like me, a luscious rib-eye piled high with pomme frites. Now, aren't you starving?!

Your season won't be complete without a trip to Henry's. [Year round, Weds.-Sun Oct. to May, 7 days May-Oct. reservations a must, V/MC/AMEX, $$$]

✪✪✪✪ **World Pie** (Pizza/Italian/and other specialties) ("Casual Dining"), Main Street, across from Bobby Van's, 537-7999. Wonderful spot to sit and relax, have a brick oven pizza or a cool and delicious cocktail. The Dutch Fries, served in a paper cone are outrageous! Great bar! Casual yet elegant atmosphere. Marvelous spot to snuggle into on a cold winter's evening, but the outside patio is the place to be in summer.

✪✪✪✪ **Bobby Van's,** (American/Steak) ("Fine Dining") Main St., 537-0590. This is just a really pleasant place to spend a leisurely lunch or dinner. The openness of the restaurant and its casual but elegant atmosphere make for a fine dining experience. They offer more than steak, but it is the fabulous Porterhouse and excellent rib eyes that have a lot of us repeating at Bobby Van's. It's also a hangout for some of the famous local literati and some of our resident "stars." You might catch a glimpse of, well, I better not say. They might shy away. Lunch, dinner and Sunday brunch. [Year round, 7-days, all major credit cards, reservations suggested]

✪✪✪ **Yama-Q** (Eclectic with Sushi Bar) ("Casual"), 2393 Montauk Hwy., 537-0225. There are veterans of the wonderful "Sen" restaurant in Sag Harbor here and, like "Sen," Yama-Q is serving up some very fine sushi along with a smattering of other dishes: mostly whatever the chef feels like cooking! Small and cozy. Take out, too. [Year round, 7-days, MC, V, no Reservations]

✪✪ **95 School Street** (American) ("Fine Dining"), 95 School Street, just to the right of the Candy Kitchen, 537-5555. This is a true veteran of the Hamptons restaurant scene. I know lost of folks who hold this place near and dear. I fret about it. There are times when it's really good and there are times when, well, let's just say they're back in the

'Guide" this year after an absence of a couple of years. Steaks, seafood and lots of specials. Good wine list, friendly bar. [Year round, 7-days lunch & dinner, reservations suggested, V/MV/AMEX, $$]

✪✪ **Poxabogue's Café** (Breakfast) ("Casual") at the Poxabogue Golf Course, Montauk Hwy., 537-7195. One of the best-kept secrets for a wonderful and incredibly inexpensive breakfast (but they also have lunch and dinner). [Year round, 7-days, AMEX only, No Reservations taken]

East Hampton

✪✪✪✪✪ **The Farmhouse**, (French/American) ("Fine Dining") 341 Montauk Hwy., East Hampton, 324-8585. Service here is exceptional. It's nice to see people who like what they do and enjoy where they work. The wine list is excellent and if you like martinis I think they make the best in The Hamptons. The overall ambience is fabulous and spread across several different rooms, each with it's own charm. The menu is exciting! Adventurous salads and entrees woven around a French/American theme, but no matter what they're posting, there will be something to enjoy. The last time we were there they put out a potato-encrusted salmon that was out of this world. And speaking of "out of this world," you absolutely have to have the brownie "flying saucer" for dessert (if it's on the menu). You will not have had one of The Hamptons very best dining experiences if you do not visit The Farmhouse this season. But, Please! Call well in advance for reservations, especially if you are going to be a party of four or more. [Year round, 7 days, AMEX, MC, V, Reservations strongly suggested]

✪✪✪✪ **Della Femina Restaurant** (Contemporary American with Italian Influences) ("Fine Dining") 99 N. Main, East Hampton, 329-6666. Still one of our favorites and still one of the best. As we have said in this Guide for several years now, Della Femina's provides fabulous food and equally great service. I have never been disappointed by any soup, salad, entrée, dessert, or drink that I have ever had here. The pastas and fish dishes are particularly grand, but I had a venison steak last time I was here that was simply the best I have ever had. I'm also glad to see that Della Femina's is staying open year 'round, now, because it's darn near impossible to get a table in season! [Year round, 7 days, 6 PM on, AMEX, MC, V, Reservations a must!]

✪✪✪✪ **East Hampton Point** (American) ("Fine Dining") 295 Three Mile Harbor Rd., East Hampton, 329-2800. For sheer volume of good food in an atmosphere that feels like your own private Yacht Club, this is the place to be on Sunday morning and early Sunday afternoon. Absolutely the best brunch in The Hamptons. The food is superbly prepared, reasonably priced, and the bar dispenses some of the best Bloody Marys and Mimosas around. Call for reservations! It's packed—and try to get a table on the deck (unless it's windy). [Year round, 7-days In Season, weekends only off-season; AMEX, MC, V, Reservations suggested]

✪✪✪✪ **(the) Laundry** (American/Regional) ("Fine Dining") Restaurant, 31 Race Ln., East Hampton, 324-3199. You've got to really look for this place but if you do, you will be more than pleased. The Laundry is located up by the East Hampton railroad station, just a little past it, actually, and down Race Lane. One small black and white sign that simply says "Laundry" marks a spot that will make you feel warm, comfortable, and as invited as an old friend. There's a comfy bar, some couches around a fireplace, quiet nooks, booths, and an atmosphere of conviviality that is truly exceptional. The menu ranges from pasta to fish to meats. The soups are wonderful (if they have the pureed mushroom, don't miss it!), and the salads, especially the baby beets with goat cheese, are the best. If you like calves liver, theirs is the best I have ever had. The strip steaks are as good as you'll find anywhere. The wine list is extensive and features some of our own homegrown Long Island wines. [Year round, 7-days, AMEX, MC, V, DC, D, No Reservations except for parties of 6 or more]

✪✪✪✪ **The Maidstone Arms** (Continental) ("Fine Dining") 207 Main, East Hampton, 324-5006. Excellent food, often with different and exciting main dishes, all served in the warmth and charm of an old Colonial Inn—which it is. Sunday brunch, too, after which you can take the paper and find a rocking chair on the front porch. [Year round, 7-days, AMEX, MC, V, Reservations suggested]

✪✪✪✪ **Nick & Toni's** (Mediterranean) ("Fine Dining") 136 North Main Street, East Hampton, 324-3550. Nick & Toni's launches into their 12th season this year—with some re-modeling to boot. They certainly qualify as "venerable" in a restaurant community where some of the "also-rans" don't even last a season. It's a wonderful spot, with fine Italian cuisine as well as other local favorites like roasted chicken and fresh caught fish. Now I know, and you probably know, that this is a spot where a number of the "stars" of both coasts are prone to hang out. Don't go there just to see Brad Pitt or the Baldwins or Ron Perleman. Go there to have a wonderful meal. If Cindy Crawford or Leonardo DiCaprio happen to stroll in, well, you got a bonus. [Year round, Fri–Sun, AMEX, MC, V, Reservations needed]

✪✪✪✪ **Peconic Coast** (American/Mediterranean) ("Fine Dining") 103 Montauk Highway, East Hampton, 324-6772. Veterans of (the) "Laundry," across town, have taken this spot and turned it into a first class operation. Great pastas, mouth-watering burgers, baskets of skinny French fries, perfect grilled vegetables, herb crusted chicken to die for, and more! Peconic Coast also has a very attractive bar. Service was impeccable and the Peconic Coast people clearly enjoy their work. Peconic Coast does not take reservations; so, show up and be prepared to wait, but it'll be worth it. [Year round, 7-days but dinner only, AMEX, MC, V, No Reservations taken]

✪✪✪✪ **Santa Fe Junction** (Southwest) ("Fine Dining") 8 Fresno Pl., East Hampton, 324-8700. Some folks would classify this as "Mexican," and there is much that may seem like Mexican, but Santa Fe Junction is, to a purist, Southwestern. And there is a difference. No matter. Whether you like Mexican or Southwestern, you'll LOVE Santa Fe Junction. Located near the East Hampton train station, Santa Fe Junction is small and does not take reservations; so, get there early. The bar is inviting and you can wait for your table in convivial comfort. Try the Onion Blossom! The nachos are great, the Fajitas are wonderful, and just about everything on the menu is mouth watering—enhanced by whiffs of mesquite-fired smoke wafting from the kitchen. If you're itching for a taste of the Southwest (or, c'mon, Mexico) it is the best place in the Hamptons for this type of cuisine. [Year round, 7-days, MC, V, No Reservations taken]

✪✪✪ **Bostwick's Seafood Grill & Oyster Bar** (Seafood) ("Casual") 39 Gann Rd., East Hampton, 324-1111. Bostwick's is way off the beaten path, about a half mile beyond East Hampton Point. But if you want excellent seafood, a great bar crowd, and the best sunsets while dining in The Hamptons, you'll jump in your car and find Bostwick's. [May through September, MC, V, call for hours]

✪✪✪ **Café Max** (American) ("Casual"), 85 Montauk Highway, near the Red Horse Plaza, 324-2004. [May through September, MC, V, call for hours]

✪✪✪ **The Palm** (American/Steak) ("Fine Dining") at the Huntting Inn, 94 Main St., East Hampton, 324-0411, continues the Palm tradition from The City in a magnificent fashion. The restaurant is lovely, well laid out, the service superb, and, the steaks, well, the steaks. If you're a steak lover or are trying to escape the vegetarian world for just a few hours, you need to check into The Palm. [Year round, 7-days, AMEX, MC, V, DC, D, Reservations taken for 4 or more]

✪✪ **Mary Jane's** (Italian/Seafood) ("Fine Dining") 126 N. Main St., 324-8008. Mary Jane's is smack in between two of The Hamptons finest restaurants. Della Femina's is kitty-corner across the street and Nick & Toni's is right next door. And Mary Jane's isn't so bad, either; in fact, it's pretty darn good. (For those of you who've been around here a while, this used to be "IL Monastero.") Mary Jane's is cozy with a warm, inviting bar and lounge. The two main dining rooms are open and airy with the appropriate candlelit glow at night. Delicious homemade garlic "knots" start off the meal, and there are a host of delightful pasta and seafood dishes. You should try the stuffed portobello mushrooms, too! [Year round, 7 days, AMEX, V, MC, Reservations suggested, $$]

✪✪ **Sam's Restaurant** (Italian/Pizza) ("Casual") 36 Newtown Ln., East Hampton, 324-5900. If you like your pizza thin, slightly charred, and crusty, Sam's has the best. Have a fresh salad and a sip of wine while you wait for "the pie." This is a warm, comfortable, unpretentious spot. Good for all the family—bring the kids! [Year round, closed Mon., AMEX, MC, V, No Reservations taken]

✪✪ **Rowdy Hall** (American/Burgers and Stuff) ("Casual") 10 Main St., East Hampton, 324-8555, tucked in the alley between London Jewelers and Book Hampton. A really neat little place for a great burger, fries, or a salad. It's also one of the places where you can take the kids without worry. [Year round, 7-days, AMEX, MC, V, No Reservations taken]

✪✪ **Zizzi Balooba's** (Varied) ("Casual"), 47 Montauk Hwy., 329-9821: The best description of the food here at Zizzi's is that it's a "menu of favorites." The whole idea behind the restaurant is that this is a place where you can have your favorite lobster Napoleon or tuna steaks with mango salsa while the kids have burgers and chicken wings. You should give it a try, if only to find out what the name means! [Year round, 7-days, AMEX, MC, V, Reservations accepted]

Hampton Bays

✪✪✪✪ **Edgewater's** (Italian/Continental) ("Casual") Montauk Highway, near the Shinnecock Canal, 723-2323. Last year this was "Galea's." This year, it's a ten times better! First, you can't beat the location. Right on the highway and just across the road from a lovely water view. In season, a table on the deck would be perfect. Fresh mozzarella and tomato, portobello mushrooms, great burgers and pasta. Roomy, airy and delightful with a very welcome bonus: these folks are not out to empty your wallets. Prices here are very reasonable for the quality of food available on the menu. [Year round, closed Feb., closed Mondays, reservations for 6 (+), V, MC, $]

✪✪✪✪ **Hampton Maid** (Breakfast) ("Casual") Montauk Highway, Hampton Bays, 728-4166 (just before the Shinnecock Canal going west). Now known as having the best country breakfast in the Hamptons, the folks at the Maid will stuff you with delightful egg dishes, pancakes fresh coffee, yum! Best cure for one of "those" Saturday nights… [April-Oct., Breakfast only, 7 days, CASH ONLY]

Montauk

✪✪✪✪✪ **(The) Harvest** (Seafood/Continental) ("Fine Dining"), 11 South Emery St., 668-5574. [Year round, Thurs.–Sun, AMEX, MC, V, DC, D, Reservations suggested]

✪✪✪✪ **The Lobster Roll** (called, simply, "Lunch") (Seafood) ("Casual") Montauk Highway., the Montauk side of Amagansett, 267-3740.

Imagine the typical, hectic, old New England-style clam chowder and lobster hut and you've got a pretty good picture of The Lobster Roll. And, man, their stuff is good! So, if you've got that hankering for fried clams and chowder, get on down! Their lobster salad is to die for, even at $24 (+) per pound ("market price")! Another great spot to bring the kids, too. [April–Oct, 7-days, AMEX, MC, V, No reservations taken]

✪✪✪✪ **the Pig 'n' Whistle** (Irish) ("Casual"), Montauk Highway, 267-6980. An Irish pub in a sandpit, full of brass, etched glass, and Irish hospitality. It reminds me of Runyon's…lots of deep-sea appetizers, great soups and salads, fish & chips, shepherd's pie, and Gaelic chicken! The kids will love it, too! [April–Oct, 7-days, AMEX, MC, V]

✪✪✪ **Gosman's Dock Restaurant** (Seafood) ("Casual") West Lake Dr., Montauk, 668-5330. There's not much that can beat an ocean-side dining experience, especially when the seafood is fresh, superbly prepared and served in a warm, cozy atmosphere. Gosman's is the place to go if you want that kind of experience. The "catch of the day" was caught that day—probably that very morning and hauled back to Gosman's in time for lunch. Gosman's Dock also has a fine group of specialty stores where you can shop before or after your meal. There's a great fish market, too. [April–Oct., 7-days, AMEX, MC, V, Reservations suggested]

✪✪✪ **Mr. John's Pancake House** (Breakfast) ("Casual") Main Street, 668-2383. Flap jack heaven! Crepes, waffles and homemade donuts, too. In summer, the line is out the door, so get there early (they open at 6:30 AM). You can't possibly walk away from here hungry. If you do, it's your fault. Best breakfast on this part of the East End. They also have great burgers, chowders, soups, and fish for lunch. [Year round, 7 days, breakfast & lunch ONLY, Reservations not needed—just show up and wait! Cash only, $]

✪✪ **Surfside Inn** (Seafood/American) ("Casual") Old Montauk Highway, Montauk, 668-5958. This little spot is hidden from most of the rest of the world out here because you have to cruise down Old Montauk Highway to find it. If you do, you'll be very happy. It's perched above the beach, has a nice little bar, and offers first rate seafood at very reasonable prices (sometimes two-for-ones!).

[Year round, 7 days April 1 to Nov. 1; Thurs.–Sun. Nov. to April, AMEX, MC, V, Reservations suggested for large parties]

The North Fork

✪✪✪✪ **Cliff's** (Steak, for sure!) ("Casual"). There are actually three locations: Cliff's Elbow Room, on the Main Road (Route 25) in Jamesport, 722-3292; Cliff's Elbow Too, Main Road in Laurel, 298-3262 and Cliff's Elbow East, Kenny's Road and North Sea Drive in Southold, 765-1203. They are all equally good. And if you're a vegetarian, don't bother crossing any of Cliff's transoms. You won't be happy because Cliff's is Nirvana for local steak lovers. Thick, juicy steaks, pepper encrusted steaks, rib eyes slathered in homemade sauce, prime rib as thick as a set of IRS regulations. Always crowded and you just have to show up and wait. But it's worth it. [Year round, 7 days, noon to 10PM, Weds., 3 to 10 PM, V/MC,AMEX, no reservations, $$]

✪✪✪✪ **Legends,** (American) ("Casual") 725 1st Street, New Suffolk, down by the water, 734-5123. And they are a local "legend." Follow the signs from Route 25 to find this lovely spot. Convivial, nautical and delightful. Excellent sandwiches, fresh seafood, great soups and many daily specials. [Year round, 7 days, lunch & dinner, V/MC/AMEX, Diners, Discover, reservations accepted, $$]]

✪✪✪✪ **The Seafood Barge** (Seafood) ("Casual") on the Old Main Road in Southold (Route 25), on the water, 765-3010. Really one of the nicest dining spots on the North Fork. Dine on the water and enjoy an excellent bar and wine list, too. Many daily specials, great sandwiches, wonderful seafood. Soft-shell crabs and crab cakes are some of my favorites here. [Year Round, 7 days, lunch & dinner, V/MC/AMEX, Diners, reservations accepted, $$]

✪✪✪ **Jamesport Country Kitchen** (American) ("Casual") on the main Road (Route 25) in Jamesport, 722-3537. This is where the locals on the North Fork hang out. And if the locals hang out here, you should, too. Cozy, warm, inviting. Lots of specials, homemade dishes, and great prices. [Year round, 6 days, closed Tues., lunch & dinner, brunch Sunday, V/MC/AMEX, no reservations, $$]

✪✪ **O'Donnell's** (American/Pub-style) ("Casual") 212 Front Street, Greenport, 477-9577. Slip in here for a quick brewski and a great burger. Eat at the bar or sit in comfort in the spacious dining room. Daily specials, too. Convenient to all downtown Greenport and the North Ferry terminal is right down the block. [Year round, 7 days, lunch & dinner, V/MC/AMEX, Diners, reservations accepted, $$]

Noyac

✪✪✪ **Coast Grill** (American) ("Casual") Noyac Rd., Southampton, 283-2277. Unpretentious, this gem sits by the roadside next to a small bay and marina on Noyac Road. The Coast Grill consistently gathers solid reviews for the quality of its food and the laid-back, waterside atmosphere. No summer in The Hamptons would be complete without a trip (or two, or three!) to The Coast Grill. Very good seafood selections! Great prices! [Year round, 7 days June 15 to Sept. 15; weekends only. Sept. to June, diner only, AMEX, MC, V, Reservations suggested for large parties]

Quogue

✪✪✪ **Inn at Quogue** (Regional American) ("Fine Dining"), 52 Quogue Street, Quogue, 653-6560. A gracious, wainscoted dining room centered on an old brick wood-burning fireplace—traditional New England atmosphere. Signature dishes include: New Zealand venison, lamb Wellington, and horseradish, herb-encrusted salmon. [Year round, 7 days May-Sept. Weds.-Sun. April-Oct., dinner only, V/MC/AMEX/Discover, reservations requested, $$$]

Sag Harbor

✪✪✪✪✪ **Serafina** (Italian) ("Fine Dining"), 29 Main St., 725-0101: Think: warm, traditional Italian food, a great bar and—in summer—sidewalk dining and you've got Serafina. Abundant pasta dishes, polenta with grilled shrimp that's astoundingly good, veal dishes like Grandma's in Abruzzi. It's all home cooking masterfully presented by the lovely couple that owns and run this gem of a spot. Myra and I spent New Year's Eve here to open our new Millennium, so you know how great we think it is. Serafina has expanded to stay open more of the year, but they are closed some days and weeks in the off season. Best to call ahead. [Seasonal, 7 days, AMEX, MC, V, Reservations suggested]

✪✪✪✪ **American Hotel** (French with Nouveau Cuisine) ("Fine Dining") 725-3535. A truly lovely spot that we don't get to often enough. The main dining room is all oak and tradition, and filled with warmth, great service, and grand food. To me, this is a perfect spot to begin a moonlit summer evening. Sip a cocktail on the front porch then walk down the block for the evening show at Bay Street Theatre. After the show slip back into the American Hotel's dining room for late supper. Doesn't get too much better. [Year round, 7 days, lunch Sat & Sun, AMEX, MC, V, DC, D, Reservations suggested]

✪✪✪✪ **La Superica** (Mexican) ("Casual") Main St., Sag Harbor, at the foot of the bridge, 725-3388. Arriba! Don't miss this place if you like frozen margaritas, chilled Coronas, and four-star Mexican. La Superica's beans are not "paste," the rice is not sticky, the chips are hot and crisp, the salsa is fresh, and all the entrees are lovingly prepared. You need to be prepared, though, to stand at the bar on a busy night. No reservations, first come, first served. Do go. It's a treat. [Year round, Thurs.–Sun., AMEX, MC, V, No Reservations taken]

✪✪✪✪ **Sen** (Japanese) ("Casual") 23 Main, Sag Harbor, 725-1774. If you have a "yen" for great sushi, sashimi, or mouth-watering tempura, Sen will satisfy you quite nicely, thank you. No reservations and you may end up standing outside on the sidewalk for an hour, but it'll be worth it. Best Japanese food in the Hamptons. Great place to grab a bite before or after the theater—Bay Street Theatre Festival is just a couple of doors down and the Sag Harbor Theater is across the street. [Year round, closed Tues., AMEX, MC, V, No Reservations taken]

✪✪✪ **Beacon** (Asian Inspired French & American) ("Fine Dining"), West Water St., Sag Harbor, 725-7088: The emphasis here is on seafood prepared with a French-Indochina flair—and a few fairly traditional American seafood dishes. You won't be disappointed with much here, if anything, especially since dinner comes with a spectacular water view; and, these are the same folks that run the very excellent Red Bar in Southampton. [March-Dec., 6 days, closed Tues., dinner only, V/MC/AMEX, no reservations, $$$]

✪✪✪ **B. Smith's** (Southern) ("Fine Dining"), Long Wharf, Sag Harbor, 725-5858. Yes, the very same Barbara Smith of modeling, TV fame, and restaurants in The City and Washington. "B," as she is known, and her husband Dan, secured what is absolutely the most beautiful waterfront restaurant location in The Hamptons and opened up a lovely, tastefully decorated restaurant. "Everyone" shows up: Billy Joel, Calvin Klein, and all the rest. This will be the third season and you should go, just for the atmosphere plus some great lobster, marvelous salads, homemade dishes that "B" whips up, and more. [April–Oct., 7-days, AMEX, MC, V, Reservations suggested]

✪✪ **Spinnaker's** (American) ("Casual") Main Street, Sag Harbor, 725-9353. A favorite spot for my wonderful in-laws and it should become one of your favorites, too. It's just solid, comfortable, tummy-warming cuisine. Lots of specials, great sandwiches, tasty chowders, good salads, and a comfortable bar. [Year round, 7 days, lunch & dinner, V/MC/AMEX/Diners, reservations accepted, $$]

Sagaponack

✪✪✪✪✪ **Alison by the Beach** (Country French) ("Fine Dining") 3593 Montauk Highway., Sagaponack, 537-7100. Same talented Alison who runs Alison on Dominick in Manhattan. Unfortunately, it's not right "by the beach" but close enough. The surf is about a mile away. The food is simply phenomenal. The cuisine tends toward light fish dishes, summer soups, salads, etc. I, of course, barbarian that I am, went right for the "steak frites"—a very nice strip steak with bordelaise sauce and skinny French fries that were even better than McDonald's. Wine list is good, service is excellent. The atmosphere is warm, cheery, and very romantic. Open nights only, 6 to 11. [Year round but closed mid-Feb. to mid-March, mostly weekends, AMEX, MC, V, DC, D, Reservations a must!]

Shelter Island

✪✪✪✪✪ **Michael Anthony's** (American/Continental) ("Fine Dining"), at the Dering Harbor Inn, 13 Winthrop Road, Shelter Island, 749-3460. Views of the water that are matched by absolutely scrumptious food. We've been spending quite a bit of time on Shelter Island of late, and we love this spot. Yes, it's a hike to get here, but if you take the time, trouble, and the ferry, you won't regret it. Make a day of it on the Island, then get to Michael Anthony's for dinner. You will not be disappointed. Michael takes the time, each day, to carefully select the ingredients for his menu, which, by the way, is delightfully crafted to please just about any palate, but is purposefully limited to not overextend and dilute. [Seasonal, April–Oct., 7 days, AMEX, V, MC, Reservations recommended]

✪✪✪✪ **Old Country Inn** (American) ("Fine Dining") Shelter Island, 749-1633: Sometimes I think these folks want to keep their light under a bushel. First, they're hard to find (call ahead for directions). Next, they don't advertise much nor do they publish their phone number! If you track them down you won't be disappointed. Small and intimate, in the dining room of an old country inn, the food is lovingly prepared and served expertly. The menu is a little eclectic, but when you call to make reservations (and you should!), ask what's cookin'. One of the Island's best kept secrets! [Seasonal, 7 days, lunch, dinner, brunch, V/MC/AMEX, Reservations required, $$$]

✪✪✪✪ **Sunset Beach,** (Seafood/American) ("Casual") 37 Shore Rd., Shelter Island Heights, 749-3000. Can't go to St. Bart's this year? No problem. Boogie on over to Sunset Beach on Shelter Island. Sure, it's a pain to get to Shelter Island since you have to take a ferry, but you won't be disappointed. Plan a whole day on the Island: Hike the Mashomack Preserve or park yourself on the beach in front of this restaurant until cocktail time. Sunset Beach is a cross between the tree house in Swiss Family Robinson and Carl Gustaf's spectacular hillside restaurant in St. Barth's Gustavia Harbor. If you're lucky enough to get a table prior to sunset, you'll see why this place is so aptly named. The open air and up-tempo Island music will absolutely transport you to the Caribbean—for a few hours, anyway. The staff is, well, "hippie chic," but they are wonderful, spirited, and capable. The food is fabulous. Great steak, shrimp, fresh fish and hearty salads stand out. The bartenders, I swear, can make any exotic drink you can name; and, they have a wonderful wine list. This is one terrific place. Don't miss it. [April–Oct, 7 days., AMEX, MC, V, Reservations suggested]

✪✪✪ **Chequit Inn** (American) ("Casual") 23 Grand Avenue, Shelter Island Heights, near the North Ferry, 749-0018. The Chequit ("Chee-quit") is the sister inn to The Ram's Head Inn and owned by the same good folks. A little more casual than the Ram's Head, but the same quality of food and service. In the warmer months there's a beautiful, flower bedecked outside patio available for dining. Music on most weekend nights. [Year round, 7 days, lunch & dinner, V/MC/AMEX, Reservations requested, $$]

✪✪✪ **Ram's Head Inn** (American) ("Fine Dining") Ram Island Drive, 749-0811. You just can't beat the Ram's Head for ambiance. It's nestled on a hillside overlooking the water. The dining room is open all year and continually proffers meal after excellent meal. The adjacent bar provides a languid respite form the cares of the world. This is a true escape and as romantic a restaurant as we have in the Hamptons. [Seasonal, closed in March, 3 days Apr-May, 7 days late May-Dec., dinner & brunch, V/MC/AMEX, Reservations requested, $$$]

Southampton

✪✪✪✪✪ **Savanna's** ("Contemporary American") ("Fine Dining") 268 Elm St., Southampton, 283-0202, fax 283-6034. The menu is wonderful: fresh local seafood, veal, pork, steaks, and homemade pastas. They have their own wood-burning oven, where they bake their own bread, rolls, and roasted entrees. All of the produce is organic. In the summer they have pavilion dining in an outside rose garden. You can step off the train in Southampton, walk across the street, and be on one of Savanna's comfortable barstools and a million miles away from the stress of The City in about a minute. Savanna's is cigar friendly, but you'll have to puff away in the pavilion or the rose garden. Oh, by the way, a wonderful brunch on weekends and lunch 7 days in season. [May–Nov., 7 days., AMEX, MC, V, DC, D, Reservations suggested]

✪✪✪✪ **basilico** (Italian/Mediterranean) ("Fine Dining") 10 Windmill Lane, 283-7987. (Yes, Philip, the owner, prefers the small "b" for "basilico"). This is another enduring—and endearing—restaurant that does not get its due. Basilico has a loyal following, as well it should, but if you have not yet experienced its charms I suggest you go there soon. Superb pasta dishes prepared in Philip's own signature style. Absolutely excellent breads, soups, salads, and desserts to accompany the many special dishes that Philip and his staff try so hard to provide. I also love the candlelit atmosphere, the great service, and the bar. When they're available behind the bar try the PineHamptons. Not quite as good as mine, but close. [Year round, 7-days, AMEX, MC, V, Reservations required on weekends]

✪✪✪✪ **The Golden Pears** (Gourmet/Health/Coffee/Takeout) ("Casual") Four Hamptons stores: 97-99 Main St., Southampton (283-8900); 2426 Montauk Hwy., Bridgehampton (537-1100); 34 Newtown Lane, East Hampton (329-1600); and Westhampton,103 Main St., (288-3600). The Golden Pear restaurants have established a well-deserved reputation for providing hearty, flavorful, and absolutely delicious casual fare. These four storefront operations are the best places in The Hamptons to zip into for a quick bite. Whether it's a hot bowl of homemade soup on a chilly winter day, a scrumptious sandwich and salad as you shop, or a quick muffin and coffee in the morning, you cannot beat any of the Pears. You might also try them for catering. (Westhampton closes for the winter, the other locations are open year 'round.) [Year round, 7 days, AMEX, MC, V, No Reservations taken]

✪✪✪✪ **La Parmigiana** (Italian/Pizza/Takeout) ("Casual") Hampton Rd., Southampton, 283-8030. "La Parm," as we locals call this spot, has been one of my personal favorite places for almost ten years now. There is just not a finer, family, home-style eatery in the Hamptons. This is like going home to Mama's kitchen in whatever part of Italy you claim as "home." The pasta is always "al dente," the peas, broccoli raab, sun dried tomatoes, eggplant, or whatever you like to toss in your pasta is always fresh and tasty. The pizzas are the best on the East End. Homemade soups abound with aroma and fresh ingredients. Huge antipastos and salads brimming with fresh Gorgonzola cheese will also delight. Order a carafe of house wine to go with your meal and top off this gastronomic extravaganza with a fresh cannoli or some other delightful dessert from the pastry case out front. The place is crowded and noisy but that is part of the charm. Get there early on summer nights—La Parm will be packed. [Year round, closed Mondays, AMEX, MC, V, walk-in reservations only]

✪✪✪✪ **Le Chef** (Continental/French) ("Casual") 75 Jobs Ln., Southampton, 283-8581. Le Chef is a very solid and commendable place. You'll always get an excellent meal at a good price. I also like the bar. It's a warm and cozy spot. Grab a stool and park your fanny for a while. The soups are wonderful and most of the entrees have a Gallic touch (i.e., a bit of garlic, but never too much). It's a wonderful location for lunch before or after the beach and a great spot to rest up after the exhausting shopping trip tromping up and down Jobs Lane. In the off season you can't beat their prix fixe meals. [Year round, 7-days, AMEX, MC, V, Reservations suggested]

✪✪✪✪ **Plaza Café** (Italian) ("Fine Dining") 61 Hill Street, behind the Southampton Cinema, 283-9323. This spot has been through several iterations over the past few years but the Plaza Caf=E9 has been here three years now and it looks as if it's going to stay. It's a Tuscan style eatery with many fine pasta and seafood dishes. The atmosphere is warm and pleasant, complimented on cool nights by a cozy fireplace. [Year round, 7 days, dinner only, V/MC/AMEX, Reservations requested, $$$]

✪✪✪✪ **Sant Ambroeus** (Northern Italian) ("Fine Dining") 30 Main St., Southampton, 283-1233. Refined, elegant, and oozing atmosphere. Superb food, well prepared, and served with style. Prices to match, of course, but not too much different than a comparable place in The City. After dinner check out the gelatto fountain in the front of the restaurant! (You know, for some reason, this place doesn't get as much credit as is due. It really is a treat. You should try it.) [April–Nov., 7-days, lunch and diner, AMEX, MC, V, Reservations recommended]

✪✪✪✪ **Red Bar** (French Inspired/Continental) ("Fine Dining") 210 Hampton Rd., 283-0704. Red Bar is the new "King." After opening two summers ago the team that runs this very fine place has done a superb job of turning this formerly staid and steady spot into the best eatery in the Hamptons. (For 27 years prior, this was Balzarini's.) The bar is tiny, but it is cozy and warm. The food, served in an atmosphere to equal the great bistros in Manhattan, has improved steadily and it's now our choice for the "best-of-the-best." Here you will find carefully crafted fish entrees, steaks to delight the most discriminating beef lover, soups and salads of exceptional quality and style, plus a tantalizing wine and champagne list. The Red Bar team has also expanded its horizon and, last year, opened another fine restaurant, the Beacon, in Sag Harbor. These folks are doing it right. This is the must-do place for fine dining in the new Millennium. [Year round, closed Tues., AMEX, MC, V, Reservations a must]

✪✪✪✪ Southampton Publick House (American/Microbrewery)

("Casual") at Bowden Square, 283-2800. I like this wonderful place a lot—for many reasons. First and foremost, as far as you folks that are reading this are concerned, the food is delightful. The menu tends toward sandwiches and salads, but there are many fine entrees and a number of superb specialties. The herb encrusted salmon is excellent: pink, moist, just a touch of herbs and garlic. If your cardiologist says OK, go for the fish and chips. Tasty, never greasy, just like in ol' London Town. And then there are the ribs. Oh my…the best ribs in the Hamptons. Beyond the food there are the fine folks who run this place. Sully, Kevin, and Charlie are just the best. Great hosts. They truly do care that you have a pleasant dining experience. Thirdly, there's the bar. Personally, my favorite bar in the Hamptons. But, hey, that's just me. You try it for yourself and tell me what you think. [Year round, 7 days, AMEX, MC, V, Reservations not required]

✪✪✪ Fellingham's (Continental/Burgers and Stuff) ("Casual") 17

Cameron St., Southampton, 283-9417 or 9674. Located just off Main Street, behind and to the left of the Chase Bank building. This place is a treasure. We're talking jalapeno poppers, popcorn shrimp, succulent baby-back ribs, marinated porterhouse, and an array of burgers named after famous sports personalities (I found the Cosell burger particularly amusing: "Plain, with nothing on top.") The service was excellent and Millie Fellingham, co-owner and hostess, was going from table to table greeting people and making them feel at home. Well, as Executive Director of the

Southampton Chamber of Commerce, Millie knew most of the patrons anyway. Hey, if you want linen and candlelight, we've got many other listings. But if you want solid, tasty, hearty, friendly and fun, go to Fellingham's. [Year round, 7-days, AMEX, MC, V, Reservations not required]

✪✪ **75 Main** (Continental) ("Fine Dining"), 75 Main Street (what a surprise!), 283-7575 (get it? " 75-75"? clever): The lady who owns this comfortable and inviting affair has been wondering for years now why I haven't put her in this book. Well, now she can stop wondering. You're finally "in." Why? Because you finally got a good chef and a menu worthy of your truly nice location. This place has always been an enigma to me. I mean, what a lovely spot! The bar is beautiful, the ambiance fine and the service is pretty good, too. But the food never made it for me. Now it does. Congratulations! You're doing great! Keep up the good work! [Year round, 7 days, dinner & brunch, V/MC/AMEX, Reservations requested, $$$]

✪✪ **Barrister's** (American) ("Casual") 36 Main Street, 283-6206. Venerable is a word I'd use here at Barrister's. They've been around a long time. But it's not stodgy. In fact, we've started to come here more often in the past few months. When you review as many places as we do, it's hard to get to them all as frequently as we would like (and your waistline takes a beating, too!). We haven't paid as much attention to barrister's as we should. It really is delightful. Lots of specials, very good prices, excellent chowders, sandwiches, and desserts. Great place to take a break from shopping or the daily grind in general. [Year round, 7 days, lunch, dinner, brunch, V/MC/AMEX/Diners/Discover, reservations accepted, $$]

✪✪ **The Driver's Seat** (American/Burgers and Stuff) ("Casual") 62 Jobs Ln., Southampton, 283-6606. In the summer, the place is jumpin'—especially at the back bar. In season there are some outdoor tables in the back where you can bask in the warm sun, weather permitting. The menu is eclectic and there are a number of "blue plate special" type entrees, but it's the burgers you want, served with a frosty mug. This is also an excellent place to bring the kids. Expand their horizons past McDonald's. [Year round, 7 days, AMEX, MC, V, No Reservations taken]

✪✪ John Duck's (German/Steaks) ("Casual") Prospect St., Southampton, 283-0311. I'm fudging a little on this one because (1) John Duck's serves more than German food and has been doing it well and consistently for many years; and (2) it's just about the ONLY place that serves German food anywhere here in The Hamptons. In any case, if you want a good sauerbraten, and you don't want to drive 25 miles, you can feel very comfortable at John Duck's. Walking into John Duck's is like stepping into a time warp: one that has the old red naugahyde chairs, a real piano player (Saturday nights) and waitresses that still stick pencils behind their ears! Order the prime rib, regular cut (it's huge!) and sample their locally famous chopped coleslaw. [Year round, closed Mondays, AMEX, MC, V, Reservations suggested]

✪✪ Paul's (Italian/Pizza and Sandwiches) ("Casual") 21 Hill St., Southampton, next to the Southampton Cinema, 283-1861. Paul's pizza is very good. You can have a slice before or after the show, or order the whole pie. The calzone is also exceptional. I like to pick up dough from Paul's, take it home to and make my own pizza, too. [Year round, closed Tuesdays, AMEX, MC, V, D Reservations not required]

Water Mill

✪✪✪✪✪ Mirko's ("Eclectic European") ("Fine Dining") Watermill Square, just behind the Post Office, 726-4444. Mirko's repeats as one of our favorite spots (all five years, now, as a matter of fact!) The bar is small—as is the entire restaurant—but its heart is big. I have seldom had finer meals, and the consistency impresses me, too. There are some exotic and wonderful central European dishes from time to time (the owner has roots in the former Yugoslavia), but everything they serve will knock your culinary socks off. The fish dishes and meats are truly exceptional. I also like the fact that whether you are a Captain of Industry, a Wall Street Tycoon or just plain folk like me, you will feel very special with Elaine's warm greeting and personal service. Reservations are extremely difficult to get in summer, but planning ahead will get you there. [In Season, Wed.–Mon, 5:30 til?; Oct.–April is Thurs.–Sun., 5:30 til? AMEX, MC, V, Reservations a must!]

✪✪✪✪ **Robert's** (Italian Coastal) ("Fine Dining") 755 Montauk Hwy., 726-7171: Located in what once was the old stagecoach stop in Water Mill. If this beautiful old colonial could talk, what stories it could tell. In the meantime, today's story is this: fabulous Italian Coastal cuisine prepared with an expert touch. We're talking whole roasted sea bass, shrimp and artichoke salad, handmade pastas and aromatic foccacia served piping hot. Even if you don't have a stagecoach, this is a must stop on your dining card. [7 days Mem. Day-Labor Day, 5 days off-season, dinner only, V/MC/AMEX, Reservations strongly suggested, $$$]

✪✪✪✪ **The Station Bistro** (Country French) ("Fine Dining") Station Rd., Water Mill, 726-3016, located in what used to be the LIRR Water Mill Depot. It feels like you've come home to dinner after being away far too long. On top of that, you're served an incredible country French meal! Do not fail to try one of Erica's home made soups—even if you don't like soup. The paté is to die for. The hearty French stews, country peasant chicken, and local seafood served French style will transport you gastronomically to Provence. Call ahead. The Station is a consistent winner and another Hamptons restaurant you should not miss. [Seasonal, 7 days; Oct–Dec, Thurs.–Sun; closed Jan–Mar; MC, V, Reservations preferred]

✪✪ **Meghan's Restaurant,** (American/Burgers and Stuff) ("Casual") Montauk Highway., Water Mill, 726-9657, across the street from the Water Mill Green. Big, juicy, succulent burgers topped with whatever you want in cheese, vegetables, chili, etc. They even have an excellent veggie burger and a decent turkey burger. Served with home fries. You'll soon forget about fast food burgers. [Year round, 7-days, cash only, No Reservations needed]

Westhampton

✪✪✪✪ **Belle's Café** (Caribbean/Cajun) ("Casual") at the Westhampton Airport, Gabreski Field, 288-3927. Hidden away in the airport's main administration building is this little gem of a restaurant with great food and extraordinarily reasonable prices. Great burgers, tuna sandwiches, daily specials, and soups. The iced tea is like nothing you've ever had! Every Thursday, year round, there's a free Blues jam and usually some live jazz Friday and Saturday, too. Sunday brunch is "mah-vell-us" as Billy Crystal might say. Well, you might not see Billy Crystal here but Tom Hanks has been by. So have all the Spielbergs. They park the jet there, you see, just outside the café door. [Year round, 7-days for breakfast & lunch, Thurs.–Sat. for dinner & Sunday brunch, cash only, no reservations needed)

Westhampton Beach

✪✪✪✪✪ **Atlantica** (Seafood) ("Fine Dining") 231 Dune Road, 288-6577: Amazingly, for a resort community that is water-oriented, we have very few good restaurants with water or ocean views. Atlantica is a spectacular exception. Here, you are right on the beach and the food matches the view—spectacular. This is also one of the few premier restaurants in the Hamptons that is equipped to handle large parties, weddings and the like. I love the outdoor deck—in good weather of course! Seafood par excellence! [Year round, 7 days, lunch & dinner, brunch on weekends, V/MC/AMEX, Reservations suggested, $$$]

✪✪✪✪ **Baby Moon** (Italian) ("Casual") Montauk Highway, 288-6350: Owned by the same family that owns La Parmigiana, another of our favorite places. And Baby Moon is just as great! This is superbly prepared Italian food in a home-style atmosphere. You can slip into a table in the deli section without too much of a wait or slide over to the slightly more formal dining room, but you may have to wait a little longer. The "pies" are grand, the fresh fish dishes delight, and the pastas..ooh..the pastas! Abundant and delicious. [Year round, 7 days, closed Mondays in winter, lunch & dinner, V/MC/AMEX, Reservations a must on weekends, $$]

✪✪✪✪ **Johnny Chih's** (Chinese) ("Casual") 85 Montauk Hwy., Westhampton Beach, 288-9191. Want the best, most intoxicating Chinese food in The Hamptons? Here's where you need to go. Served with Johnny's very own smile. [Year round, 7 days, AMEX, MC, V, No Reservations taken]

✪✪✪✪ **Starr Boggs** (Regional) ("Fine Dining") 379 Dune Rd. (in the Dune Deck Hotel), Westhampton Beach, 288-5250. Starr Boggs (that's the owner's name) is a consistent top pick on The Hamptons restaurant scene. Absolutely wonderful. First rate seafood. And the restaurant is right on the dunes, so on a good day, the view is pretty spectacular. [April through October, 7 days, lunch and diner, AMEX, MC, V]

✪✪✪ **The Post Stop Café** (American/Burgers & Stuff) ("Casual") 144 main St., Westhampton Beach, 288-9777. Whaddya do with an old Post Office? Well, in this case, you turn it into a pretty decent café. The food is warm, hearty, and made from really fresh stuff. Some of the best burgers in The Hamptons can be ordered here. Cozy bar, too, for those cool Fall evenings. In the Spring and Summer it's one of those rare spots out here where you can eat outside and watch the world stroll by.

Which of our Rated Restaurants are the "Most Romantic"?!

Here they are: (We wouldn't steer you to a spot that is simply romantic. It must have good food as well. In my family, food is love, so you know how important food is to us! Here are The Guide's recommendations for those spots that are "most romantic" and also have great food):

Alison by the Beach, Wainscott, 537-7100	French
American Hotel, Sag Harbor, 725-3535	French
Atlantica, Westhampton Beach, 288-6577	American
basilico, Southampton, 283-7987	Italian
Beacon, Sag Harbor, 725-7088	American
B. Smith's, Sag Harbor, 725-5858	Southern
Bobby Van's, Bridgehampton, 537-0590	American/Steak
Della Femina's, East Hampton, 329-6666	Continental
East Hampton Point, 329-2800	Brunch
Henry's, Bridgehampton, 537-5665	American
Farmhouse, East Hampton, 324-8585	French
Inn at Quogue, 653-6560	American
(the) Laundry, East Hampton, 324-3199	American
Maidstone Arms, East Hampton, 324-5006	Brunch
Mary Jane's. East Hampton, 324-8008	Italian
Michael Anthony's, Shelter Island, 749-3460	American

Mirko's, Water Mill, 726-4444	Continental
Nick & Toni's, East Hampton, 324-3550	Mediterranean
Old Country Inn, Shelter Island, 749-	American
Pacific East, Amagansett, 267-7770	Seafood
(The) Palm, East Hampton, 324-0411	American/Steak
Peconic Coast, East Hampton, 324-6772	Mediterranean
Ram's Head Inn, Shelter Island, 749-0811	American
Red Bar, Southampton, 283-0704	French
Sant Ambroeus, Southampton, 283-1233	Italian
Savanna's, Southampton, 283-0202	Continental/Italian
Serafina, Sag Harbor, 725-0101	Italian
Station Bistro, Water Mill, 726-3016	French
Starr Boggs, Westhampton Beach, 288-5250	Seafood
Sunset Beach, Shelter Island, 749-3000	Seafood/Steak

"We Love Kids!"

These are the Restaurants that we would rate as the most "kid friendly" places in the Hamptons (by location):

Location	Restaurant	Cuisine	Award
Amagansett	Mt. Fuji	Japanese	✪✪✪
Bridgehampton	Golden Pear	Soup/Sandwich	✪✪✪✪
	Poxabogue Café	Breakfast	✪✪
	World Pie	Italian	✪✪✪✪
	Yama-Q	Eclectic/Japanese	✪✪✪
East Hampton	Bostwick's	Seafood	✪✪✪
	Golden Pear	Soup/Sandwich	✪✪✪✪
	Rowdy Hall	American	✪✪
	Sam's	Italian	✪✪✪
	Zizzi Balooba's	Varied/Casual	✪✪
Hampton Bays	Edgewater's	Italian	✪✪✪✪
	Hampton Maid	Breakfast	✪✪✪✪
Montauk	Gosman's	Seafood	✪✪✪
	Lobster Roll	Seafood	✪✪✪✪
	Mr. John's Pancake House	Breakfast	✪✪✪✪
	Surfside Inn	American/Seafood	✪✪
North Fork	Jamesport		

			Rating
	Country Kitchen	American	✪✪✪
	Legend's	American	✪✪✪✪
	Seafood Barge	Seafood	✪✪✪✪
Sag Harbor	La Superica	Mexican	✪✪✪✪
	Spinnaker's	American	✪✪
Southampton	Driver's Seat	American	✪✪
	Fellingham's	Cont./Casual	✪✪✪
	Golden Pear	Soup/Sandwich	✪✪✪✪
	La Parmigiana	Italian	✪✪✪✪
	Mt. Fuji	Japanese	✪✪✪
	Paul's	Italian	✪✪
	Publick House	American	✪✪✪✪
Water Mill	Meghan's	American	✪✪
Westhampton	Belle's	Caribbean/Cajun	✪✪✪✪
West. Beach	Baby Moon	Italian	✪✪✪✪
	Johnny Chih's	Chinese	✪✪✪✪
	Post Stop Café	American	✪✪✪

RUBBISH & TRASH REMOVAL

Hmmm…Interesting that this follows right behind "Restaurants." Anyway, if you don't want to "mess" with taking your own garbage to one of the local dumps, er, I mean "Recycling Centers" (see "Dumps & Dumping" or "Garbage & Trash"), you can hire a local Carter. Here are some folks who can clean up after you.

✪✪✪✪ **S & P Sanitation,** Water Mill, 726-9500. S & P services the entire East End, picks up on a regular schedule, and also does debris removal (like that big pile of brush in your back yard!).

✪✪✪✪ **Norsic,** Henry Rd., Southampton, 283-0604. Also has full residential service, plus commercial service, but serves mostly Southampton and Bridgehampton areas.

S

SAILING

Sailing is a wonderful sport—a delightful hobby; but, as the old salt once said, the classic definition of a sailboat is: "a hole in the water surrounded by fiberglass into which one pours money." How true, how true. In any case the East End is a sailor's heaven. There is everything from the challenge of the pounding Atlantic to the safe havens of Peconic Bay. If you already have a boat, there are lots of marinas and service providers. If you don't own a boat, there are a number of reliable boat dealers (see "Boats"). If you want to charter or rent a boat for a day here are some suggestions.

✪✪✪✪**Tompkins Yacht Sales**, Ltd., Bay Street, Sag harbor, 725-5100. Jim Tompkins has a small fleet of 20-foot day sailers for rent as well as a couple of larger boats, a 28-footer and a 34-footer, that are available for charter. You can join his sailing club for a flat fee for the season which will get you a number of day rentals at a better price.

✪✪✪✪ **Uihlein's,** Montauk Harbor, Montauk, 668-3799. Uihlein's can arrange just about anything for you right up to the 50-foot motorsailer. They are a reliable company and one that also believes in giving you the boating instruction that you need to have a safe and enjoyable time.

✪✪✪ *Alyan,* a 45-foot Sparkman & Stephens sloop, is available for everything from day charters to long cruises to New England. Sleeps up to 8, lessons available. Call Bruce Tait, 24-hours, 725-7253 (Sag Harbor).

SCHOOLS

(See also "Colleges and Universities" for schools of higher education) The local schools are probably of great concern to you if you're moving out here and have school age children. The scores and quality of the public schools out here varies from district to district. Frankly, some districts are better than others. What's the best measure? Standardized test scores on the State exams are probably the only universal measure of all our districts. In that regard, the Sag Harbor, Shelter Island, and Tuckahoe School Districts are better than the others, but, candidly, none of the districts will really knock your socks off when it comes to Statewide test scores. I wish it weren't so and I don't understand why it isn't so, but, there you have it. Beyond the "numbers," talk to your real estate broker and any friends or acquaintances you might have out here—folks with school age children. Then you'll get the real low-down. For information and enrollment call the appropriate local school district. We also have a number of parochial and private schools. They, too, are listed after the public schools.

These are the local public school districts. If you're unsure which one may apply to you, just call your first choice, and give them your address. They can tell you if you have the right one.

Amagansett:
Amagansett Schools: 267-5372 and 267-4049
Bridgehampton:
Grades K–12, Office & School: 537-0271
East Hampton:
District Office: 329-4100
Montauk:
(call East Hampton number, above)
Sagaponack:
Grades 1–4, Office & School: 537-0651
Sag Harbor:
District Office: 725-5300
Pierson High School (grades 6–12): 725-5302
Sag Harbor Elementary (grades K–5): 725-5301
Shelter Island:
Island Schools Office: 749-0302
Southampton:
District Office: 283-6800
Southampton High School (grades 9–12): 283-6800
Southampton Intermediate School (grades 5–8): 283-6800
Southampton Elementary School (grades K–4): 283-6661
Springs:
Springs Public School: 324-0144
Tuckahoe (Southampton):
Pre–K thru 8: 283-3550

Westhampton Beach:
District Office: 288-1503

Here are some of the parochial and private schools. I say "some" because the picture seems to change yearly. Little schools and "academies," some of which are nothing more than "at-home" schools or small classes in someone's living room, do pop up once in a while. Best to check these out with the local school district office or get solid recommendations. Please note: this is a listing of parochial and private schools for your convenience. These are not recommendations. We don't have school age children; so, it's best that you do your own "due diligence" and check these folks out for yourselves. You should…you'll be paying a pretty penny for them.

Parochial Schools:

Immaculate Conception Pre-School, Westhampton Beach, 288-9128
Our Lady of the Hamptons Regional Catholic School, Pre-K thru 8, Southampton, 283-9140
South Fork Christian School, N–8, Water Mill, 726-4987
Stella Maris Regional School, N–8, Sag Harbor, 725-2525
St. Therese Parish School, N, Montauk, 668-5353

Private Schools:

Child Development Center of the Hamptons:
Amagansett: 267-0133
East Hampton: 324-3229
Country School, Amagansett, 267-6995
Hampton Bays Children's Center, 728-2064
Hampton Day School, Bridgehampton, 537-1240
Hayground School, Bridgehampton, 537-7068
Peconic Montessori School, Southampton, 287-4022
Pioneer School, Bridgehampton, 537-7122
Raynor Country Day School, Westhampton, 288-4658
Ross School
East Hampton, 329-8168
Sag Harbor, 725-7198
Tuller School, North Haven (Sag Harbor), 725-1181

SEAFOOD (see "Clambakes," "Fish Markets" and peruse the "Restaurant" listings to find great seafood places!)

SECURITY COMPANIES—HOMES (see also "Alarm Companies")

We have an alarm system connected to a central monitoring station. The staff at the station contacts a list of folks we specify or calls the police if we cannot be reached. We also have a "panic button" and a special voice code. If the alarm goes off and we don't respond with the right code over the phone or if we just don't answer, they dispatch the police immediately. The local gendarmes are pretty good at responding, by the way. What happens if it's a false alarm? You get, maybe, two "free" mistakes a year. After that the local police start charging for false alarms: it's $25 a pop in Southampton Town!

Alarm Service (only):

✪✪✪✪ **General Security** (central monitoring—no patrols): 349-8989, and about $300 per year.

Alarm and regular patrol service:

✪✪✪✪ **Bellringer Communications**: 283-3400
✪✪✪ **Holmes Protection**: 283-0569

SECURITY COMPANIES—PERSONAL SECURITY

With all the rich and famous out here, there is a need for personal security (i.e., "bodyguards"). When fans of the Guide start mobbing me on the street for my autograph (Right!) I'm going to call.

✪✪✪✪ **Mike Zimet Enterprises, Inc.,** 718-601-2984 or beeper at 917-759-8012. Ask for my friend Mike Zimet. Mike's a great guy and even though his office is in Riverdale, he does a ton of work out here. And he's the best. Lots of high profile celebrity parties, Presidential security cooperation, Hamptons International Film Festival, armored limos, etc. You'll feel safe with Mike and his troops around.

✪✪✪✪ **New York Security Group,** Southampton, 287-5426. Another good choice: These folks tend to a number of high-profile clients and secure high-profile events, like the Bridgehampton Mercedes polo matches. They specialize in private parties, body-guarding, film production security and even do video surveillance.

SELF STORAGE

There are a couple of good places out here where you can dump the bikes, store the plastic pool toys, and put up the lawn furniture.

✪✪✪✪ **Mark Press Moving & Storage, Inc.,** Southampton, 283-2110. M. Press is one of our top-rated moving companies, and they have excellent storage facilities as well.

✪✪✪✪ **Despatch Self Storage,** 229 Butter Ln., Bridgehampton, 537-4500. These folks have heated indoor storage, electronic gates, sprinklers, and on-site managers.

✪✪✪ **Southampton Mini-Storage,** Mariner Drive, Southampton, 283-2211, near the Southampton railroad station. Climate controlled, elevators to multi-level storage, computerized gate access.

✪✪ **Hampton Bays Self Storage,** Montauk Highway, Hampton Bays, 728-1000, near Sterns Department Store and next to Hampton Bays Diner. Climate control, alarms, fireproofing, controlled gate access.

✪✪ **East Hampton Self Storage,** right off Route 114, near Cove Hollow Road, 329-5000. New facility, climate controlled, video surveillance, computerized gates.

SEPTIC TANKS (see "Cesspools")

SHERIFF'S DEPARTMENT

The Suffolk County Sheriff has jurisdiction in the entire county we live in. They cooperate extensively with the local police departments. The Sheriff is the "super cop" for Suffolk County and they handle the really serious stuff, major investigations, or tragedies, and they run the county jail. They have a very fine police academy and that's where most of the local "PD's" send their new officers for training. The Riverhead headquarters office is 852-2200.

SHOES

Madonna has 3,500 pairs of shoes in her closet. Wow…her closet must be bigger than our whole house! Even if you're not Madonna, here's where to go to keep your tootsies warm and fashionably shod.

The best Athletic Shoes:

✪✪✪✪ **Gubbins Running Ahead,** 7 Windmill Ln., Southampton, 287-4945; or, 86 Park Pl., East Hampton, 329-7678. A complete selection of training and cross training shoes and equipment. Nice store.

✪✪✪ **The Athelete's Foot,** Bridgehampton Commons, 537-1930, offers all the latest and greatest in footwear for the athelete—or those of us who like to think we are.

The best for Men's and Women's Dress & Casual Shoes:

✪✪✪✪✪ **Sak's,** in Southampton, corner of Main Street, 283-3500. The expanded shoe selection at Sak's is the absolute best in The Hamptons.

✪✪✪✪ **Bass Shoe Outlet** at the Tanger Mall, Riverhead or the Bass Shoe Outlet in Amagansett, Hedges Ln., 267-1029. One of my favorite stores! Been wearin' them Weejuns for thirty years.

✪✪✪✪ **Joan & David,** Hedges Ln., Amagansett, 267-3358. Joan & David is an institution out here and they have consistently offered the best in women's footwear.

✪✪✪✪ **Stubbs & Wooton,** 14 Jobs Lane, Southampton, 283-7332. (Also in The City and Palm Beach). The best dress and casual shoes, hands down. Or, better put, "hand crafted." These folks are so traditional and meticulous they still consider themselves to be cobblers. (My personal favorites are the "devil shoes"—go and see for yourself!)

✪✪✪ **Timberland,** Tanger Mall, Riverhead, 369-5282 (see also "Malls"). Great outdoor shoes and boots. Excellent prices.

SHOE REPAIR

Here's what we have and remember: these folks are often good in a pinch to repair anything leather (handbags, leather pants, etc.) as well as market umbrellas, canvas backing, seat cushions and so forth.

✪✪✪ **Cobbler Shop of East Hampton,** 84A Park Pl., East Hampton, 324-3248

(Bronze—but not for "bronze shoes") **Luciano Shoe Repair,** 48 Park Pl., East Hampton, 329-0287

SHOPPING

Shopping is an Olympic Sport here in The Hamptons. And there are lots of great places to shop. First, let me direct you to our "10 Most Fun Things to do in The Hamptons" section. This entry describes what we think is the ultimate Hamptons shopping trip—and it can all be done in one long day. It features our top award-winning shopping spots. You'll have a blast! Next, I will refer you to some specific categories elsewhere in the Guide that offer wonderful shopping experiences. Check these out:

- **Antiques**
- **Ceramics**
- **Children's Wear**
- **China & Glassware**
- **Department Stores**
- **Gift Shops**
- **Malls**
- **Men's Clothing**
- **Shoes**
- **Women's Clothing**
- **Thrift Shops**

SMALL CLAIMS COURT (see also "Bad Checks")

If you have a monetary dispute with someone who resides or owns a business in Suffolk County and the dispute originated in Suffolk County, and the value of that dispute is $3,000 or less, you can have a day in court. You must file in person. In Southampton Town, call 283-6000 ext. 248. In East Hampton Town, 324-4134.

SMOKING

The state prohibits or strictly limits smoking in nearly all public indoor settings. The Clean Indoor Air Law prohibits smoking in elevators, auditoriums, theaters, and on school grounds. Smoking is allowed only in restaurants with separate, ventilated sections. It's only allowed in bars if your sales are more than 60% booze. After June 30th, 1998, all of Suffolk County became (God forbid!) like California; that is, NO SMOKING anywhere indoors! But who the $%$#$@# wants to be like California!!! The land of the "fruits and the nuts," as they say. And California isn't too thrilled about the new total smoking ban in public places, either. The local Chambers of Commerce and a group of County merchants have sued to block enforcement of the law. They have not been very successful. What they are striving for is no smoking in dining rooms and smoking allowed in bars if there is "outside ventilation." In the meantime, some restaurants are setting up private, enclosed (or vented) smoking areas if it's economically feasible for them to do so. Most, however, have given up. It's a rare place in the Hamptons these days that'll let you puff away indoors. About the only place I know of is the Cigar Bar in Sag Harbor.

SNAKES

Don't need to worry a great deal about this one. We don't have any poisonous snakes to deal with out here. You will see big garter snakes and a few noxious reptiles that look pretty big and mean, but they're good for your garden. They engage in natural, environmental pest control (they eat mice, for example. Ugh!). And they're just as afraid of you as you are of them. Unfortunately, the nastiest snakes we have on the East End tend to have two legs.

SNOW REMOVAL

Generally, the best folks to remove the snow from your driveway (or roof if the winter is particularly bad) are your landscapers. They know your property and they obviously aren't doing much landscaping with three feet of snow on the ground! Most of them buy and/or have snow removal equipment to augment their businesses.

✪✪✪✪ **John Leuthardt,** 878-1387.

✪✪✪ **Tom Tillinghast,** 19 Woods lane, East Hampton, 324-6555

SPAS (as in spas and hot tubs)

✪✪✪✪ The company and the supplier we'd turn to so as not to get "soaked" so to speak would be: **Sparkling Pools and Harbor Hot**

Tubs, Division St., Sag Harbor, 725-3983. Ask for Gus. Competitive prices, terrific service, quality construction.

SPAS (as in spa treatments)

✪✪✪✪ **Naturopathica,** in the Red Horse Plaza, Montauk Highway, east Hampton, 329-2525. Think soft, quiet, perfume scented evenings…think of exotic places like a Sultan's palace in ancient Persia…a Mandarin's private residence in ancient China…think: warm oils and fragrant herbs being rubbed all over your back…Mmmm. Wonderful! That's what you'll find here at "Natch-ro-path-ica," the finest spa treatments on the East End. Ginger and lemongrass massage, cranberry body polish, green tea herbal wrap, seaweed body wraps and more. After all those oils and herbs you'll not only feel rejuvenated you'll look good enough to eat!

SPRINKLER COMPANIES/IRRIGATION

Most places out here, whether owned or rented, have sprinkler systems—and this is generally the one household system people screw up the most. Almost everyone sets the timers wrong or waters too much or too little. Believe me, you'll do yourself a favor if you take the time to read the *$@&!^% instructions on the sprinkler box and consult with a good irrigation specialist. You should also have an irrigation professional purge or "blow out" your system before the ground freezes in the Fall. This involves shooting high-pressure air through all your sprinkler pipes, valves, and sprinkler heads. This "blow out" service costs a lot less than letting water freeze in your irrigation pipes. If the frost goes deep enough (as it does most winters) it will burst the pipes. Remember that these are plastic pipes! You'll have to dig up your yard and replace the pipes in the Spring if you're not conscientious about this. The best company I know is:

✪✪✪✪ **Bradie Sprinkler**, 653-4142. Quick, efficient, reliable work by a team that is truly expert. I've been working with these good folks for a bunch of years now. I've had them add, subtract, replace, retrench, service, and purge the heck out of two residences now and they do it well for a fair price. Honest, too!

STATIONERS/STATIONERY STORES

✪✪✪ **Lemarc's Hallmark,** Bridgehampton Commons Shopping Center, Bridgehampton, 527-2855. Excellent selection of greeting cards and small gifts plus a terrific selection of cards you can easily customize for all types of occasions (weddings, bar mitzvahs, graduations, all types of birthday parties, etc.).

✪✪✪ **Dunkerly's,** 137 Main Street Southampton, 283-5061, as well as 134 front Street in Greenport, 477-2710. Pretty good selection of standard stationery supplies as well as forms, folders, labels, pens, envelopes and more. They also do repairs on a wide range of small office machines.

✪✪ **Southampton Stationery,** 18 Hampton Rd., Southampton, 283-1964. Located down the street from Sak's, this small but well stocked stationery store has a great selection of greeting cards, small gift items, legal forms, a notary service, fax service, UPS service, party supplies, organizers, pens, lottery tickets and some stationery.

STEREO

✪✪✪✪ **Charos Custom Audio/Video,** 28 Cameron St., Southampton, 283-4428, has been on the local scene for a long time and has a reputation for fair prices and good service. They do just about everything from wiring up your new stereo system to installing complete home theaters. They also have satellite dishes, cellular phones, and audio supplies.

STOCKBROCKERS

If you've teamed up with a broker in The City, it's likely that you'll stay with that broker as you laze away your summer hours in The Hamptons. But remember: your broker may be out here, too, since he or she needs to spend the money you've been forking over in commissions.

If you want to make a permanent arrangement with a broker in The Hamptons or if you want a local outlet for your city account, there are some first rate firms with top-notch offices out here.

✪✪✪✪ **Mary Ellen Kay of Prudential Securities,** 3 Railroad Ave., East Hampton, 329-7290. Mary Ellen knows the business and has established a very firm reputation for customer service (I've talked with some of her clients!). She is also a very active member of the community and supports a number of worthy causes. In addition, she does a very clever and insightful daily stocks report on both Beach Radio (104.7 FM) and WEHM, 96.7 FM. Stop by her office on Hampton Road by the train station. Get the latest quotes, a hot cup of coffee, and Mary Ellen's smile.

✪✪✪✪ I like a good, solid local firm with feet firmly planted in the home soil. Call me old-fashioned. If you agree, call my friends at **Tucker Anthony** in Southampton, 131 Main St. (across from Sak's), 283-4731. See Richard or Brian Nydegger (father and son team, and that's nice to see in the business, too!). These folks know the area, its special needs, and offer a relationship-oriented approach to serving your financial requirements. Good guys—go talk with them.

STORAGE (see "Self Storage")

SUPERMARKETS (see also "Grocery Stores")

We don't have too many SUPERmarkets, in the traditional sense. Lots of "local markets" or "grocery stores," yes, but not too many large or "super-sized" markets. The old IGA chain has one or two outlets still clinging to life in The Hamptons but by far the BEST supermarkets are.

✪✪✪✪ America's first supermarket chain, Long Island's own **King Kullen.** The local King Kullen stores are in the Bridgehampton Commons Shopping Center, 537-8103, and in Hampton Bays, 260 W. Montauk Hwy., (just past south of Exit 65 off Rte. 27), 728-9621. These stores represent as fine a supermarket group as you'll find anywhere. The Bridgehampton store recently finished a bold expansion program, taking over more space in the Commons and adding a dry cleaners as well as a new dairy section. The produce department is not as good, naturally, as stopping by one of our many farm stands, but not bad. The meat department provides cuts better than many specialty meat stores we've been to. The Hampton Bays store is new and very well laid out. They are both clean, attractive, and offer everything you could find in supermarkets "up island"—and maybe more.

✪✪✪ **Waldbaum's,** two stores locally, Newtown Lane, East Hampton,

324-6215 and Main Street, Southampton, 283-0045. Waldbaum's took over two aging and dowdy A&Ps at these locations; the changes have been welcome. The stores are cleaner, better laid out and better stocked.

SURFING

Well, this is one area where The Hamptons is not always paradise. We don't have any big "pipelines" or major surfing beaches. We'll get a few 3–4 foot waves once in a while, but our beaches tend to be much too gently sloped to get any big wave action. Except during hurricanes. And if you're out surfing in a hurricane you need this Guide only to help locate a "shrink." I am told that this is a great place to learn to surf, though, because it is seldom too frightening to be intimidating. I am not the expert, but these folks are. They can give you all the latest and best on this subject.

✪✪✪✪ **Main Beach Surf & Sport,** Montauk Highway, Wainscott, 537-2716. Boards, wet suits, kayaks, canoes, rollerblades, beach accessories, sunglasses, lessons and rentals. They also sponsor the local beach and surf report on Beach Radio (FM 104.7).

✪✪✪ **Bridgehampton Surf,** Bridgehampton Commons, 537-5663. A complete line of surfboards and accessories, also providing rentals, repairs, and lessons. You can also catch a daily surf report provided by Bridgehampton Surf at 537-5623.

✪✪✪ **Sunrise to Sunset,** 21 Windmill Ln., Southampton, 283-2929. A full line of water sports products, boards, suits, beachwear, etc.

✪✪ **Espo's Surf & Sport,** 57 Main St., East Hampton, 329-9100. Complete line of boards and accessories, plus lessons, service, and rentals.

SWIMMING—FOR FUN

There are so many homes our here with pools that we tend to forget, well, what if you don't have a pool? Where can you take a swim? There are no public pools that I'm aware of anywhere in The Hamptons. We had a ballot proposal in '98 to build a YMCA pool in Hampton Bays but it lost by a wide margin. Some of the Health Clubs have indoor pools (Omnihealth). Some of the beach and tennis clubs have outdoor pools (Bridgehampton Surf & Tennis and East Hampton Indoor Tennis). Many of the larger hotels and motels have pools (Gurney's, Montauk Yacht Club). Best swimming advice I can give you, if you don't have access to a pool, is: Go to the beach! The ocean waters around here, even in Summer, are not tropical, with temperatures mostly in the 50s, but sometimes it'll creep into the 60s and every once in a blue moon, we'll have a 70 degree day. Now, that's bliss!

SWIMMING POOLS—SERVICE (see "Pool Service")

SWIMMING POOLS—
CONSTRUCTION & SUPPLIES
(see "Pools—Construction")

SYNAGOGUES

For our friends of the Jewish Faith, there are three choices for religious activities here on the East End.
- (1) **The Jewish Center of The Hamptons**, 44 Woods Lane, East Hampton, 324-9858, Rabbi David Gelfand.
- (2) **Temple Adas Israel** (Conservative-Reform), Elizabeth St., & Atlantic Ave., Sag Harbor, 725-0904, Rabbi Dr. Paul Steinberg.
- (3) **Congregation Tifereth Israel,** 519 Fourth Street, Greenport, Rabbi Harold Spivak, 477-0232

T-SHIRTS

A sure sign that we have become a tourist community will be when we have a T-shirt shop on every corner. Thank goodness we aren't there—yet. But we do have a couple of good T-shirt shops.

✪✪✪✪ **Breezin' Up,** 54 Jobs Lane, Southampton, 283-5680 and 21 Main St., East Hampton, 329-9370. This is where you find your "signature" Hamptons T-shirts, tank tops, sweatshirts, shorts, etc. Rack after rack of product with some version of "The Hamptons" stamped on it will allow you to select that piece of outer wear that's just right for cousin Bob in Idaho or sister Lucy in San Diego. It is, by the way, where you buy the T-shirt that you want to flaunt when you're walking about in Central Park. Breezin' Up closes down at the end of the season, and when they do (usually by Thanksgiving) that's when they unload everything that hasn't sold during the season. Shorts for $5, T-shirts, too. And sweatshirts for less than half price.

✪✪✪✪ **Montauk Clothing Co.,** 787 Main St., Montauk, 668-1281. HUGE selection of first-rate imprinted T-shirts, "sweats," shorts, and casual gear. Excellent selection of bathing suits, too.

TAILORS

✪✪✪✪ I like **Joseph's Tailor Shop,** 8 N. Main St., Southampton, 283-0244. I tried Joseph for the first time last year and he did a very fine job taking in three of my suits (Yes! Finally! Taking in instead of letting out!). Delivered on time, as promised.

TAXES

Well...as you might expect, taxes out here aren't low—especially property taxes. But compared to what you might think—since this is, after all The Hamptons—even property taxes aren't terrible; not considering the wonderful quality of life. Assessed values are meaningless—incomprehensible, really. They have no relation to "market value," i.e., what you're going to pay for a home. The Assessors first establish what they call "full value." My experience is that it's about 50% of market value. Your assessed value is 4–8% of "full value," depending on the Town in which you live. Your tax rate is about 30% of assessed value. Confused yet? I am! OK, here's an example (for Southampton Town): A house with a market value of $750,000 (average these days for a 1-acre, single family home) is going to pay about $6,750 in property taxes. If you don't happen to know the appraised value of a property, especially if you're looking to buy and wondering how much you're going to get socked with in property tax, here's a pretty good rule of thumb: estimate property taxes at 1% of the purchase price.

Property tax valuation could change, though, if the move to create Peconic County actually happens. The backers of Peconic County claim that property taxes could go down by as much as 50%. Don't hold your breath—the Peconic County Initiative got seriously slammed in '98.

By the way, if you're a Veteran (combat or not), be sure to apply for the homeowner's exemptions for veterans! The forms are available in the local Assessor's offices.

Another new—and wonderful—property tax exemption is the STAR (School Tax Relief) program. School expenditures are a BIG chunk of our property tax bills! The state passed a school tax exemption plan for all homeowners that is being phased in over the next three years. It doesn't matter whether you have kids or not. Property taxes lost to schools are being replaced from State revenues and to qualify you must fill out a simple, one-page form and provide proof of residency for the property you are exempting. The average STAR savings is going to be about $700. If you're over 65 with an income less the $60,000, there's an enhanced version of STAR that will save you even more. You must apply for and file this exemption through the local assessor's office by March 1 of any year.

Sales taxes are a pain. The current rate is 8.5%. The rate is going to stay this high for awhile, most likely, so our "benevolent legislators" can continue to pay off the disaster that was previously scheduled to become the Shoreham Nuclear Power Plant.

TAXIS

We're talking regular old cabs here, not limos, which are covered under the "Limousines" category. So if you need a regular ol' cab here are some folks to call.

✪✪✪✪ **Hampton Coach Taxi,** 283-0242. I have found these guys to be the most reliable at pick-ups and being on time; 24-hours, 7 days.

✪✪✪ **A Taxi,** 725-8900 or 324-3377. (as in "call a taxi"…cute!) 24-hour service, local and long distance, corporate accounts.

✪✪ **Hampton Town Taxi,** Southampton, 283-1900

✪✪ **Pink Tuna** (Yes, the cabs are pink!) Montauk, 668-3838

TELEPHONE (services)

Bell Atlantic (ex-NYNEX) dominates the local phone market, and they're actually not too bad. If you need service or installation call 890-6611 for home service, 890-1598 for business service, or toll free 1-800-722-2300. Locally, we now have call waiting, caller ID, three-way calling and *69 service (to get the number of the last incoming call), but we've yet to get voice mail. Would be nice, Bell Atlantic.

TELEVISION (as in local TV)

Since we are so close to the one of the world's most saturated television markets (New York City), there hasn't been a big impetus to develop much of a local TV market. But that's changing. Channel 12, ("News 12 Long Island") broadcasting from up-island, does very well as our local 24-hour news channel. WLIW, Channel 21, is likewise doing respectable programming as the Long Island PBS affiliate. Out here, on the East End, the choices are more limited. Our local access channel is WVVH, Channel 23, in East Hampton (537-0273). You really should watch it sometime. It is, as they say, a "hoot." There is some pretty respectable and credible programming here, as in Bill Fleming's "Our East End" show, but some of the other what I call "Ego-Vision" is absolutely hilarious. What some people won't do to get on TV.

TELEVISION (as in production)

Only one place to turn to but they are the best.

✪✪✪✪ **Black Sheep Television**, Westhampton Airfield, 288-5477. If you're interested in producing that corporate video, training tape, television show, radio commercial, voice-over, or whatever call these guys. Their rates will be much better than in The City and the quality will be just as good.

TENANTS RIGHTS (see "Renters Problems")

TENNIS CLUBS, COURTS

The best way to get a tennis game is to find someone who has a tennis court and make friends; or, alternatively.

✪✪✪✪ **East Hampton Indoor Tennis,** 175 Daniel Hole Rd., across from the East Hampton Airport, East Hampton, 537-8012. Tennis is one of my passions, and it hurts not being able to play in January and February. East Hampton Indoor Tennis can be the cure! But don't just go in Winter. The outdoor courts are great, too. In fact, these folks probably have the absolute best indoor and outdoor Fast Dry courts in the area. This is a place for people who really love—and live—tennis. Scott Rubenstein runs the club with a firm but gentle hand, and if you arrive without a playing partner, he'll line you up with someone at your level. A friend of mine who is a dedicated and terrific player said she has never had so much great tennis available—year round—in her life. If you're new to tennis or want to take some lessons they have a first rate training program headed by Paul Annacone who is, if you didn't know, Pete Sampras' coach. The head pro is Vincent Horcasitas. There are women's leagues, summer day camps for kids, and they're added an outdoor pool! In Summer there's always a waiting list, so move fast! Also check out their website at www.peconic.net/ehit/.

✪✪✪✪ **Bridgehampton Tennis & Surf Club,** 747 Mid Ocean Dr., Bridgehampton, 537-1180. 14 Har-Tru courts located on the ocean. Fully equipped pro shop, lessons, Olympic sized pool, cabanas and lockers, Club House (where you can have private parties), lunch and snacks overlooking the beach, exercise classes, nursery, and sports camps. Private beach and "beach boys" (yikes! I mean "beach persons"!) to haul chairs and snacks to and from the sand, set up your umbrellas, etc. Membership limited: A family member-ship (parents, all children under 21, and the "Nanny") for tennis, beach, and pool facilities runs about $7,700 for the season (May 29–Labor Day). Full, single memberships are also available for $3,300. Private cabanas are extra and range from $1,650 to $3,300 (but can be shared with up to two families).

✪✪ **Hither Hills Racquet Club,** Montauk Highway, Amagansett, 267-8525 (in season). 5 Har-Tru courts, limited membership, club-house, reasonable rates.

TENNIS COURT CONSTRUCTION/REPAIR

✪✪✪✪ **Court Order, Inc.,** P.O. Box 1764, Quogue, 653-0132. They build, resurface, maintain courts and stock all sorts of supplies. We used them last year to fill some post-hole cracks and partly resur-face our 5-year old court. They were on time, professional and rea-sonably priced.

TENNIS LESSONS

A lot of really serious tennis gets played out here; therefore, there is a lot of good instruction available. There are a number of good pros at the local tennis clubs, but since so many people out here have their own courts at home, there are also a number of instructors who will travel to your place. Here are some of the best of both.

✪✪✪✪ **Paul Annacone Tennis Academy** at East Hampton Indoor tennis, 175 Daniels Hole Rd., East Hampton, 537-8012. Private lessons, clinics for both juniors and adults, on 19 beautiful, outdoor courts and 6 indoor courts.

✪✪✪✪ **Drew Green,** Tennis Professional, 287-6424. I hate looking like a tennis idiot while a dozen people stand around in their tennis whites snickering at my lousy backhand. After several tries, we found a local instructor who is fair, patient, and excellent. Drew improved my game 100% in one lesson. No kidding. Drew also offers a "ten-pack" of very affordable lessons. Give him a call.

THEATERS

Stage and Professional:

✪✪✪✪ **Bay Street Theatre Festival,** Long Wharf, Sag Harbor. Box Office: 725-9500. This will be Bay Street's 8th season. The original founders of Bay Street, Sybil Christopher plus husband and wife team of Steven Hamilton and Emma Walton, took a huge risk in opening an equity theater that was so close to and at the same time so far away from Broadway. Would patrons used to getting the variety and quality of Broadway come to a "country theater" in Sag Harbor? Well, in a nutshell, the risk has paid off. Helped in great measure by some very talented and very well known actors, who were willing to work for next to nothing, Bay Street was a critical success in its first season. They have continued to grow and have put on some first-rate productions. I haven't always liked everything they've done, but, hey, that's just me. My tastes in theater are pretty traditional. I do know that whatever they are doing will be done well, and I really love the intimacy that can be achieved in a 300-seat theater. Call the box office for details on tickets and the shows. Better yet, support truly professional theater in our community. Become a member of Bay Street! Call the development office for details at 725-0818.

✪✪✪✪ **Westhampton Beach Performing Arts Center,** Main Street, Westhampton Beach, 288-2350. There's a good buzz building about this Playhouse. Three years ago this was a seedy, run-down old movie theater in the middle of Westhampton's Main Street. It has been lovingly refurbished and the theater is attracting some really great acts. Call the box office for details and watch the local papers for shows and times.

Community Theater:

✪✪✪✪ **The John Drew Theatre of Guild Hall** in East Hampton, 158 Main St., East Hampton, 324-4050. Yes, this is "community theater" but you know what? There's an awful lot of good stuff going on here. And once in a while, the pros get involved (Billy Joel, for example). There's always something going on here in summer, so call the box office get an earful.

Movie Theaters:

✪✪✪✪ **East Hampton Cinemas,** Main St., East Hampton, 324-0448. Currently the reigning box office champs for movie theaters here on the East End. Their six screens do offer all the latest in first run features. The Cinema also supports and screens productions for the Hamptons International Film Festival (see "Events"). Good news! The 777-FILM number has been re-activated so you can pre-order and pre-pay for tickets up to three days in advance!

✪✪✪ (United Artists) **Southampton Cinema,** Hill St., Southampton, 287-2749. The Southampton Cinema was refurbished and up-graded three years ago and is once again a really pleasant place to go to the movies. All shows before 6 PM are bargain matinees.

✪✪ There's a new **United Artists Cinema** in Hampton Bays, Montauk Highway, 728-8676. The only drawback is the parking, which can get pretty cramped on hot theater nights.

✪✪ **Sag Harbor Theater**, Main St., Sag Harbor, 725-0010. If your tastes in movies lean toward the avant-garde, or the boutique productions, or some of the real classics, then the Sag Harbor Theater is for you! You won't find any first-run mega-hits here, but it can be fun!

✪ **Loews Hampton Arts Twin Theater,** Brook Rd., Westhampton
Beach, 288-2600

THINKING: BEST PLACES TO SIT AND THINK

Need a refuge away from the office, the screaming kids, a spot to just sit and think? Here are the best places for contemplating one's navel or just grabbing a few peaceful moments of bliss:

Beaches are always good, but some of them can get crowded. Try Flying Point Beach, way down at the end of the beach, where it abuts Mecox Bay.

Then there's the strand toward the old lighthouse at Cedar Point County Park.

Stroll around the ground at the Montauk Lighthouse.

Park in the lot at Hither Hills State Park in Montauk and go sit on a dune.

Take the Cross Sound Ferry from Orient Point to New London and Back. Sit on the top deck in the sun with a soda. Maybe have lunch in New London. Guaranteed a peaceful day.

And my personal favorite: An Adirondack chair on the lawn of the Ram's Head Inn on Shelter Island.

THRIFT SHOPS

"Oh, c'mon! I'm in The Hamptons, for Heaven's sake! You can't possibly be recommending thrift shops!" Why not? The second hand stuff of this crowd out here might be pretty good! I'll sure take a look. These are the best Thrift Shops.

Southampton Hospital Thrift Shop, 79 Main St., Southampton, 283-9709

The Daffodil Thrift Shop (American Cancer Society) 4 North Main St., Southampton, 283-6789

TIRES

✪✪✪✪ **Southampton Tire Center,** North Sea Rd and County Rd. 39, Southampton (next to McDonald's), 283-4205. This is a very complete tire store, with just about every type of tire you can name. They have to stock darn near anything. They run into all kinds of exotic requests: Maserati tires, Rolls tires, Bentley tires, etc. The only problem is, you have to get there. If you're stuck somewhere and can't change the tires or get the car to a tire center then call:

✪✪✪ **East End Tire Service,** 99A Mariner Dr., Southampton, 283-2600, the East End's only 24-hour radio dispatched tire service. They do truck service, too.

TOILETS— PORTABLE/TEMPORARY (see "Bathrooms," too)

Would you like to keep those 500 guests out of your bathroom at your next lawn party? Then call:

✪✪✪✪ **Island Portables**, P O Box 284, Main Road, Greenport, 477-2427. Clean "potties" for all occasions: weddings, fund raisers, sporting events, construction sites, etc. I mean, you've got to be dedicated to be in this business.

TOYS

✪✪✪✪ **Lillywhite & Son Toys & Sporting Goods,** 68 Jobs Lane, Southampton, 283-2111. No guns allowed! More amazing than that, no Barbie dolls either! This kids toy store is devoted to educational toys. Expand their minds instead of mindless expanse of their toys.

✪✪✪ **Penny Whistle Toys,** Main St., Bridgehampton, 537-3875. Cute selection of oversized toys, including many outdoor toys. The kids will love this place: they can test drive toys in the store's front yard. They also do helium balloons, which the kids will promptly untie, stick in their mouths, let out the helium, and try to sound like Donald Duck.

✪✪✪ **Recreational Concepts,** Butter Lane, Bridgehampton, 537-5055. BIG toys! Here's where to go for all your swing sets, basketball hoops, trampolines, Ping-Pong tables, air hockey tables and more!

✪✪ **I'm Puzzled,** 50 Park Pl., East Hampton, 329-5104. Brain toys for kids—especially if we get a rainy day and there's nothing for them to do outside. You'd better get on down here and stock up.

TRAINS (see "Railroads")

TRANSPORTATION
(see "Railroad," "Ferries," "Airports," "Taxis," "Rental Cars")

TRAVEL AGENTS

My favorite travel agent sign in the world is the one that hangs over the door of Crimson travel in Harvard Square in Cambridge. It's been there for years and simply says: "Please! Go Away!" The travel business here on the East End is a little thin. First, we are a destination, so most people, once they're here, aren't thinking about going much of anywhere else. Second, the permanent population is not large enough to sustain a large travel agency community. Third, there's the Internet. I wouldn't want my son or daughter to be aspiring to a career as a travel agent these days. In any case, here are our suggestions for local travel agent help.

East Hampton:
✪✪✪✪ **Cook Travel,** 20 Main St, 324-8430
Southampton:
✪✪✪✪ **Cook Travel,** 30 Nugent St., 283-1740
✪✪✪ **Sunshine Travel,** 184 N. Main St., 283-7800

TREES, TRIMMING & SERVICES

This is a service category where you can hang out a shingle (or a limb?) and start your own business fairly quickly. So who are the best? First, I'd look for a certified arborist. This ensures you that the folks have gone through a fairly rigorous certification and training process. Here are some folks we have heard good things about. They are all certified arborists and have been around awhile.

✪✪✪✪ **Sav-A-Tree,** Southampton, 283-1155, Long Island, NY State and National Arborists certified.
✪✪✪ **Ray Smith & Assoc.,** Southampton, 287-6100, Long Island, NY State and National Arborists certified.

UNIVERSITIES (see "Colleges & Universities")

UTILITIES (see also "Cable," "Electricity," "Fuel," "Telephone," and "Water")

The utility situation out here is dominated by Cablevision for cable TV, LIPA for electricity, Suffolk County Water Authority (SCWA) for water, Bell Atlantic for telephone service, and, by 2001, Brooklyn Union for natural gas. Each of these utility areas has an individual listing in the Guide. The only other utilities you will need are fuel oil and maybe propane. Oil heat has been the fuel of choice and pretty much still is (see "Fuel"). Propane (see "Gas") is used mainly for heating the pool—some for cooking.

VETERINARIANS
(see also "Animal Shelters," "Animal Hospitals")

We don't have any pets ourselves, so we had to use "spies" in this category. Here are what our trusted pet owners say are the best bets for Vets, by community.

East Hampton:

Dr. Laura J. Corrado-Glennon, 4 Good Friend, 324-7900

Dr. Mark S. Davis, Montauk Highway, 537-0035

Sag Harbor:

Dr. Susan M. Thompson, Bay Rd., 725-5803

Southampton:

Dr. Daniel Duberman, Bishop's Ln., 283-1094

Dr. Charles N. Gould, 380 Cnty. Rd. 39, 283-0611

Dr. Claude D. Grosjean, 380 Cnty. Rd. 39, 283-0611

Dr. Carol L. Popolow, 380 Cnty. Rd. 39, 283-0611

VIDEO (Editing and Production)

No doubt about it, if you need that demo tape sliced and diced or if you want to edit out Uncle Harry's drunken lamp shade dance from your wedding video, you need to call my friends.

✪✪✪✪ **Black Sheep Television,** Westhampton Airfield, 288-5477. The most creative video team in The Hamptons—maybe even the known universe!

VIDEO STORES

Is a video store a video store unless it's a Blockbuster Store (we have two now, one in Hampton Bays and one in Water Mill)? You tell us. Here's a handy list of video stores by location plus our favorites:

Amagansett:

Video Store of Amagansett, 136 Main, 267-3200

Bridgehampton:

Bridgehampton Video, Montauk Highway, 537-2589

East Hampton:

East End Video, 100 Pantigo Rd., 324-4688

East Hampton Video, 108 N. Main, 324-2441

Springs Fireplace Video, East Hampton, 324-5980

Take II Video, 514 Three Mmile Harbor Rd., 324-8023

Hampton Bays:

Blockbuster Video, 250 W. Montauk Hwy., 723-3600

Montauk:

Montauk Video, S. Elmwood, 668-4824

Sag Harbor:

Harbor Video, Long Island & Water Aves., 725-7025

Long Wharf Video, Long Wharf, 725-9090

Shelter Island:

Geojo Video, 80 Menantic Rd., 749-2324

Triple A Video, 21 N. Ferry Rd., 749-3347

Southampton:

✪✪✪✪ **Windmill Video,** 20 Hampton Rd., 287-1144. A nice store with lots of selection.

North Sea Video, 1336 N. Sea Rd., 287-2244

Water Mill:

✪✪✪✪ **Blockbuster Video,** Montauk Hwy., at the Water Mill Shoppes, 726-0099. New store, nice and clean, and they have all the latest releases. "Frequent Flyers" club now, too.

Westhampton Beach

Video Kingdom, 204 Montauk Hwy., 288-3333

VOLUNTEER PROGRAMS (see "Clubs & Organizations")

VOTER REGISTRATION

There's no excuse not to register! If you need general information on how and where to register, call the Suffolk County Board of Elections.

General Information: 852-4500

Absentee Ballots: 852-4512

WATCH REPAIR

Do NOT take your prized Rolex, Patek-Phillipe, Tag Heuer or whatever to someone who simply "repairs watches." If that someone is not certified, you'll void the warranty. Do it the smart way. Take your watch to reliable folks like:

✪✪✪✪ **London Jewelers,** 2 Main St., East Hampton, 329-3939. They are authorized for Rolex as well as for repairs on many other fine watches.

✪✪✪✪ **Jobs Lane Jewelers,** 50 Hampton Rd., Southampton, 283-2841. I find Jobs Lane to be perfect for watch repairs, replacement batteries, watchbands, and so forth.

WALKS (see also "Hiking")

Check out our "Hiking" category for the best walks on the East End, but if you'd like a really fun hosted walk, go see the East Hampton Town Crier Hugh King. (Yes! We do we still have "town criers"!) This year's schedule of walking tours has already started, but they will continue through Christmas. There are historic building tours, cemetery tours, romantic winter lantern tours, and so on! For a complete schedule, call the East Hampton Historical Society at 324-6850. Each walking tour will cost $10 per person.

WATER

You're either on well water or town water. The Suffolk County Water Authority (SCWA) controls the flow for all of us with town water and sewer facilities. (If you're on well water, see below, "Wells & Well Drilling.") I have to say that water is the best bargain we have out here in utilities. Unless you fill your pool five times a year or water your yard every day, you'll not find the water bills unreasonable. If you need general information or a hookup call: 324-0959. After 5PM and for emergencies call 665-0663.

But here's a problem! Anyone see the "60 Minutes" report on MBTE? Methyl-butyl-tri-ethelene? Or some such gobbledygook? MBTE is the additive that the EPA so gleefully mandated be added to the gasoline we use in our cars. It was supposed to cut down on emissions—smog, don't you know. It did! But just like thalidomide, it's come back to haunt us. As it turns out, MBTE is very toxic—even in minute parts-per-million. To make matters worse, MBTE is an oxygen-based compound. When it comes into contact with other predominantly oxygen based compounds—like water—it takes to water like a duck! Even the smallest of spills—like someone accidentally dumping a gallon can of gasoline, or an underground gasoline storage tank springing even a very small leak—will send this poisonous stuff into the groundwater. And in case you didn't know it, the entire East End is hovering over an aquifer that is all ground water. It, in turn, supplies a huge portion of our drinking water supply. Bummer. There are now over 200 wells on Long Island that are contaminated with MBTE—50(+) alone in the Hamptons! And those are the ones we know about.

If I were building a house, I'd sure as heck want to try and get it hooked up to city water. If that's not possible I'd sure as heck want to get the ground around my new abode tested.

WATER SKIING

As popular as this sport is in many other water accessible parts of the country, it hasn't developed a large following out here. Perhaps it's because of the many places on or near the water that are marine or wildlife sanctuaries. Perhaps it's because there are many more fisher-persons than water skiers. Perhaps it's because there are many more sailors. Whatever...most of the water skiing is done on Peconic Bay, Three-Mile Harbor, and sometimes Mecox Bay. There is also a water ski course in Quogue on Quantuck Bay.

For information and supplies, call:

✪✪✪✪ **Main Beach Surf & Sport,** Montauk Highway, Wainscott, 537-2716

For Information on the Quantuck Bay Course, call:
Westhampton Ski Club, Westhampton Chamber of Commerce, 288-3337

WEB SITES

These are absolutely the best web sites in The Hamptons for getting your latest local info. So, rotor heads, fire up your PC or your laptop and take a look at:

www.hamptonsurvivalguide.com: This is our very own web site, and we think, of course, that it's THE answer to information on The Hamptons. Check it out.

www.cablevision.com: See what's shakin' on Cable TV tonight, plus get the scoop on pay-per-view movies offered, cable rates, etc.

www.easthamptonchamber.com: official site of the East Hampton Chamber

www.montaukchamber.com: All the latest on Montauk from the good folks at their Chamber of Commerce.

www.southampton.com/chamber: Southampton's Chamber of Commerce web site, and it's a good one!

WEDDINGS (as in "Hurry Up Let's Get Married")

For that all important marriage license, check out the "Licenses—Marriage" category. For everything else you're going to need, including a very fat checkbook, I'm going to refer you to the one best company we know that will do it all for you:

✪✪✪✪ **Hampton Wedding,** P.O. Box 2227, East Hampton, 537-3833, fax 324-8343: These talented professionals provide a custom planning program that includes consultation, budget breakdown, planning schedules, entrée to the best sources and The Hampton Wedding Guide which contains a bevy of useful information for the wedding weekend. Also available, a menu of additional services including comprehensive wedding design and coordination, on-site event management, ceremony design, and Hampton Wedding gift baskets.

Hamptong Wedding will offer its clients personal referrals to the following services: locations, invitations, caterers, décor and floral design, tents, lighting, rentals, music, accommodations, wedding cakes, hair and makeup artists, valet parking and transportation, rehearsal dinner arrangements, weekend activities and everything else to make the wedding weekend a success.

Referrals will be tailored to the client's budget and vision and the vendor's proven quality and reliability.

✪✪✪✪ **Jill Gordon Celebrate,** P.O. Box 2227, East Hampton, 324-2422, fax 324-8343, jgcelebrate@hamptons.com: Jill's goal is to help you celebrate all the momentous occasions of your life, but she loves to do weddings—and has been doing them for 14 years. She is an expert in doing them in The Hamptons and can help you plan that wedding if it's just the two of you or the two of you and 1,200 friends! She coordinates locations, invitations, catering, flowers, tents, lighting, rentals, music, photographers, and everything else. The goal is: maximum joy, minimum stress.

If you're a real masochist and want to do it all yourself, I'm going to refer you to some of our winning merchants who can help. All of these folks appear elsewhere in the Guide under the appropriate category, if you want more detail on what they do and how well they do it.

Announcements/Invitations
Lemarc Hallmark, Bridgehampton, 527-2855
Balloons/Novelties
see "Florists," Artistry in Flowers, 283-8200
Banquet Facilities
Call some of our top-rated restaurants; but, for size and ambiance, I'd also recommend you call some of our local wineries: Castello di Borghese/Hargrave Vineyard on the North Fork (734-5111) and Sagpond Vineyards on the South (537-5106). There's also Whitefields Condominiums in Southampton (283-4640). Whitefields has a big, beautiful main house that's a real Stanford White designed Colonial with a ballroom for rent. For restaurants with room enough for a good-sized wedding party I'd try:

East Hampton Point
Maidstone Arms
Della Femina
Alison By-The-Beach
Southampton Publick House
Savanna's
Rams Head Inn (Shelter Island)
The American Hotel
The Palm
The Farmhouse

(the) Cake: see "Bakeries"

Caterers: see "Catering," call any one of our several winners

Chairs & Tables: see "Party Supplies," Water Mill Rentals, 726-6664

Florists: see "Florists," Yardley Florist, 725-0470

Jewelry: London Jewelers, East Hampton or Hollis Reh, Southampton

Limos: Hampton Jitney, Southampton Limos

Liquor: Herbert & Rist, Southampton (best deals on case buys, etc.)

Make-Up: see "Beauty Salons": Salon East, Kevin Maple Salon, or Oak Street Salon

Music: Troy Grindle Entertainment (see "Musicians")

Nails: Nails by Joann (see "Beauty")

Party Supplies: see "Party Supplies," Water Mill Party Rentals, Bar Boy

Photographers: see "Photographers"

Security: Mike Zimet Enterprises or New York Security Group (see "Security—Personal")

Tents: see "Party Supplies," P.J. McBride

Travel: see "Travel Agents"

Wedding Ceremonies: see "Churches" or "Synagogues" and then contact a local cleric for rules, procedures, and so forth.

WELLS & WELL DRILLING

Many new homes going up today on the East End are still going in with well water. Most of the older homes are certainly on well water. So, if you buy or rent a place that was built more than a decade ago, there's a pretty good chance you're getting your household water from the aquifer that runs everywhere beneath the surface of the East End. If your new place is close enough to one of the many sewer systems that Suffolk County Water is developing all over the East End you may luck out and get city water. Whether you rent or buy be sure to find out from the seller or landlord what kind of water you're on! If the shower suddenly starts spitting nothing but small flakes of rust or there are noxious bubbles rising to the top of the pool that remind you of the stink bombs from high school chem class, it would be nice to know whether you need to call Suffolk County Water or a local well driller. If you need a new well, well service, or if you have a water problem of any kind relative to a well, call:

✪✪✪✪ **Casola Well Drillers,** 1706 North Highway, Southampton, 283-5553 or in East Hampton at 329-0808.

WILDLIFE

No, no, no...we're not talking about that kind of "wild life." This kind has wings and paws, and stuff like that. We have abundant wildlife out here. Thankfully, most of it is benign. Deer are plentiful. So are fox, rabbit, pheasant, Canadian geese, grouse, small mammals, many types of wild birds (see "Birds") and even a few wild turkeys (other than the drunk who tried to grope you at last year's benefit ball). No bears or mountain lions—they're long gone—migrated to upstate, just like cousin Hal from the

Bronx. No poisonous snakes, either. The deer are majestic and compelling, but they can be pests (see "Deer"). If you run across an endangered wildlife specimen, call Animal Rescue, and please refer to that category herein.

WINDOW TREATMENTS (see also "Interior Decorators")

✪✪✪✪ **Windows & Walls,** 375 North Hwy, Southampton, 287-1515. My friends Paul and Linda have been running a wonderful shop specializing in window treatments for many years. Although they do many other decorative assignments (like "walls"—it's part of their name!) making your windows into reflections of your good taste and style has been their specialty. They hold up extraordinarily well—and they're beautiful. Windows & Walls also has very, very good prices on everything.

WINE SHOPS (see also "Liquor")

✪✪✪✪ **Herbert & Rist,** 63 Jobs Ln., Southampton, 283-2030—just the best selection, best prices, and really knowledgeable people. See John. He's always ready with a wine special that you wouldn't find unless you ask. And if they don't have something you need, they'll find it and, in most cases, deliver it to you. They even deliver to the City!

✪✪✪✪ **Morell's Wines,** 74 Montauk Hwy., Red Horse Shopping Plaza, East Hampton, 324-1230. NOT the same Morell's as in Manhattan.

But it doesn't matter. These folks are terrific. Great shop, excellent selection. And they're expanding, too. You really should check out their spectacular collection of library wines!

✪✪✪ **Amagansett Wines & Spirits,** Main Street, Amagansett, 267-3939. Perhaps the best fortified and most interesting wine shop in this part of the way-out-east East End. Selection is excellent and they have some of those wonderful but harder to find Long Island wine buys. Often have specials, too. Watch the windows for "deals" as you drive through Amagansett.

WINE & WINERIES

Volumes could be written about the wine industry that has arisen on the East End. Most of it happens to be on the North Fork, but the South Fork is coming along. And several of our wineries are producing very fine wines. I am not an expert, but, as they say, "I know what I like," and there is some true wine magic happening out here. There are now 21 major wineries on the East End, with another three or four in various stages of planting and development. That's truly remarkable since the wine scene really only started to happen here in '70s. It was, in fact, 1973 when the true pioneers of the business, Alex and Luisa Hargrave, first put vines in our soil. Speaking of which, Alex and Louisa, after 27 years of truly hard work, sold the winery last October to Ann Marie and Marco Borghese. Marco comes from an Italian family that has roots going back to the 9th Century. Marco is, himself, a Prince, but does not use the title. The Hargrave sale (which was consummated at a price of $4 million) comes on the heels of the purchase of Corey Creek for $2 million by Michael Lynne, Chairman of New Line Cinema. Then, after the Hargrave sale, Mr. Lynne came right back to the table and bought Bedell Winery for $5 million! Whew! Everyone wants to own a vineyard! As I look at this scene I can only tell you that the wine business seems to be coming into its own. Look for more acquisitions, more start-ups and lots more money being tossed around. And it's all thanks to the Hargraves.

If you're not quite ready to shell out a few "mil" to buy a vineyard, you can still enjoy a sybaritic experience any day by just jumping in your car and taking our wine tour. If you're not careful, you can be swacked by the third stop; so, try and pace yourself. There's a lot of good stuff to sample! First we'll give you a list of all the wineries.

Winery List by location:

North Fork:

Bedell, Rte. 25, Cutchogue, 734-7537

Bidwell, Rte. 48, Cutchogue, 734-5200

Corey Creek, Southold, 765-4168

Gristina, Main Rd., Cutchogue, 734-7089

Castello di Borghese/Hargrave., Rte. 48, Cutchogue, 734-5111

Jamesport, Rte. 25, Jamesport, 722-5256

Laurel Lake Vineyards, Laurel, 298-1420

Lenz, Rte. 25, Peconic, 734-6010

Macari Vineyards, Mattituck, 298-0100

Martha Clara, Mattituck (not yet open)

Osprey's Dominion, Rte. 25, Peconic, 765-6188

Palmer, 108 Sound, Riverhead, 722-9463

Paumanok, Rte. 25, Aquebogue, 722-8800

Peconic Bay, Rte. 25, Cutchogue, 734-7361

Pellegrini, Rte. 25, Cutchogue, 734-4111

Pindar, Rte. 25, Peconic, 734-6200

Pugliese, Rte. 25, Cutchogue, 734-4057

Raphael, Peconic (not yet open)

Schneider Vineyards, Cutchogue, 734-2699

South Fork:

Channing Daughters, Bridgehampton, 537-7224

Duck Walk, Montauk Highway, Water Mill, 726-7555

Sagpond Vineyards, Sagaponack, 537-5106

Now, I have to say, there isn't a bad winery out here, so choosing the best of the best for you has been difficult, but here are the wineries that we would especially commend to you.

✪✪✪✪ **Castello di Borghese/Hargrave Vineyard,** Rte 48 at Alvah's Lane, Cutchogue, 734-5111. Yes, the vineyard that started it all is still among the very the best. Even though the winery has changed hands, the same steady hands from the Hargrave era are still making the wines. Alex and Luisa are still around—hired as consultants for the first two years after the sale. Mark Terry, the principal winemaker is still there, too, as are the "Hargrave Kids," Zander and Ann. The winery is likely to have a few changes this year, though, including some cosmetic changes to the tasting room, the planting of some new vines, and a gradual name change on the labels. One thing they're not changing is their commitment to their wines. Their Chardonnays are among the best I have ever tasted. Then there's my favorite Blanc Fume and a wonderful Pinot Blanc. The reds are lov-

ingly crafted, too, topped off by their incredibly rich Merlots. *The New York Times* loves the wines, *Newsday* loves the wines, *Gourmet* magazine loves the wines, *Wine Spectator* praised the wines, and so will you. Oh, by the way, they even sell wine futures at Castello di Borghese/Hargrave. You can actually buy future vintages that are still aging in the barrels at reduced prices. Castello di Borghese/Hargrave also has excellent indoor and outdoor venues for weddings, special parties, corporate retreats, and so forth. And we must all say thanks, again, to the Hargraves for really starting this industry moving here on the East End.

✪✪✪✪ Even though the South Fork has only three of the twenty-plus wineries, one of the best wineries, in my view, is on the South Fork: **Sagpond Vineyards,** Sagaponack. First, the property is absolutely stunning. Second, the people are very nice. Third, and most importantly for wine lovers, the wines are marvelous. The main building and tasting room are inside a multi-million dollar Tuscan Villa. The tasting room itself is vaulted in old beams and Italian floor tiles. There is no bar. The folks helping you sample Sagpond wines do so from behind a large table. The winemaker, Roman Roth, says that this helps develop "relationships" between their customers and the winery. The winery has a German slant (but no Rieslings) and produces fabulous regular and reserve Chardonnays. Believe it or not, they also make cheese! As it turns out, the farmer next door to the winery had cows but was not marketing the milk. Mr. Roth wanted to try making some cheese. Viola! You can now get a slice of Ementhaler (Swiss) with the bottles of wine you buy here. If you are going to have a very special dinner party, business event, or wedding, I'd sure ask these folks about renting their hall, too.

✪✪✪ **Pindar**—The largest of our local producers, but it's not just quantity that makes them special. They are producing some very good wines. Two of my favorites are "Autumn Gold" and "Winter White." These light, white wines are perfect for drinking with just about any meal. Pindar's tasting room is fun and informative (But you may have to pay a couple of dollars to sample some of the premium wines and champagnes). Pindar is also the owner of Duck Walk in Water Mill.

✪✪✪ **Paumanok**—A family run business that works hard at producing some exceptional vintages. One of their wines was even served at a White House dinner last year!

✪✪✪ **Bidwell**—These folks have always done a fine job, and we always stock a case or two of their wines at the beginning of summer. Wonderful Chardonnays.

✪✪✪ **Bedell**—Classy, smooth, consistent. I love their basic, hearty "Main Road Red."

✪✪✪ **Macari**—New from the ground up and a beautiful facility. They are starting some champagne production here. Well worth a visit.

✪✪ **Channing Daughters**—What I like about this winery is its lack of pretense. They produce good wines that are meant to be consumed now!

✪✪ **Osprey's Dominion**—Opened in '96. Excellent fruited wines and they also make a delightful spice wine. Buy a few bottles of spice wine to keep on hand for winter holiday parties.

If you wanted the perfect wine-tasting afternoon, here is how you could do it:

1. Hire a driver or a limo (See "Limos") or at least designate a driver.
2. Pack some cheese, crackers, fruit, bottled water, ice, and extra wineglasses. Better yet, stop at Razzano's in Bridgehampton and pick up sand-

wiches, salads, cheeses, cold cuts, whatever.

3. Start your day at Channing Daughters in Bridgehampton, right down Scuttle Hole Road heading toward Sag Harbor. Beautiful little winery with eminently and immediately drinkable wines. Picnic tables, too!

4. Go back to Montauk Highway via the Bridgehampton–Sag Harbor Turnpike, turn east (left). Go up the road a couple of miles to a stoplight and turn left at the big green winery sign to Sagpond Vineyards. You will fall in love with this Tuscan Villa that rises out of the vineyard. Sample both the wine and the cheese!

5. Head back to Sag Harbor, but be sure to take the signs to Route 114, North Haven/Shelter Island. Take the South Ferry to Shelter Island to the North Ferry. Take the North Ferry to Greenport, get on Rte. 25 West. Next stop:

6. Osprey's Dominion in Peconic: try the strawberry wine and, if it's the right time of year, the hot, mulled wine made from their Spice Wine.

7. Next, Pindar in Peconic: Forget the "Dollar Bar" for tasting. Just sample the regular wines, especially the light whites like "Autumn Gold".

8. Next, Bedell in Cutchogue: arguably some of the finest red wines made out here. Try "Main Road Red," their great red table wine, and definitely try the Merlot.

9. Next, turn right on Depot Lane, go over to Route 48, turn left.

10. Stop at Bidwell in Cutchogue: These folks make some very good whites as well as respectable reds.

11. Stop at Hargrave in Cutchogue: Ahh! My favorite! Start with the Chardonette, their light white table wine, then proceed through the Blanc Fume, Pinot Blanc, the extraordinary lattice-label Chardonnay, then go to red with a little Petit Chateau, some Cabernet Franc, and last but not least, a rich, red Merlot. Take at least one bottle home with you!

12. Stop at Macari in Mattituck: Stand up to the lovely Vigioner and a glass of champagne (if you're still sanding!).

By now, you're totally "juiced"—thank goodness for the limo or designated driver. Head on back to the South Fork via Route 111 and Route 27. If you're still reasonably vertical, go out to dinner at one of the fine spots highlighted in our restaurant section.

WINTERIZING

What do you do with all your cherished possessions if you're spending the winter in Palm Beach, a couple of months in St. Barth's (lucky you!). Let's treat this like a checklist for winterizing your home.

The House:

Sprinklers: If you have a sprinkler system, get it winterized! This means having someone come and blow out the pipes, usually with pressurized air. If you don't do this, you stand a pretty good chance of having frost bust a pipe or two.

Hoses: Take them inside.

Outside showers: drain and secure them (see above). You won't want to be taking many more outside showers after the first of October—not unless you really want to freeze your you-know-what off.

Pool: Pools do NOT need to be drained—especially if they are gunite. In fact, it's better to leave some water in gunite pools. I also recommend a cover, although it's not mandatory to have one. Covers do keep debris and the occasional wandering animal out of your pool. The water stays cleaner and it's a lot easier to get the pool ready next spring if it's been covered. And don't forget your pool heater! You should remove the heater element and store it in the garage or basement. The pool pump is generally detachable and, like the heater element, it should be stored where it won't freeze. Shut off your propane tanks if you heat the pool with propane. When it comes to all this stuff, have a pro do it. Believe me, it's easier. (See "Pool Service.")

Tennis Court: If you're lucky enough to have one, there are no particular precautions you need to take. Just take down the net and store it. Nets last longer that way. If you see any cracks in the surface of the court, especially around the fence posts, it's a good idea to get them filled before the frost and winter winds make them worse. If you have a Har-Tru (asphalt base) surface, these surfaces should last many years without major surgery.

Windows and doors: Check the weather stripping around all the windows and doors. If it's cracked, frayed, or missing, replace it. If you have storm windows, you'll want to put them up before November 1st. Note: if you're in a newer home, you probably have double-pane-insulated windows. If you have these type windows, you don't need storm windows, so don't let anyone sell them to you! If you have a Bilco door, make sure it's locked. Inside, the house can be better sealed from the elements if you put those long, sand-filled draft protectors at the base of each outside door.

Utilities: If you're on town water, I see no need to stop the service. It's more trouble than it is worth. If you're on well water, call your well servicing company for a winterization. Electrical? Up to you, but I'd leave it on—especially if you have an alarm or think you might come out at the spur of the moment for a winter weekend. Water heater: turn it off or to a minimum setting (120 degrees or so). Thermostat: leave it set to a temperature that will keep the pipes in the house warm—at least 40 degrees. If you have a freeze alarm, the setting will probably be higher, like 50 degrees. If you have oil heat, be sure that your supplier sets you up on a monitored or regular delivery so you won't run out of fuel. The phone: Bell Atlantic offers a service that shuts down your system while you're away but keeps your service minimally active. Much better than the re-connection fees they charge if you shut it down completely. Oh, and don't forget the Post Office! Have your mailed stopped, held, or forwarded.

Alarm system: be sure to have it on when you leave and be extra sure you update the notification list, especially if you'll be travelling.

Your Goodies: There are a couple of places that offer winterized storage and self-storage. See "Self Storage" category.

Your Indoor Plants: If you want to leave your precious indoor plants in good hands over the winter see our "Plant Sitters" category.

The Car:

Leaving a car out here for winter? There are a couple of places where you can have a professional winterization done, including storage (see "Auto Detailing"). If you do it yourself, put the car up on cinder blocks to protect the tires, check the coolant levels (don't forget antifreeze even if you're not going to drive the car!), and disconnect the battery.

For help with any of the winterizing challenges mentioned above, check the individual categories in this book for the professionals that can serve you best!

WOMEN'S CLOTHING & ACCESSORIES

Hey! I'm a Guy! What do I know about this stuff? Plenty! I live with a lady who knows how to shop! Here are the winners.

✪✪✪✪ OK, shoppers! Here we go. Let's start with—**Sak's Fifth Avenue,** 1 Hampton Rd. and also on Main Street, 283-3500. Both the main store and the new men's store further down the block on Main Street are absolute winners. The selection, even in limited space is the best of the best. Can you say: "Giorgio Armani," "Ungaro," "Max Mara"? The friendly staffs at both locations also make this a wonderful shopping experience.

✪✪✪✪ **Blanc Bleu,** Main St., East Hampton, 329-2552. Men's and women's casual clothing; and, everything is just as the store's name suggests: "white" or "blue." Wonderful, French-style sportswear: classical, updated, and nautical. The chain originated in Paris. There are only two stores in the US: this one, in East Hampton, and one on Rodeo Drive in Beverly Hills. Does that give you a clue as to what we have here?

✪✪✪✪ **Steven Stolman,** 83 Main St., 283-8602. A Hamptons shopping "experience." Truly elegant resort clothes, both resort formal and resort casual. (Great clothes to take on a cruise!) One of the very best stores in The Hamptons.

✪✪✪✪ **Titano,** 22 Nugent St., Southampton, 287-4123, on-line at www.titanoonline.com. Men's and women's custom-made shirts, hand stitched from pure Egyptian cotton—French cuffs, too! Great knit sweaters, cashmere, and a "traveling jewelry" collection. A lot of their goods are imported from Italy. Not inexpensive, but you deserve it!

✪✪✪✪ **TJ Maxx,** Bridgehampton Commons, 537-1591. Boy is this a cool place! The whole idea behind TJ Maxx, in case you didn't know, is that they take on and sell a lot of other designers overstocked items. Myra got a $280 Tahari gown for $88!

✪✪✪ **The Gap,** also at Bridgehampton Commons, 537-2762. Would we be complete without a Gap? Jeans, carpenter pants, shirts, sweaters and more.

✪✪✪ **Tutto Bene II,** Main St., Bridgehampton, 537-3320. Don't be confused. There are two stores. One is on Main Street about half way down the block and is a pretty good accessories store. This is the "II" part and that's the one we're featuring. It's at the end of Main Street, next to Penny Whistle Toys and across the street from the Candy Kitchen (by the stoplight as you come into town). This half of Tutto Bene has some wonderful women's clothes, sweaters, scarves and jackets—excellent prices, too on quality merchandise.

✪✪ **DMC Accessories Outlet,** Jobs Lane, Southampton, 287-1212. Fun store! And it's all accessories: brushes, straw bags, scarves, sunglasses, hats costume jewelry and inexpensive gifts.

Photos: Tom Ratcliffe

22 Nugent Street
Southampton
631.287.4123
www.titanoonline.com
Open 7 Days

TITANO

Italian shirts & blouses
in pure Egyptian Cotton.
Silk Ties, Accessories
and Fine Knits for men,
women and children.

www.BestSelections.com/Titano

X

I tried like heck to find something to put in the "X" category. "X" spouses? That's a big topic out here... "X" Files? One of my favorite shows... "X" istentialism? Man, now I'm really reaching... Well, here's one "X" and hopefully you'll not have to use it much, but if you do:

X-RAYS

Wainscott Walk-In Medical Care, 537-1892

y

YOUTH ORGANIZATIONS (See "Clubs & Organizations")

z

ZIP CODES

Amagansett 11930
Bridgehampton 11932
East Hampton 11937
Hampton Bays 11946
Montauk 11954
Noyac 11963
Quogue 11959
Riverhead 11901
Sag Harbor 11963

Sagaponack 11962
Shelter Island 11964
Shelter Island Heights 11965
Shinnecock Hills 11946
Southampton 11968 & 11969
Wainscott 11975
Water Mill 11976
Westhampton 11977
Westhampton Beach 11978

1. Go to the Beach

Isn't this what a lot of us live for when we come out here? Of course it is! Review the section on "Beaches." Our favorites are: Flying Point Beach, Hither Hills, and Sagg Main Beach. And here's a way to go to the beach that I call "The Best Morning of Your Hamptons Life": Set your alarm some summer morning for 5:00 AM. Pack a basket of hard-boiled eggs or deviled eggs, cheese, bread, a little pate, some hot coffee and a bottle of champagne. While it's still dark, drive to Flying Point or Sagg Main Beach and park (if you get there early enough, the guards won't be around to charge or ticket you!). Pick a comfortable dune, spread a blanket, and watch the sun come up. You'll never get a day off to a better start, but check the Weather Channel first.

2. "Wine-ing" Is Allowed!

One of the most fun things to do in this part of the world is set aside a Saturday or Sunday, rent a limo with a couple of close friends, and go "winery hopping." Take our suggested winery tour! Reserve time for a hearty lunch. You can either pack a picnic or stop at any number of the little diners and restaurants that dot the North Fork (my personal favorite is "Legends"). See the "Wineries" section, above, for details on all the wineries and our recommendations on the very best of them.

3. The Great Hamptons Pub Crawl

Definitely, definitely rent a limo or have a serious designated driver. This crawl can start in either Southampton or East Hampton. Our description starts in Southampton, but if you start in East Hampton start at number 7 (The Palm) then go 8-9-6-5-4-3-2-1-10. The crawl is best-done starting at about 6:00 PM. [NOTE: If you've been doing our pub-crawl faithfully each year, and this is our 4th one, you'll see it's changed this year!]

1st stop: Start at The Driver's Seat, Job's Lane, Southampton. Get "liberated" with a Strawberry Daiquiri in the back bar.

2nd stop: basilico, at the end of Jobs Lane and Windmill Lane: Time to try the PineHamptons! That's the great stuff marinating in the large glass jar behind the bar…zowie!

3rd stop: Southampton Publick House, Bowden Square. Tip a brewski! These guys are making some fabulous specialty brews, so don't miss a chance to sample their wares. Have a quick appetizer, too, to combat the gathering alcohol haze.

4th stop: Savanna's, across from the train station in Southampton. A clear and perfect Chardonnay or a glass of house champagne will do nicely. Sit out back, in the great outdoors, under the canopy and enjoy the gathering dusk. Cigar? Smoke 'em if you got 'em.

5th stop: World Pie, Main Street, Bridgehampton: What a great bar! Superb ambience, lots of "bar crowd," if you know what I mean. Try shots of Pekonica (our best local vodka, made from our best local potatoes!).

6th stop: Motor on to East Hampton. Stop at Peconic Coast. Perhaps a simple gin and tonic will do here, or a Manhattan, straight up. But while you're sitting in one of The Hamptons' most attractive bars, check out the menu for the next time you want to take someone out for a special dinner.

7th stop: The Palm at the Huntting Inn, Main Street, East Hampton: If you've forgotten what an elegant and cozy bar full of polished wood and soft chairs feels like, the bar at the Palm is for you! I'd order a rum and Coke or something like that.

8th stop: To help you recover a bit, you're going to motor for a while, out past Amagansett, straight toward Montauk, and stop at the Pig n' Whistle—a real Irish pub in the middle of the Hamptons! So, what are you going to order? You've got to be kidding…It's an Irish pub!

9th stop: Keep heading east all the way past downtown Montauk, then turn left to the Montauk Marina. You're looking for Star Island and the Montauk Yacht Club. Settle into their delightful indoor bar for a Margarita or step outside if the weather's good and lounge by the outdoor bar.

10th Last stop on the crawl. This "shtop" (hic!), sorry, "stop" should always be last. You're motoring way back to Sag Harbor and the Cigar Bar, at the end of Main Street. Plunk yourself down on one of their stools or just drop into one of the overstuffed chairs. Have a last cigar and order a Cosmopolitan. Your driver will have a last coffee and get you safely home and contentedly tucked away. (Don't forget to take your aspirins before you go to bed.)

4. Hiking and Shelter Island

The hiking here is really wonderful and too little appreciated. The terrain is blessedly flat and the scenery is magnificent. Refer to our "Hiking" section above for the best hikes, but our favorites are the Eastland Trails and Mashomack on Shelter Island.

If you want a truly wonderful day of outdoors exertion combined with some fun try this: Go to Shelter Island. This is one of the last places in America that cannot be directly accessed by car—not even by 4-wheel drive, unless that 4-wheeler has a snorkel. The only way you can get to the island is by ferry or by swimming. Presuming you decide not to swim, you'll arrive by car from either the South Ferry from Sag Harbor or the North Ferry from Greenport. Come early—preferably on one of those balmy summer days that are awash in the filtered light for which the East End is rightly famous. You'll spend the morning lolling away the hours at Crescent Beach. Next, you'll journey to the Ram's Head Inn for lunch. Following the midday repast you'll stroll the grounds and end up napping for an hour in one of the convenient Adirondack chairs scattered about the property. Then, since you're really not the sloth you've been so far all day, you'll head to the Mashomack Preserve and take the five-mile hike through some of the most pristine coastal scenery available in the eastern US. Finish off a fabulous day by having cocktails and dinner at Sunset Beach up on Shelter Island Heights (see "Restaurants"). Don't miss the ferry, though! Last one leaves at 1:45 AM.

5. "Take a Flyer"

How about this to get your blood pumping? Go out to Westhampton Airport (Exit 58 off the Sunrise) and check into Sky Sailors Glider School (288-5858). Spend a glorious summer afternoon soaring with the eagles. Feel the gentle updrafts that roll in off the beach taking you to a higher level, both physically and mentally. Don't do it after lunch, though, because you might be taking some "barrel rolls." An introductory soaring lesson can be had for $69.95. There are also beginner packages for as little as $199; or, go all the way and get a FAA Private Glider License for approximately $1,195.

6. Whale and Seal Watching

"Thar she blows!" Whale watching of the finest kind can be had in Montauk via the good folks at the Viking Fishing Fleet Line, West Lake Drive in Montauk, call 668-5700. There are generally lots of whales cavorting in the seas around Montauk in the summer and fall. The east end of our island is right on their migratory highway, but for some reason the whales are coming a little closer to shore these days, and the opportunity to see them has increased dramatically. Viking works closely with the Cornell University Extension program that is conducting whale research—and they are the only whale watch cruise that is so sanctioned. Oh, in case you're wondering about "bothering" the whales, you need not worry.

During the winter and early spring months (December through April) you can see the shy but fascinating Harbor Seals play on the rocky shores of Montauk State Park. The Riverhead Foundation for Marine Research and Preservation (Boy! There's a mouthful!) sponsors guided walks for a donation of $5 per person. Call 369-9840, extension 10, for dates, times, and other details.

7. Be Here in Autumn

Pick a late September or early October day that is crisp and clean. Journey on out past Water Mill. Go right on Mecox Road, following the "Apple Picking" signs to the Halsey Apple Farm. Bring the kids. Spend a delightful couple of hours picking ripe apples off the trees. John Halsey will also lecture you on apple growing and apple picking etiquette based on his 20 years of successful growing here on the East End. There are pumpkins, too, filling the patches next to the apple groves. Select a giant orange jack-o-lantern to be carved later. Once your trunk is filled with sacks of apples and a pumpkin or two, head back down Mecox Road to Montauk Highway and stop at The Milk Pail, the Halseys' roadside stand, for fresh pressed cider and mouth watering cider doughnuts. Head back to your house and start a fire in the fireplace. Maybe Mom will turn some of those fresh picked apples into a gorgeous pie while Dad and the kids carve up the pumpkins!

Another pumpkin attraction that popped up last year that proved to be very popular with the kids was Hank's Pumpkin Farm, right on Montauk Highway in Water Mill, across the street from Duck Walk Vineyards. This whimsical pumpkin patch (September–November) was piled high with pickable pumpkins and wonderful wooden sculptures that the kiddies could climb all over (airplanes and pirate ships!).

8. Block Island

One of the most fun things to do in The Hamptons isn't even in The Hamptons! In fact, it's not even in New York! But you can get there from The Hamptons. Go to Montauk Harbor to Viking Landing. Get there by 8 AM so that you have a spot aboard the Viking Ferry Lines boat to Block Island. In less than two hours, you'll be on the island, which is part of Rhode Island. Block Island is 11 square miles of pristine beaches and breathtaking landscapes. There are shops and superb restaurants. Best to rent bicycles or a moped to get around. You can stay overnight in one of the few but exquisite hotels, if you like. If you're not staying over, get back to the ferry for the 4:30 PM sailing. You'll be back in Montauk by 6:30. Ferry tickets are about $32, round trip, for adults and $16, RT, for children (ages 5–12). You can rent bicycles on board the ferry. For information on the Island itself, call the Block Island Chamber of Commerce at 401-466-2982. (The ferry does not run year round from Montauk, by the way!)

9. 'Shop 'till you Drop…'

Here's the dream Hamptons Shopping Trip. We've really pared this down to the very best places. The trip is designed for one shopping day. Start at Tanger Mall at 9:00 AM sharp and get out your Gold card—it's going to be warped and limp by the end of the day!

Stop 1: Tanger Mall, Riverhead: You could spend a whole day here alone, and you might want to some other time, but here are the absolute best stores to hit: **Tommy Hilfiger**—Men's & Women's fashions • **Off Fifth** (Sak's Outlet) • **Brooks Brothers Outlet Store**

Stop 2: Job's Lane and Main Street in Southampton: **Sak's Fifth Avenue,** 1 Hampton Rd. and also on Main Street, 283-3500: Both the main store and the men's store further down the block on Main Street are absolute winners. • **Steven Stolman,** 83 Main St., 283-8602: Women's clothing; we rate this one of the very best stores in The Hamptons. • You also need to stop by: **Fishs Eddy**—china and glassware—on Job's Lane, **Breezin' Up**—T-shirts, etc., also on Job's Lane, and **Hildreth's** Department Store on Main Street.

Stop 3: Bridgehampton Commons in Bridgehampton: **GAP and GAP Kids, Eddie Bauer, Banana Republic, Talbot's, TJ Maxx,** and **Williams-Sonoma.**

Stop 4: Main Street, Sag Harbor: The gift shop adjacent to the **American Hotel** in Sag Harbor, Main Street, 725-3535. This place must not be missed! • **Carriage House Antiques**, 12 Main St., Sag Harbor, 725-8004, fax 725-8006: A superb selection of antique furnishings, and fine linens. • **Latham House,** 117 Main St., Sag Harbor, 725-1973: This is what I would call "distinguished weekend country clothes" for men.

Stop 5: Main Street in East Hampton: **Blanc Bleu,** Main St., East Hampton. Men's and women's casual clothing. Everything is, just as the store's name suggests, in "white" or "blue." Wonderful, French-style sportswear: classical, updated, and nautical. • **The Coach Factory Store,** 69 Main St., 329-1777: Coach is one of the defining stores of The Hamptons. Coach cannot be beat for the quality of their leather offerings in belts, handbags, portfolios, briefcases, gloves, and so forth. • **London Jewelers,** 2 Main St., 329-3939: Rolex, Tiffany items, fine jewelry, crystal, gift items and floral arrangements blended together in an atmosphere of pure Hamptons elegance. This is a truly beautiful store.

10. The Club Scene

No question about it. The Hamptons finally has a real Club Scene. There are some really hot spots that are beginning to attract loyal crowds. At the top of the list would be Jet East and NV Tsunami. Get the details in our "Clubs" section.

HAILS, FAREWELLS, RELOCATIONS & RUMORS ??!!

In this section of The Guide we will "Hail" those spots that are new for this year. We will also list those places that bit the dust last year-the "Farewell" part. Each season also brings some shifting around, so we have some "Relocations." Lastly, there are the intriguing "Rumors" that we've heard-from the usually reliable sources, of course!

"Hail"

The A-Lounge Club: 1271 North Sea Road, Southampton. Happy Hour 5 to 7 PM, with a full dinner menu and (gasp!) shareable dishes! They'll also have a DJ and dancing. Outdoor terrace, which sounds great, and they'll be open to 4 AM!

Blue Duck Bakery: Hampton Rd., Southampton, 204-1701: This looks promising—Excellent cookies (reminds me of Brooklyn) and specialty cakes.

BookHampton in Paradise: Hal Zwick, the creative new owner of BookHampton, is adding another store to his growing empire. He's bought the old Paradise Cafe in Sag Harbor and is turning it into a combination bookstore and restaurant. Thus: "BookHampton in Paradise," which I think is pretty cute! One-third of the old downstairs and all the upstairs area will be devoted to books. Hal's adding an outdoor patio on the back for dining in the fresh and wonderful Sag Harbor air.

Bridges: The Hamptons newest restaurant, bar, cabaret and function room. Open year round. Live music and Continental fusion cuisine. 964 Sag Harbor Turnpike, Bridgehampton, 537-9105.

Goldberg's Bagels: County Road 39, Southampton, 204-1046: Took the spot formerly occupied by one of the Hampton Bagels stores. My in-laws think it's pretty good

Hamptons Concierge: (see "Concierge Services")

K-Mart: Bridgehampton Commons, Bridgehampton (see "Department Stores")

Phao: A new Thai restaurant at 62 Main St., Sag Harbor, 725-0055). Phao has taken over the spot formerly occupied by "Citron."

Reflections, a new floor maintenance company in Hampton Bays, 723-1236. Free estimates and service throughout the Hamptons.

Starbucks: see "coffee".

Utopia Lifestyle Inns, The Atlantic, the Bentley, and the Capri: Yes, three new hotel/motel properties have been unveiled by Utopia. The Atlantic is already open, on County Road 39 in Southampton, just before Southampton College. I stopped by to visit and it looks pretty promising. The Bentley will open up just down the road with 39 more rooms and shortly after that the nearby Capri will offer another 31 rooms, most able to comfortably accommodate 4 people. Call them at 287-0908 or check out the properties on line at www.utopiainns.com.

World Pie: (see "Restaurants," Bridgehampton)

"Relocating"

Court Order: From County Road 39 in Southampton to Quoque (653-0132).

Doug & Besim's: from one of Jobs Lane in Southampton to just up the block. (see "Cigars")

Chrysalis Art Gallery: from 92 Main Street, Southampton to 2 Main Street, Southampton, (spot formerly occupied by "Aveda").

Fountain of Youth Day Care from Sacred Hearts Church to David White's Lane, Southampton, 287-8734

The Medicine Shoppe on Jagger Lane in Southampton has changed its name to SouthThrifty Drugs.

"Farewell"

American Pacific Enterprises: As we go to press this Jobs Lane specialty store is clearing out to the walls.

Aveda: Pretty good natural cosmetics store at the end of main Street in Southampton—up and gone!

Caldor: (Bridgehampton) Replaced by a new K-Mart (see "Department Stores")

Concert at the Ranch: Usually every year in Montauk in early August—big blast put on by Paul Simon and friends; but, alas, they seem to have given up. The promoters say it got too "crazy," too rowdy, too "druggy".

Encore: This chain of bookstores went belly up and dragged this local branch in Bridgehampton down with them.

Fish Net Restaurant: North Highway, Southampton, is gone. Not once in all my time out here did I ever wander into this seedy looking place. Not even Karaoke Nights could save the place. Well, too late.

Kathleen's: Can you believe this?! Kathleen's! As in the best baked goods in the Hamptons, that Kathleen! Well, it seems she had a falling out with her partners. It's a big mess and Kathleen is having a tough time of it. There have been picketers in front of her building on North Sea Road. As we go to press, the lawyers have taken over. There are suits and claims flying in all directions. I talked with Kathleen and her hope is that she'll be able to reclaim her landmark building (she owns it after all)! and start over. She wants to and she should! Go, Kathleen! We wish you the best and we love ya!

Margot: A trendy dress store tucked into an alley off of Jobs Lane: Poof! Gone!

Maya: The folks who own the high society restaurant of the same name in St. Bart's came to East Hampton last summer and took over the old Sappore di Mare site. They didn't last the season. The food was wonderful but the prices were out of control, even for the Hamptons! What were they thinking?

Red Marq: This beautiful card and stationary shop on Main Street in Bridgehampton disappeared without a trace last winter. It is being replaced by King-Beck Stationery store, moving to this location from down the block.

Sedona: Nice little coffee shop on Main Street, Bridgehampton. Starbucks is opening down the block and I guess that proved to be just too much.

Stubby's: This was the Hamptons Literary Society's annual awards dinner. Pretty good event, but in the last year it lost one anchor in the death of Joe Heller and another anchor, Kurt Vonnegut, was seriously burned in a fire in his Manhattan apartment last winter. The event has been canceled for this year.

Vermont Farmer's Market: This was a great country market, the anchor tenant in the new Water Mill Shoppes. Only lasted one summer. Too bad. The baked goods were exceptional and the deli was first rate. I think they failed from lack of name recognition more than anything else. The market is being replaced with a Hamptons of "Citarella's" (see above). Welcome Home AIDS Thrift Shop, 70 Main St., Southampton, has closed.

Wilke-Rodriguez: Hip men's clothing store that first appeared on Jobs Lane in Southampton, then moved to Main Street in East Hampton and has now (Poof!) vanished!

"Rumors"

Ian Robertson Fine Furniture: the for sale signs are up. Hmmm.

The Station: Is for sale. Another one of our favorite places. I hope someone with a loving touch will buy it.

Montauk Playhouse Community Center: Is there another major playhouse in the offing for the Hamptons? Perhaps. There's a group in Montauk promoting the resurrection of the old "barn" at the foot of Montauk Manor as a combination playhouse and community center. A very worthy cause. call the Montauk Chamber at 668-2428 for details or write the Playhouse people at P. O. Box 1612, Montauk, 11954.

ABOUT THE AUTHOR

Phil Keith is a Harvard graduate, ex-Naval Aviator, Vietnam Vet and sales and marketing consultant who now lives full-time in Sag Harbor with his wife, Myra.

ABOUT US

Here at City & Company we publish beautifully designed and illustrated guidebooks on subjects of interest to our fellow New Yorkers and sophisticated travelers: culturally affluent, intellectually curious urbanites who lead active and varied lives.

Our little volumes are collections of the city's jewels. They take you to the wonderful little hotel tucked away on a side street in SoHo; a tranquil garden hidden behind a Chelsea seminary; a Gramercy Park salon for a sumptuous five-course tea; a romantic midtown restaurant for a caviar brunch; a place in Chinatown to play tic-tac-toe with a talented chicken; and now to nearby communities to weekend or summer. These are places to indulge, inform, amuse, and just enjoy for the discerning city dweller.

City and Company guidebooks are necessary additions to your bookshelf, at home and in the office. Whether you're setting off solo, with a friend, as a couple, parent or family, these companions guide you to the best of where to go, what to see and what to do in this city of infinite choices, this capital of the world, this city we choose to call home.

Helene Silver

Publisher

GUIDES
TO THE
BEST OF
NEW YORK

City Baby $15.95

CityTripping New York $15.95

City Wedding: A Guide to the Best Bridal Resources
   in New York, Long Island, Westchester, New Jersey
   and Connecticut $17.95

Heavenly Weekends: Travel Without a Car $14.95

New York's New & Avant-Garde Art Galleries $14.00

New York's 50 Best Art in Public Places $12.00

New York's 50 Best Places to Go Birding $15.00

New York's 50 Best Places to Have Brunch $12.00

New York's 50 Best Bookstores for Book Lovers $12.00

New York's 50 Best Places to Discover & Enjoy
  in Central Park $12.00

New York's 50 Best Places to Take Children $12.00

New York's 60 Best Wonderful Little Hotels $15.00

New York's 75 Best Hot Nightspots $12.00

New York's 100 Best Party Places $14.00

New York's 50 Best Places to Find Peace & Quiet $12.00

New York's 100 Best Little Places to Shop $14.00

The New York Book of Tea $18.00

The Ultra Cool Parents Guide to All of New York $14.95

You can find these books at your local bookstore, through
booksellers on the web, or by contacting City & Company.

City & Company
22 West 23rd Street   New York, NY 10010
tel: 212.366.1988   fax: 212.242.0415
e-mail: cityco@bway.net   www.cityandcompany.com